POW

WINDOWS

POWER
WINDOWS

Maximizing the

Speed and Performance

of Windows 2.0

& Windows/386

J I M   H E I D

PUBLISHED BY
Microsoft Press
A Division of Microsoft Corporation
16011 NE 36th Way, Box 97017, Redmond, Washington 98073-9717

Library of Congress Cataloging in Publication Data

Heid, Jim.
Power Windows.
Includes index.
1. MS-DOS (Computer operating system)   2. Microsoft Windows (Computer programs)   I. Title.
QA76.76.063H45   1988   005.4'3   88-5227
ISBN 1-55615-008-3

Printed and bound in the United States of America.

1 2 3 4 5 6 7 8 9   FGFG   3 2 1 0 9 8

Distributed to the book trade in the United States
by Harper & Row.

Distributed to the book trade in Canada by General
Publishing Company, Ltd.

Distributed to the book trade outside the United States
and Canada by Penguin Books Ltd.

Penguin Books Ltd., Harmondsworth, Middlesex, England
Penguin Books Australia Ltd., Ringwood, Victoria, Australia
Penguin Books N.Z. Ltd., 182-190 Wairau Road, Auckland 10, New Zealand

British Cataloging in Publication Data available

Project Editor: Ron Lamb   **Technical Editor:** Michael Halvorson

To Maryellen,
to my mother,
to my grandmother,
and to Duncan.

Contents

Acknowledgments

My sincere gratitude goes out to the many people who helped to make this book possible. Among them are John Butler, for providing technical assistance and a wealth of information on Windows' history; Tandy Trower, for reviewing Chapter 1 and providing valuable insights on Windows' history; Phil Hermann and Don Hasson, for reviewing the chapters and answering technical questions; Paul Grayson of Micrografx, for technical assistance and historical information; and the entire Windows 2.0 and Windows/386 development teams, for creating such a superb operating environment.

At Microsoft Press, thanks go to Ron Lamb, for his expert editing, his patience, and his ability to keep track of myriad inserts and last-minute changes; Mike Halvorson, for his attention to detail and his excellent suggestions for tips; Roger Shanafelt, for technical assistance and for providing the latest prerelease copies of Windows and Microsoft Excel; and Susan Lammers, for her support and assistance in developing the book's outline.

My deepest thanks and my undying love go to Maryellen Kelly, my wife and best friend, who read and edited the first drafts, tried the exercises, and took me to Hawaii when it was all over.

INTRODUCTION

You can learn the basics of Microsoft Windows in a day, but understanding its intricacies takes time. That's where *Power Windows* comes in. This book is your guide to mastering Microsoft Windows version 2.0 and Microsoft Windows/386. It is intended for intermediate to advanced Windows users and assumes that you're familiar with Windows terms such as MS-DOS Executive, icon, and drop-down menu and with mouse terms such as click, double-click, and drag. If any of these terms are new to you, review Chapters 1 through 5 of the *Microsoft Windows User's Guide* before continuing with this book.

Chapter 1 of this book deals with the history and underlying technology of Windows 2.0, including how it differs from version 1.0, how it runs programs, and how it interacts with MS-DOS. Chapters 2 through 9 begin with a summary of the chapter's contents, followed by a series of tips, each numbered and clearly titled for quick reference.

Chapter 10 examines the considerations involved in assembling the hardware needed to run Windows efficiently. Chapter 11 looks at a sampling of released and soon-to-be-released Windows applications. Chapter 12 focuses on the differences between Windows 2.0 and Windows/386, the version of Windows designed for 80386-based computers. Unless otherwise noted, all the material in this book applies to both Windows 2.0 and Windows/386.

Generally, this book follows the style used in the *Microsoft Windows User's Guide.*

A plus sign (+) between two key names means you press the keys at the same time. For example, the phrase "press Alt+Tab" means you press and hold down the Alt key while you press Tab, and then you release both keys.

This book uses the phrase "direction keys" to describe the cursor-movement keys on the numeric keypad of your keyboard (as well as the separate cursor-movement keys on IBM enhanced keyboards). The Left direction key, for example, is the key that moves the cursor one character to the left.

Text that you must type appears in italics.

Text instructions are not specific to the keyboard or the mouse. For example, instead of saying, "Double-click on the file CLIPBRD.EXE," this book says, "Choose the file CLIPBRD.EXE."

With this book, you'll learn how to make Windows run faster, how to customize it, and how to combine programs to get more done in less time.

And I promise to keep the window puns to a minimum. They are, after all, a pane.

Jim Heid
January 1988

CHAPTER 1

INSIDE WINDOWS

Windows' gestation was longer than Microsoft had expected—so much longer that when Windows finally was released in 1985, Microsoft hosted a comedic "roast" at the COMDEX computer-industry trade show to poke fun at the pace of Windows' development.

Behind the delays was an obstacle course riddled with technical land mines. The story of Microsoft Windows is one of remarkable programming feats and breakthroughs in how people interact with computers.

A Brief History of Windows

The tale begins not in Bellevue, Washington, in 1985, but in Cambridge, Massachusetts, in 1962. There, at the Massachusetts Institute of Technology, a doctoral student named Ivan Sutherland developed a drawing program called Sketchpad for his dissertation. With Sketchpad, you used a light pen to draw straight-line geometric shapes, move them, alter them, and attach them to one another.

Sketchpad's graphic display and interactive operating style contrasted sharply with the programs of the day, which received instructions from punched cards and responded on teletype terminals.

Another stepping-stone was laid at the Stanford Research Institute (SRI) in Stanford, California, in 1964, when Douglas Engelbart invented the "X-Y Position Indicator for a Display System," or, as it's come to be known, the mouse. The mouse's birth was part of SRI's research into office-automation systems that employed pointing devices and special function keys for issuing commands and that relegated the keyboard to information entry.

Those concepts impressed other visionary computer scientists, including Alan Kay, who, with hardware designer Edward Cheadle, built a desktop computer called FLEX that offered windowing capabilities, a pointing device, and graphics—in 1969. But Kay's real dream was to build the Dynabook, a $1,000 computer that would be the size of a large book with the power of a mainframe computer. In 1970, he joined Xerox's new Palo Alto Research Center (PARC). At PARC, he persuaded fellow researchers that his dream warranted investigation, and in 1971 he formed his Learning Research Group. The next year, Kay created the Smalltalk programming language, which was designed to run on a desktop computer that had a pointing device and high-resolution graphics.

Elsewhere within PARC, researchers led by Larry Tesler (who had worked with Kay on Smalltalk) were creating a version of Douglas Engelbart's office-automation system for PARC computers. Tesler's group found that the system's many abbreviated commands—such as typing *DW* to enter delete-word mode—made it difficult to learn. His solution was significant: Instead of requiring users to choose a command and then specify the information on which the command should act, he required the reverse. Users would first mark, or select, the information (such as a word to be deleted) and then choose a command from a list of supplied choices.

One result of this research was a computer called Alto, which combined Smalltalk, high-resolution graphics, a mouse, and Xerox's Ethernet networking system. Developed between 1972 and 1974, Alto was the first of the new breed of computers to leave PARC. Xerox sold a few of the machines to government entities, including the White House and Congress, which used them to create the *Congressional Record*. But Alto was never a commercial product. Only 2000 of the $32,000 machines were built.

In 1977, Alto co-designer David Liddle was assigned the task of crafting the Alto into a commercially viable product. Charles Simonyi, a Hungarian-born scientist who learned programming on a Russian computer built around vacuum tubes, joined the team that created the Xerox Star, a $16,595 workstation.

Basic Tenets of User Interface Design

The Alto and the Star were the culmination of PARC's research into person-machine interaction, research that resulted in several tenets of software design. One is that a computer user shouldn't have to memorize and type commands but should be able to choose commands from pull-down or pop-up menus. Another principle is that the user should "select, and then act." Whether editing text, deleting files, or starting a program, the user should first select the information or object he or she wants to work with and then tell the computer what to do with it. Another precept is that programs should not be modal. Instead of having to work within and switch among various modes—an edit mode, an entry mode, a print mode—the user should be able to access any program feature at any time. People generally don't operate in modes in real life; having to do so with a computer adds a hurdle to the course of mastery.

Because they were certain that computer newcomers would find issuing commands and viewing text on a screen unfamiliar, PARC researchers pioneered the use of high-resolution graphics to display pictures, or icons, representing program functions or computer components. An iconic approach replaces abstract actions, such as typing a command to view a disk's directory, with the more concrete process of pointing to a disk drive icon, as shown in Figure 1-1.

FIGURE 1-1.

Yesterday versus today: two approaches to summoning a directory listing.

High-resolution graphics also let a display show text and graphics much as they appear on paper—another key to making the computer a less-alien place.

Finally, because people often work with several different pieces of paper at once, shuffling them about as they work, PARC researchers felt computer users should be able to work with numerous files at once, each in its own viewing area, or window.

The Marketing of Graphical User Environments

The significance of PARC's user-interface breakthroughs combined with the microcomputer industry's snowballing momentum guaranteed that PARC concepts and mass-market microcomputers would soon meet. They did, through several channels. Apple cofounder and then-chairman Steve Jobs toured PARC in 1979 with several engineers. He saw the Xerox Star and Smalltalk in action, and the seeds for the Lisa were planted. Frustrated by what he felt was Xerox's indifference toward the personal-computer market, Larry Tesler joined Apple to help the seeds germinate. They did, and the $10,000 Lisa was unveiled in 1983. The Lisa embraced many PARC precepts. High-resolution graphics allowed it to display documents as they would appear when printed. Icons replaced typed commands for disk and file management—for example, users could "throw" files into a trash can icon to delete them. Pull-down menus placed all of an application's commands just a mouse movement away, setting the stage for a new generation of modeless software. And overlapping windows and a multitasking operating system allowed multiple documents and applications to be shuffled about on an electronic desktop. The Lisa was critically acclaimed but overpriced, and it sold poorly. The Macintosh, which had most of the Lisa's capabilities but was faster and cost only $2,495, was introduced a year later and has grown to become the microcomputer industry's second standard.

Meanwhile, several software firms were crafting PARC-inspired operating environments for the first standard: the IBM PC.

The Development of Windows

Microsoft announced Windows on November 10, 1983, but the environment's beginnings date back to late 1982, when Microsoft began work on a set of device-independent graphics routines called the Computer Graphics Interface (CGI).

CGI was to be a product distributed with Microsoft's language compilers to enable software developers to create applications that could produce output on a wide variety of printers. Developers would use hardware-independent CGI instructions in their programs, and CGI would work with device drivers to translate those instructions into the commands required by a particular printer.

Shortly after starting work on CGI, Microsoft began contemplating creation of a graphical operating environment for MS-DOS computers. A number of catalysts were behind these initial musings. Microsoft chairman Bill Gates felt that microcomputers should be easier to use and that a graphical user interface would be a way of accomplishing that. Microsoft's operating-system customers began expressing interest in windowing environments—especially after another software firm, VisiCorp, announced that it was working on a graphical operating environment for MS-DOS computers called VisiOn. These factors—Gates' vision of the future and good, old-fashioned corporate competition—combined, and by February 1983, the mission was clear: Microsoft would do Windows.

Although many aspects of Windows' design changed over the next several months, some design goals were carved in stone from the outset. Windows was to be multitasking—that is, it would be able to run many applications simultaneously. Windows was to be device independent—it would be able to work with a variety of displays and printers. And because users couldn't be expected to abandon their existing, non-Windows applications, Windows was to be able to run existing applications. That last goal later became a hurdle.

The Windows Challenge

Microsoft's challenge was formidable: to extend a multitasking, memory-managing, graphics-based operating environment to a single-tasking operating system for a computer with no built-in graphics, a 640 KB memory limit (a typical machine at that time had only 64 KB), and the relatively slow 8088 microprocessor. And because 640 KB, hard-disk-equipped machines were far less common than they are today, Windows' minimum hardware requirements would be 256 KB and two floppy-disk drives.

But Microsoft was up to the challenge, and work on Windows began in earnest in early 1983. Microsoft assembled a group of designers and programmers from different parts of the company.

In the middle of 1983, Scott McGregor joined Microsoft and was put in charge of the Interactive Systems Group, the team whose charter was Windows. A veteran of Xerox PARC, McGregor was to have a significant impact on Windows' user interface. It was McGregor who proposed that Windows would use tiling, rather than overlapping, windows. Instead of windows overlapping as they did on the Lisa, the Macintosh and Xerox's pioneering machines, they would shrink and expand as needed to accommodate other windows on the screen—as did the windows on Viewers, a windowing system McGregor helped design at PARC. (Indeed, the early prototypes of Windows shown later that year looked much like Viewers.)

The Development Effort Progresses

By September 1983, Windows' development was progressing at full steam. The Windows team had grown to 15 software designers and programmers. Nearly a dozen computer manufacturers signed agreements to release versions of Windows for their machines, as Microsoft aggressively marketed the product to original equipment manufacturers (OEMs). Many manufacturers stationed engineers at Microsoft, where they could work intimately with the Windows team. Everyone was working frantically to get working prototypes of the windowing software up and running. CGI had entered the testing stage, although by then it was no longer a separate product. CGI had been redubbed GDI—the Graphic Device Interface—and became the portion of Windows containing routines that developers use not only to print, but also display, text and graphics. To meet these new requirements, the Windows team added a large vocabulary of typographic routines to GDI, as well as routines for manipulating graphics images.

Microsoft succeeded in completing a prototype in time for the November COMDEX show. This early version of Windows was well received at COMDEX and by the computer press. Software developers liked the fact that they would be able to write Windows programs on an IBM PC; VisiCorp's VisiOn, by contrast, required an expensive Digital Equipment Corporation VAX system for development.

BYTE magazine, in its December 1983 issue, described Windows as offering ''remarkable openness, reconfigurability, and transportability as well as modest hardware requirements and pricing.'' But those modest requirements also inspired a bit of skepticism. In the same article, *BYTE*'s West Coast editor Phil Lemmons wrote, ''It is natural to wonder whether Microsoft Windows' ability to run in limited memory and off floppy disks will result in noticeable delays during execution.'' Lemmons didn't speculate whether those abilities would result in noticeable delays in Windows' development. In many ways, that question was one Microsoft hadn't considered, either.

Twists and Turns on the Development Path

At Windows' COMDEX unveiling, Microsoft promised delivery in May 1984. In the spring of 1984, Windows' shipping date was revised to November. In November, the release date changed again, to June 1985. A final version of Windows shipped to developers and hardware manufacturers that month, and the developers said the product was worth the wait. The retail version of Windows didn't reach stores until November 18.

A combination of factors and events caused the delays, but all derive from the fact that Microsoft wanted to do Windows properly. Although Microsoft received its share of criticism from the computer press and some developers, it was determined to release the best graphic environment available for MS-DOS machines. Schedules took a back seat to quality.

In February 1984, Microsoft hosted the first Windows developers seminar—a symposium at which software developers could learn how to write applications for Windows. Bill Gates presented his vision for the future of MS-DOS operating environments. Several members of the Windows team discussed Windows' multitasking and memory-management techniques and explained how Windows' graphics features worked. Developers were impressed, and by June 1984, Microsoft had shipped nearly 300 copies of a prerelease version of the Windows Software Development Kit.

As developers worked with Windows, their successes and failures helped Microsoft learn where Windows' strengths and weaknesses were. Many developers had difficulty adjusting to the new concepts involved in programming for a graphical user interface. They were used to creating their own user interfaces, and the notion of tapping into the library of user-interface routines that was built into Windows was foreign to them. By listening to feedback and observing where developers were having trouble, the Windows team was able to refine Windows and the underlying structure of Window applications, thus simplifying the task of programming for Windows.

One example of the feedback the Windows team received involved the importance of being able to control Windows and Windows applications using the keyboard. Aside from avoiding the requirement for a mouse, a keyboard interface would allow a user who performed typing-intensive tasks to keep his or her hands on the keyboard, rather than having to reach between the keyboard and a mouse. The power and flexibility of those early prototypes were immediately obvious, and the now-familiar Alt+key Windows keyboard interface was born.

Immediately after the Mac's January 1984 introduction, several programmers from the Mac applications group joined the Windows team, and some aspects of Windows' design changed to reflect their influence. The Windows team was able to decide what worked in a

windowing environment and what didn't, based on a fully imple-
mented product. For example, the team briefly contemplated changing the interface to display only one menu bar on the screen at all
times, rather than giving each open application window its own menu
bar. The sole menu bar would contain the menus for the currently
active application and would change as the user switched from one
application to another. This approach was discarded as being too cum-
bersome for an operating environment that runs multiple applications
simultaneously.

Ironically, the Macintosh delayed Windows less than existing MS-
DOS applications did. Allowing Windows to run standard applications
turned out to be a far more time-consuming and complicated
challenge than originally anticipated. One of the programmers of
MS-DOS joined the Windows team in late 1984 and began developing a
system of classification for standard applications. An application's
place within this taxonomy was to determine whether it could coexist
on the screen with Windows applications and whether users could
switch between it and other running applications. After examining
the format of the program information files (PIFs) that accompanied
IBM's TopView operating environment, the Windows team decided to
adopt the TopView PIF format for Windows rather than create its own.
Doing so allowed TopView PIFs to work with Windows.

Yet another hurdle Microsoft faced was deciding on the most appropriate programming environment. The Windows team first used
Microsoft Pascal, and then Lattice C, and finally Microsoft's C com-
piler, which was under development at the same time. They finally
settled on Microsoft C, but that, too, caused delays, because it meant
building software using software that was under development and
not stable itself.

But the most significant factors behind Windows' delay were
that Microsoft had underestimated the scope and complexity of
the Windows project and that the market continued to change. Windows had grown from being a set of device-independent graphics routines to being a full graphical operating environment. Moreover,
because MS-DOS doesn't have multitasking support and memory management, those capabilities had to be built into Windows.

And that introduced a thorny problem for Microsoft's marketing
efforts, which now had the challenge of selling to IBM PC users a
non-IBM operating system extension. That challenge became even

greater when IBM declined to develop and market a version of Windows and decided instead to market its own operating environment, TopView. Microsoft's solution was to take matters into its own hands and create a retail version of Windows for MS-DOS. To make the package more appealing to users, Microsoft developed Write, Paint, and the Windows desktop applications.

This retail version of Windows finally made it to market in November of 1985. (Interestingly, however, some users got their first look at it several months before, when Micrografx, a pioneering Windows application developer, released its In•a•Vision drawing application, which contained a special, single-application version of Windows.)

Between 1985 and 1987, however, Windows' full potential wasn't being tapped. Because few Windows applications were available, most Windows users were using the environment primarily to switch quickly between standard applications—ones written before Windows, such as Microsoft Word and Lotus 1-2-3. Indeed, one Microsoft survey revealed that 51.5 percent of Windows users bought it to switch between applications, and only 11.4 percent purchased it for its graphical user interface. Less than 6 percent bought Windows for Write, Paint, and Windows' desktop applications. Essentially, Windows was a graphical operating environment that was being used primarily to switch between text-oriented programs.

But in 1987 that began to change. Aldus Corporation released a Windows version of its extremely popular PageMaker desktop-publishing software. IBM included Windows and PageMaker as part of its complete desktop-publishing package. Microsoft introduced a Windows version of Microsoft Excel, a powerful spreadsheet and graphics program that is consistently among the top ten bestselling Macintosh programs. Micrografx added Windows Graph, a business graphics program, to its growing line of Windows applications. At last, applications were becoming available that took full advantage of Windows' capabilities.

What Windows Offers

Windows gives MS-DOS computers a graphical user interface based on PARC and SRI research and similar to that of Apple's Lisa and

Macintosh. But so does another MS-DOS operating environment, Digital Research's GEM. What makes Windows the environment of choice?

Multitasking. Windows can run numerous programs simultaneously and lets you switch between them with a keystroke or a mouse click. Your computer can perform time-consuming chores such as printing, sorting data, or transferring a disk file while you work in other programs.

Data exchange. Windows can transfer text or graphics between applications through its clipboard, letting you create your own integrated workplace containing the programs you use. Windows' Dynamic Data Exchange feature (discussed in Chapter 5) can even update information you pasted into one program as the information changes in the program where it originated.

Device independence, no software obsolescence. Windows is designed to work with a wide variety of displays, printers, and pointing devices, and to adapt to technological improvements. Computers will become faster, displays sharper, printers more powerful, and pointing devices more responsive. When they do, your current Windows applications will run faster, look sharper, and produce better hard copy.

A link to MS-DOS. Windows' MS-DOS Executive lets you manage disks, files, and directories without tacking a command cheat sheet to your monitor. You can also run COMMAND.COM in a window to have direct access to MS-DOS.

Wide-ranging software compatibility. Many of today's most capable application programs were designed for Windows, including Microsoft Excel, Aldus PageMaker, and Micrografx Designer.

Ties to the past. Running Windows doesn't mean forsaking those trusty MS-DOS applications you've come to rely on. In fact, Windows improves them by letting you run more than one at the same time, switch from one to another with a keystroke or a mouse click, and exchange data between them.

A foundation for the future. Windows lays the technical groundwork for tomorrow's programs. It contains a complete toolbox of routines that programmers can tap to create applications that exploit Windows' multitasking capability and consistent user interface. With a consistent user interface, you don't have to learn how to issue commands and navigate through each new program before mastering its features. Learn how to use one Windows application, and you've started learning how to use them all. And if in the future you switch to Microsoft's OS/2 operating system, you'll feel right at home with its Windows-like Presentation Manager.

You don't have to know how Windows works to use it. However, having a basic understanding of how Windows and its applications operate will give you an appreciation for their design and can help you manage your Windows sessions more efficiently.

Setting Up Windows

Life with Windows begins with the Setup program, which asks for information about your hardware and then tailors Windows to it. Part of this assembly process involves combining numerous files from the Windows Setup disk into the files that form an installed copy of Windows, as shown in Figure 1-2. These files contain the device drivers that Windows needs to access your display, mouse, and printer. Device

FIGURE 1-2.

Windows files before and after installation.

KERNEL.EXE
   Provides task handling,
   memory management,
   resource and segment loading
GDI.EXE
   Provides graphics resources,
   routines for drawing and filling arcs,
   lines, polygons, and pies;
   loads graphics drivers
USER.EXE
   Provides user interface code for creating
   windows, icons, cursors, dialog boxes, menus;
   manages keyboard and mouse events
WINOLDAP.MOD
   Provides code for running standard
   applications; swaps code between memory
   and disk when you switch between
   standard applications and Windows
WINOLDAP.GRB
   Contains code that allows capture of
   screens from standard applications that
   cannot run in a window
DISPLAY.DRV
KEYBOARD.DRV
SYSTEM.DRV
FONT*.FON (numerous font files)
MSDOS.EXE
SOUND.DRV
COMM.DRV
MOUSE.DRV

WIN200.BIN
WIN200.OVL
WIN.COM
WIN.INI
WINOLDAP.MOD
WINOLDAP.GRB
MSDOS.EXE

drivers are portions of code that tell Windows what kind of instructions your hardware responds to and what its capabilities are. They let Windows run on different types of hardware.

Some background is necessary to appreciate the vital job Windows device drivers perform. Many non-Windows applications such as WordStar and Lotus 1-2-3 bypass MS-DOS and directly access hardware components such as the screen. By bypassing MS-DOS, they can create faster screen displays, but at a price. They risk not being able to run on MS-DOS computers that aren't 100 percent compatible with the IBM PC, they may not work with memory-resident programs that directly access the hardware in different ways, and they often require a long installation process to tell them what kind of hardware you have.

But a Windows application never accesses hardware directly, thanks to device drivers and Windows' Graphic Device Interface. GDI provides a complete vocabulary of commands for displaying text and accessing all the fonts you installed in all their styles and point sizes. GDI also tells a Windows application how to draw lines, circles, and other shapes. When a Windows application needs to send information to the display or printer, it uses GDI commands. Windows sends those commands to the device driver, and the driver translates them into the specific commands your hardware needs.

This approach means that a Windows application doesn't need to know what kind of hardware you have. One benefit is that you don't have to endure a lengthy installation process every time you get a new Windows application. Another is that your Windows applications and the documents they create will never become obsolete. If you get a new mouse or that ultra-sharp monitor you've been craving, simply reinstall Windows, and you'll be up and running. If you get a new printer, the job is even easier because you can add its device driver with Control Panel. (The reasons you can't change pointing devices and displays with Control Panel are discussed in Chapter 8.)

Working with Windows

When you start Windows, the program called WIN.COM displays the Microsoft logo and Windows version number while loading some Windows code and the device drivers for your screen and pointing device. Next, Windows reads your WIN.INI configuration file. WIN.INI tells

Windows the printer attached to each port, the applications to run or load (if any), the screen colors, the filename extension each application uses, and much more. (Chapter 8 covers WIN.INI in detail.)

After a few seconds elapse, Windows' opening screen surrenders to a display that resembles a blank desktop as Windows begins to run MS-DOS Executive. MS-DOS Executive isn't Windows itself; it's a Windows application that lets you start programs and manage files, directories, and disks. It's your link to MS-DOS. (Macintosh users might find this a rough equivalent to the Finder.) One of MS-DOS Executive's first tasks is to read the current directory and display its contents. When that's completed, Windows is up and running.

At this point, nothing appears to be happening. In reality, MS-DOS Executive is hard at work—running around in circles, so to speak. Every Windows application has a main event loop, also called a message loop. During the main event loop, the application is on the alert for messages from Windows indicating that an event occurred— the mouse moved, a button was clicked, or a key was pressed. When an event occurs, Windows sends a message to a holding area called the application queue.

The application queue is like a line at a bank: Messages line up like customers, one after another, waiting for an application to say, "Who's next?" Every application periodically does exactly that and responds appropriately to its messages. Because the messages line up one after another, you don't have to wait for an application to complete one operation (such as saving a file) before typing text or issuing another command. (Of course, a queue has a finite capacity. The application queue holds eight messages, and the system queue, which detects messages and routes them to the appropriate application queue, holds 24. If you're a fast typist or your computer is performing a particularly lengthy operation, it is possible for the queue to fill and for keystrokes or mouse movements to be lost.)

This continuous cycling for messages, combined with the fact that all of an application's commands are presented in drop-down menus, lets Windows applications honor one of the software design tenets I mentioned earlier—that an application should not be modal, but should let you access any program feature at any time. Instead of telling you, "This is what you're allowed to do now," Windows applications say, "Here are the things I can do. Take your choice."

Multitasking

Keeping a constant vigil for events sounds hard enough, but Windows really earns its keep when you tap its multitasking talents by running several applications at the same time.

Each running application is called a task, and numerous tasks can run simultaneously by sharing the computer's resources. When you start an application, Windows loads the application from disk into memory and creates the application's data area, which is a portion of memory that will hold the application's data. The data area for Paint, for example, holds a portion of the image you're drawing. The data area for Write holds a portion of the document you're editing. (I say "a portion" in both cases because both programs keep only part of their documents in memory, swapping the rest to and from the disk, as needed, to conserve memory.) After creating the data area, Windows lets the application create its windows and perform any other initialization chores such as creating temporary work files.

How does Windows divide time among applications that are running simultaneously? The secret lies in the message-gathering process I described earlier. When an application checks the queue for a message, it yields control to other applications. It's as if Windows says, "While you're checking for messages, let's give this second application a chance to run." The second application then checks for messages and, in doing so, lets a third application (or the first) run.

Windows' approach to multitasking, then, is a cooperative effort among all the applications you're running. As long as each application checks for messages periodically—and it must, because that's how it responds to your actions—each application gets a chance to run. Windows' multitasking approach is called nonpreemptive multitasking because Windows never preempts (interrupts) an application to let a different application run. Each application gets a chance to run only when other applications allow it.

Running More Than One Instance of a Program

Windows is unique among operating environments in that it lets you run the same application in more than one window. Writers can use this capability to work on several Write documents at the same time; desktop publishers can work with numerous PageMaker publications simultaneously, cutting and pasting between them. You can even run more than one MS-DOS Executive window to simultaneously view the contents of different disks or directories. (You'll learn how to do this in Chapter 2.)

Windows' ability to run the same application in more than one window is accomplished in a way that is downright clever. When you run a program in a second window, Windows doesn't load the program's code all over again. Doing so would waste memory and severely reduce the number of applications you can run. Instead, the program's second instance, as it's called, shares the program code and such resources as menus, dialog boxes, and icons with the first instance. Each instance, however, has its own data area (that part of memory that stores the data the application manipulates). It's as if Windows says, "I've already loaded this program code once, so you two (or three or more) instances will have to share. I will, however, give each of you your own data area."

You can see this for yourself by running a program such as Page-Maker in more than one window and using the About command on the File menu of MS-DOS Executive to determine how much memory is available after starting each instance. The results are shown in Figure 1-3.

As you can see, subsequent instances use far less memory than the first—about a third less in PageMaker's case—proving that each instance is sharing the program code and resources loaded by the first. If you try this yourself, your results will probably differ slightly because of the complex nature of Windows applications and Windows' memory management techniques.

FIGURE 1-3.

Impact of multiple instances on free memory.

	Free memory	Memory used
Upon Windows startup	357 KB	—
After starting PageMaker	255 KB	102 KB
After starting PageMaker a second time	190 KB	65 KB
After starting PageMaker a third time	125 KB	65 KB

Managing Memory

Its ability to run multiple applications at the same time means that Windows must constantly keep track of how much memory is available. If you close one application, Windows must be able to free the memory that application was using so that other programs can use it.

When you try to start an application, Windows must determine if enough memory is available to run it. A Windows component called the memory manager performs these jobs and more. Windows' memory manager controls where programs go so that the program uses your computer's memory efficiently—much as a hotel manager assigns empty rooms and sees to it that vacated ones are tidied up for incoming lodgers. Part of this process involves managing an application's segments.

When a large Windows application is developed, its programmers divide it into segments—chunks of program code that handle certain tasks. Think of each segment as a job specialist. One segment of Microsoft Excel, for example, contains the code that records macros. Another contains the code that creates charts. Still another handles printing tasks. When an application's code is divided into segments, Windows loads only the segments required for the task you're performing. When you choose a command or option requiring a segment that isn't in memory, Windows loads that segment from disk, discarding others if necessary to free enough memory. When it discards a segment, Windows retains enough information to reload it, should the segment be needed again.

Windows' memory management techniques are also used when you run a standard application—a program that wasn't developed for Windows. In fact, standard applications impose their own issues on Windows. Let's look at how Windows performs its juggling act between the programs of the past and those of future.

Running Standard Applications

When you start a standard application, Windows looks for the application's program information file (PIF) in the application's directory. The PIF gives Windows information it needs to run the application efficiently. (The entries in a PIF are discussed along with Windows' PIF Editor program in Chapter 9.) Windows applications don't require PIFs because the information Windows needs to run them is coded directly into their files. If Windows doesn't find a PIF for the standard application, it displays a message asking if it should make certain assumptions about the application. To tell Windows to run the application using those assumptions, choose the OK button. If you choose the Cancel button, Windows doesn't run the application.

If, however, the PIF is found or if you choose OK in the dialog box, the Windows file called WINOLDAP.MOD swings into action. WINOLDAP.MOD first moves the code that composes Windows and any running applications from memory to disk, thus freeing memory to hold the standard application. If the standard application can run in a window, WINOLDAP.MOD creates a window for it and then runs the application. The Control menu for a standard application's window contains extra commands—Mark, Copy, and Paste—that provide limited access to the clipboard from standard applications. These commands are discussed further in Chapter 5.

When running a standard application that takes over the screen, Windows loads the file WINOLDAP.GRB in addition to WINOLDAP.MOD. WINOLDAP.GRB lets Windows save and restore the application's screen when you switch from or to it. WINOLDAP.GRB also contains the software that lets you capture the screen image of a full-screen standard application (and place it in the clipboard) by using the Alt+PrtScrn key combination.

When you switch from a standard application back to Windows, WINOLDAP.MOD shuttles the necessary Windows code from disk back into memory and then moves the standard application's code to disk. The time required to perform the swap depends on the size of the application, on how much memory your computer has, and on the speed of your hard disk and computer.

Windows 2.0

Windows 2.0 is the environment's second generation. The family resemblance is obvious, but Windows 2.0 is a significant improvement.

Windows 2.0 differs from its predecessor in hundreds of ways, but the cosmetic changes are the ones you notice first. Windows 2.0 discards tiling windows in favor of overlapping ones. Your on-screen desktop can more accurately mimic a real desktop; you can shuffle and stack windows as you do papers. As Figure 1-4 shows, you can re-size most windows by dragging their borders, and you can cause windows to fill the screen or shrink to icons by clicking their minimize and maximize icons located in the upper right-hand corner of each window or by choosing the Minimize or Maximize commands from the Control menu (which in Windows 1.0 is called the System menu).

FIGURE 1-4.

Window-resizing
icons, borders,
and commands.

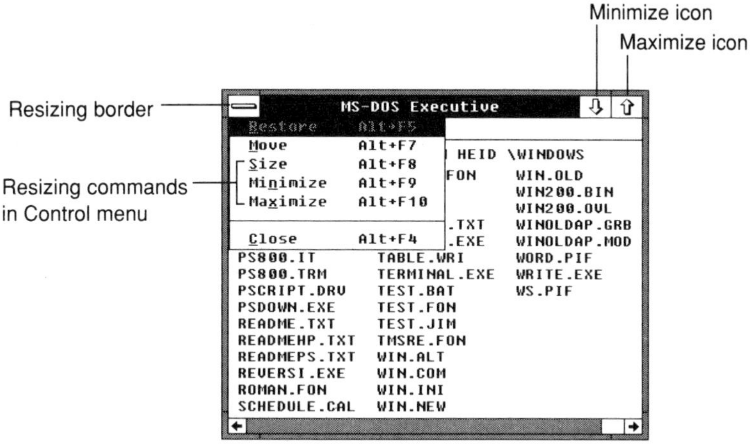

Minimize icon
Maximize icon

Resizing border

Resizing commands
in Control menu

```
┌─────────────────────────────────────────────────┐
│ ═══         MS-DOS Executive          ⇩  ⇧        │
│ ░Restore░░░░░Alt+F5░░░░░░░░░░░░░░░░░░░░░░░░░░░░░░░ │
│  Move        Alt+F7    │ HEID  \WINDOWS           │
│ ┌Size        Alt+F8    │ FON    WIN.OLD           │
│ │Minimize    Alt+F9    │        WIN200.BIN        │
│ └Maximize    Alt+F10   │        WIN200.OVL        │
│                        │.TXT    WINOLDAP.GRB      │
│  Close       Alt+F4    │.EXE    WINOLDAP.MOD      │
│  PS800.IT       TABLE.WRI      WORD.PIF           │
│  PS800.TRM      TERMINAL.EXE   WRITE.EXE          │
│  PSCRIPT.DRV    TEST.BAT       WS.PIF             │
│  PSDOWN.EXE     TEST.FON                          │
│  README.TXT     TEST.JIM                          │
│  READMEHP.TXT   TMSRE.FON                          │
│  READMEPS.TXT   WIN.ALT                            │
│  REVERSI.EXE    WIN.COM                            │
│  ROMAN.FON      WIN.INI                            │
│  SCHEDULE.CAL   WIN.NEW                            │
│ ◄═                                            ═► │
└─────────────────────────────────────────────────┘
```

Overlapping windows also make working with multiple applications more convenient. Instead of dividing the screen into small tiles, Windows 2.0 simply stacks the applications' windows on top of each other.

Microsoft switched to overlapping windows for several reasons. One is improved performance. Today's faster hardware and the faster graphics routines in Windows 2.0 are able to update, or redraw, obscured windows more quickly. Also, today's graphics hardware produces sharper images, making overlapping windows more practical and attractive. Another reason for the change is to provide visual consistency with the Windows-like Presentation Manager portion of the Microsoft OS/2 operating system. Last, Windows users wanted overlapping windows. Most Windows users did, at least: One member of the Windows development team once told me, "Tiling is superior for business applications. You will see it come back the first time a trader loses a million dollars in profit because it was hidden behind a pop-up window." Of course, that's probably an overstatement. That mythical trader could as easily lose a million dollars with tiling windows by making a window too small to see those key figures.

The overlapping-versus-tiling debate continues among graphical user interface gurus, but no one can dispute the improved command interface of Windows 2.0. Choosing commands is faster and easier, whether your link to Windows is a mouse or the keyboard. When you click on a menu title or press Alt and its underlined letter, the menu appears *and* remains visible, with its first command selected. You can then choose the selected command with another mouse click or a press of the Enter key. To choose a different command, move the mouse pointer to it and click, or press the key corresponding to its underlined letter.

In Windows 1.0, using the keyboard to choose commands feels awkward sometimes. The problem is that menus often contain commands beginning with the same letter. Consider the MS-DOS Executive's View menu. To reach the By Kind command—the fourth command beginning with B—in Windows 1.0, you must press the B key four times or press it once and then press the Down direction key three times. Either way, you do more work than you should have to.

With Windows 2.0, each menu command can have a direct-access key, a unique letter that appears underlined within the command or option name and works in concert with the Alt key to help you select what you want quickly, as shown in Figure 1-5. To choose the View menu's By Kind command, you press Alt, and then V, and then K, not Alt, and then V, and then B four times. Dialog boxes offer similar savings. Instead of wearing out your Tab key moving to a particular set of options, you can move to them by pressing Alt along with their direct-access key.

Direct-access keys are assigned by an application's developers. If an application you use doesn't have them, it was probably developed for Windows 1.0 and, therefore, lacks direct-access key definitions. If that's the case, you can still choose commands and navigate dialog boxes using Windows 1.0 keyboard techniques. And many applications, whether written for 1.0 or 2.0, have shortcut keys that let you choose commands with key combinations. (In some applications, shortcut keys are called accelerator keys.)

FIGURE 1-5.

The MS-DOS Executive View menu in Windows 1.04 and 2.0.

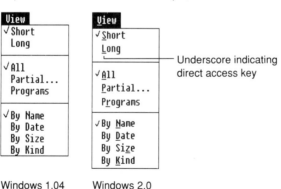

Underscore indicating direct access key

Windows 1.04   Windows 2.0

Along with the major user interface changes came several minor ones. The About command, which, when chosen, displays information about an application, moved from an application's System menu to its leftmost menu (which is usually File). The leftmost menu in Windows 2.0 applications also contains an Exit command that quits the application. The keyboard shortcuts for the Edit menu changed, as did the shortcuts for minimizing and maximizing windows, as shown in Figure 1-6.

FIGURE 1-6.

Summary of changed keyboard shortcuts.

	Windows 1.04	Windows 2.0
Edit menu		
Cut	Del	Shift+Del
Copy	F2	Ctrl+Ins
Paste	Ins	Shift+Ins
Control (System) menu		
Restore	Not applicable	Alt+F5
Move	Alt+Spacebar+M	Alt+F7
Size	Alt+Spacebar+S	Alt+F8
Minimize (Icon)	Alt+Spacebar+I	Alt+F9
Maximize (Zoom)	Alt+Spacebar+Z	Alt+F10
Close	Alt+Spacebar+C	Alt+F4

These cosmetic improvements are significant, but they represent only one aspect of Windows' evolution. Windows 2.0 boasts performance and memory-management improvements that give it a fast, responsive feel, especially on Intel 80286-based and Intel 80386-based computers. These improvements include:

Faster displays. I mentioned earlier that Windows' Graphic Device Interface is the key player in producing screen displays. In Windows 2.0, GDI is two to ten times faster, depending on the operation. Text appears faster, thanks to a new font format that represents characters more efficiently. Lines and geometric shapes are drawn more quickly. Gray text, which Windows uses to indicate commands and dialog box options that aren't currently available, appears four times faster. A new GDI feature lets applications save the portion of the screen that will be obscured by a dialog box and then restore it in a flash when the dialog box disappears.

Improved expanded-memory support. Expanded-memory boards such as Intel's AboveBoard can add megabytes to MS-DOS computers, but Windows 1.0 can't take full advantage of them. You can turn the extra memory into a lightning-fast electronic disk by using the RAMDrive utility, but that is of little comfort when the dreaded *Not enough memory to run* message appears. Windows 2.0 can put those megabytes to work, using them to store Windows applications through a technical trick called bank switching. With its SMARTDrive utility, Windows can also use extended memory (memory above 640 KB on an 80286-based computer) as a disk cache. These techniques and their performance benefits are described in detail in Chapter 10.

The multiple document interface. With Windows 2.0, application developers can create programs that support more than one open document at a time. Applications that use the multiple-document interface provide a workspace in which document windows can be opened, closed, moved, and resized using the same techniques you use to control application windows, as shown in Figure 1-7. The new interface makes possible a new generation of powerful Windows applications—programs such as Microsoft Excel and Blyth Software's Omnis Quartz database manager. Even if you're running an application that

FIGURE 1-7.

Multiple-document interface in Microsoft Excel.

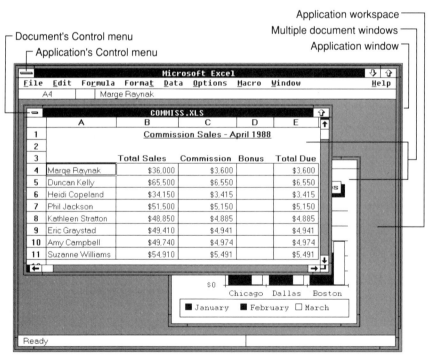

doesn't use the multiple-document interface, you can still work with multiple documents simultaneously by running the application in more than one window.

In its first generation, Windows was a significant first step toward changing the way people work with MS-DOS computers. With version 2.0, Windows has reached its stride. It's fast, responsive, and versatile. And it's much more attractive than the MS-DOS A> or C> prompt.

MS-DOS EXECUTIVE STRATEGIES

I n business, an executive is someone who manages resources and exercises administrative control. In computers, an executive is a program that manages the computer's resources and runs other programs. In both cases, a good executive manages and controls without imposing rigid working guidelines. The best executive lets you work according to the style that lets you be the most productive.

Windows' MS-DOS Executive meets those requirements. Most Windows newcomers use MS-DOS Executive for starting applications and for performing simple disk-management tasks such as copying or deleting files. This chapter explores some of MS-DOS Executive's shortcuts and subtleties and shows how to use them to streamline your disk-management and file-management chores. Many sections contain an exercise or two that you can try; therefore, you should read this chapter alongside your computer, with Windows up and running.

TIP 1: Starting Windows and an Application

This tip is for those times when you haven't yet started Windows and you know you'll be working in a particular application once you do. Instead of starting Windows and then the application, you can perform both jobs at the same time by supplying the application's name as a parameter for the command that starts Windows. At the MS-DOS prompt, type *win*, a space, and then the application's name. For example, to start Windows and Microsoft Excel, type *win excel* and press Enter. If you've already created a document with the application you're starting, you can add that document's name to the command. Typing *win excel amort* and pressing Enter, for example, starts Windows, runs Microsoft Excel, and loads a worksheet named AMORT. You can omit the application's name if you include the document's extension, as in *win amort.xls*. The extension tells Windows to run Microsoft Excel. In both cases, you must remember to type *win*; if you type only the application's name, you receive the message *This program requires Microsoft Windows.*

Another caveat: If you mistype the application's name or you specify an application or document located in a directory other than the current one and that directory isn't in your MS-DOS Path statement, Windows asks you to insert the disk containing the application or document into drive A. This means Windows could not find the application you specified. Click Cancel or press Esc. When you do, the MS-DOS Executive window appears. To have Windows locate an application in a directory other than the current one, change your Path statement to include that directory's name. (For more information about Path statements, see Chapter 4.)

TIP 2: Starting an Application as an Icon

As an experienced Windows user, you know that you can start, or run, a Windows application from the MS-DOS Executive window by double-clicking its filename or by selecting its filename and pressing Enter. You may not know, however, that you can also load an application as an icon by holding down a Shift key as you double-click the filename or press Enter. If you want to try it now, be sure the MS-DOS Executive window is active (click within it if it isn't); and then resize it so that the MS-DOS Executive window only covers the right half of your screen.

Next, locate the filename for the Clock application (*CLOCK.EXE*), and start it as you normally do. Now make the MS-DOS Executive window active again. To start Clock as an icon by using the mouse, hold down the Shift key while double-clicking *CLOCK.EXE*. With the keyboard, select *CLOCK.EXE* and then hold down Shift while you press Enter. This time, the clock icon appears in the icon area at the bottom of the screen. If you like the clock icon visible as you work, you can use this technique to start Clock without having to resize it or drag it out of the way.

Starting an application as an icon has other uses. If you know you'll be switching between two applications (or between two instances of the same application), start the second application or instance (the one you'll be switching to) as an icon. When you're ready to use it, you can quickly open the second application by double-clicking its icon. With the keyboard, hold down the Alt key while you press and release the Tab key, until the clock icon is selected. Then release the Alt key.

By starting an application as an icon, you won't have to return to the MS-DOS Executive window, you'll keep your screen uncluttered, and you'll save time when you're ready to use the application, because most of its code will already be in memory.

TIP 3: Supplying a Parameter to an Application

Some applications accept or require additional information, called options, arguments, or parameters, when you start them. When you're working with the MS-DOS system prompt, you supply a parameter by typing it after the program's filename and before pressing Enter. For example, the command *word /l* starts Microsoft Word and loads the last document you edited, leaving you where you left off. Many MS-DOS utilities that require additional parameters are discussed in Chapter 4.

You can't supply parameters when you start a program by double-clicking or pressing Enter, but you can supply parameters if you use the Load or Run commands on the File menu. Run starts the application in a window, and Load starts the application as an icon. When you select an application's filename and choose Load or Run, a dialog box appears containing the selected program's name, with the name highlighted. As shown in Figure 2-1, to supply a parameter, move the

FIGURE 2-1.

Supplying parameters to an application.(A) Application's name is selected when you choose Run or Load. (B) Click to the right of the name or press End key to deselect. (C) Type a space, type the parameters, and then click OK or press Enter.

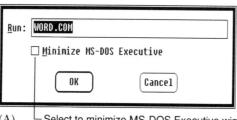

(A) └─ Select to minimize MS-DOS Executive window.

(B)

(C)

mouse pointer after the program's last character and click, or simply press the End key, and then type a space and the parameter. Finally, choose OK.

Incidentally, the Run command has something to offer even if you never supply a single parameter to an application. When you click the Minimize MS-DOS Executive check box that appears in the Run dialog box, the MS-DOS Executive window shrinks to an icon when the application you want to run starts.

TIP 4: Navigating Subdirectories

Creating and using subdirectories from the MS-DOS prompt can be grueling, with commands such as MKDIR (Make Directory) and CHDIR (Change Directory) to memorize and type correctly each time you use them. In addition, you must type lengthy pathnames that tell MS-DOS how to locate files nested in subdirectories. MS-DOS Executive simplifies working with directories by providing the commands in its Special menu and by allowing several directory-navigation shortcuts.

The standard method for changing directories with MS-DOS Executive is to choose the Special menu's Change Directory command, type the pathname, and press Enter. Several shortcuts let you bypass the command, however, and move between directories with the keyboard, the mouse, or a combination of both. The mouse is more efficient for most directory maneuvers, but even the keyboard shortcuts are faster than using the Change Directory command. I'll summarize the shortcuts and present some exercises you can use to try them.

Moving Down the Directory Tree

To move down the directory tree—that is, from the current directory to a directory within it—simply double-click the directory's name in the work area. Or, you can select the directory using the keyboard's direction keys and then press Enter. You can also combine the mouse and the keyboard: Select the directory with the mouse and then press Enter to change to it. This technique is especially effective if you use the mouse with your left hand.

Moving Up the Directory Tree

Moving up the directory tree—to directories closer to the root—is as easy as pressing the Backspace key. Doing so moves you up one level closer to the root directory. With the mouse, you can double-click on the directory you want to change to in the pathname display that appears to the right of the disk drive icons. If there isn't enough room for the path at the right of the drive icons, the path appears below them. (If you find you're not able to double-click fast enough, use Control Panel to change the double-click rate. And if you'd feel more comfortable clicking the right mouse button instead of the left one, use Control Panel's Mouse command on the Preferences menu.) When you click once on a directory name, the Change Directory dialog box appears.

To try the shortcuts, first set the stage by choosing Change Directory and changing to the root directory by typing a backslash (\) and pressing Enter. You're going to switch into the Windows directory and then into its PIF directory. With a mouse, double-click on the directory name *WINDOWS* in the work area. Now double-click on the name *PIF*. You're now in the PIF directory—it's that fast. With the keyboard, move to the name *WINDOWS* and then press Enter. (Incidentally, you don't have to tap-tap your way to *WINDOWS*. Simply press the W key, and MS-DOS Executive selects the first file or directory beginning with W. If more than one begins with W, continue pressing W or use the Down direction key to get to *WINDOWS*.) Finally, select the name *PIF* and press Enter.

Now go back to the root directory. With the keyboard, simply press Backspace until you're at the root directory. Before you try it with the mouse, step back to examine how you select directory names in the pathname display. Point to the PIF directory's name in the pathname display and then press *but don't release* the mouse button. (If you release the button and the Change Directory dialog box appears, simply press the Esc key to cancel it.) Notice how the entire pathname is selected. Now, while still pressing the mouse button, move the pointer to the left. When it reaches the name *WINDOWS*, *PIF* is deselected. When it reaches the root directory's backslash, *WINDOWS* is deselected, as shown in Figure 2-2. Drag left and right across the pathname to see how MS-DOS Executive selects directory names; then move the pointer away from the pathname and release the button. (If you release the mouse button before moving the pointer away from the pathname, the Change Directory dialog box appears. Press the Esc key to cancel it.)

FIGURE 2-2.

*Selecting
directories
in the
pathname
display.*

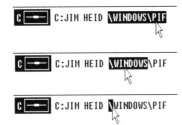

Now that you know how to select directory names in the pathname display, double-click on the name *WINDOWS* to change to it.
Then double-click on the root directory's backslash to change to it.

Accessing Directories from Within a Dialog Box

As you have seen, MS-DOS Executive offers easy, visual access to directories. But the MS-DOS Executive window isn't the only place you can
view what's in your directories. Many Windows applications have an
Open command on their File menus. When you choose an application's Open command, a dialog box appears, listing the files in the
current directory, as shown in Figure 2-3. The list of files also contains
indicators for your system's disk drives, for any directories within the
current directory, and for the parent directory—the directory one
level up from the current directory. You can navigate subdirectories
from within an Open dialog box by double-clicking these special
indicators until you reach the desired directory.

FIGURE 2-3.

Open dialog box.

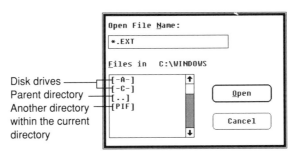

To try this for yourself, be sure the WINDOWS directory is the
current directory (switch to it if necessary) and then start Notepad.
You're going to create a short text file and bury it in the PIF subdirectory. Type a few choice words and then choose Save from the File
menu. When the Save dialog box appears, type *pif\test* and press Enter.

Switch back to the MS-DOS Executive window and move to the PIF subdirectory to verify that the file is there. Then switch back to the Notepad window and choose Open from the File menu.

When the Open dialog box appears, it lists any files in the WINDOWS directory that end with the *TXT* extension. You have two alternatives for opening TEST.TXT. You could simply type its pathname—*pif\test.txt*—in the text box. Or, you could maneuver to the PIF directory by using the list box. Try the latter route. Double-click on the entry *[PIF]* in the list box (you may have to scroll to see it). The list box changes to reflect the PIF subdirectory's contents, as shown in Figure 2-4.

You can see *TEST.TXT*, but don't open it yet. Instead, double-click the parent directory symbol—the double periods enclosed in brackets (*[..]*). You move up one "branch" in the directory tree, to WINDOWS. Now go back to the PIF directory and double-click on *TEST.TXT*.

You can use a different technique to obtain the same result. Choose Open again and then double-click on *[..]* to move up to the WINDOWS directory. Now select the text in the Open File Name text box by dragging across it. You can also select it from the keyboard by pressing Shift+Tab. Then type *pif* and press Enter. Look in the list box and at the pathname display above it. You can see that you moved down into the PIF directory. Select the text in the Open File Name text box once more and then type *\windows* and press Enter. This time, you move back up to WINDOWS. The rule is: When you specify a partial pathname in an Open dialog box, the dialog box shows the contents of the directory specified by the pathname.

Incidentally, you don't *have* to double-click the drive and directory indicators. You can use the keyboard to switch drives and directories by moving the highlight to the desired drive or directory symbol and then pressing Enter. You can also use a mouse-and-keyboard combination: Click once on a drive or directory symbol, then press Enter.

FIGURE 2-4.

Open dialog box after changing to the PIF subdirectory.

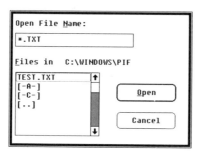

TIP 5: Selecting More than One Filename

As an experienced Windows user, you know how to select one filename at a time in the MS-DOS Executive window. (Using the mouse, you click on it; using the keyboard, you use the direction keys to move to it.) But you can also select more than one filename at a time by using one of two techniques: by extending the selection or by making a discontinuous selection. Extending the selection means adding to the selection filenames that are immediately above or below those already selected, as shown in Figure 2-5. Making a discontinuous selection refers to selecting additional filenames that are not adjacent to the ones already selected, as shown in Figure 2-6 on the next page. These techniques are helpful when you want to perform a Copy, Delete, or Get Info operation on a number of files.

Using the mouse, you extend the selection and make a discontinuous selection in exactly the same way: by Shift-clicking. To Shift-click, hold down the Shift key while you click on each additional filename you want to select.

To extend the selection with the keyboard, hold down the Shift key while you press a direction key. To make a discontinuous selection with the keyboard, hold down the Control key while you press a direction key. When you arrive at the next filename you want to select, press the Spacebar while you continue to hold down the Control key.

FIGURE 2-5.

An extended selection in the MS-DOS Executive window.

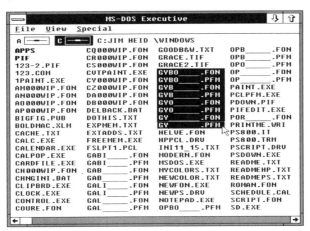

FIGURE 2-6.

A discontinuous
selection in the
MS-DOS
Executive
Window.

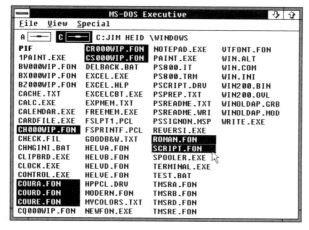

TIP 6: Running More than One MS-DOS Executive Window

Windows' ability to run more than one instance of the same application applies to MS-DOS Executive as well. By running MS-DOS Executive in more than one window, you can view the contents of two different disks or directories simultaneously. With one MS-DOS Executive window active, double-click on either *MS-DOS.EXE* or *WIN.COM*; the results are the same for either action. In a few moments, a second MS-DOS Executive window appears, as shown in Figure 2-7.

You can use this second MS-DOS Executive window exactly as you use the first—to start applications or manage disks and files. It's most useful, however, for viewing a different disk or directory. Resize and reposition both MS-DOS Executive windows so that they appear side by side and then switch to a different directory, as shown in Figure 2-8 on the following page.

The ability to view the contents of two (or more) different disks or directories simultaneously is a godsend when you're in the throes of a complex file-copying operation and you want to see where the files are and where they're going. (To see the effects of a copy operation, however, you must tell MS-DOS Executive to update its directory display. To do so with a mouse, simply click on the current drive icon.

FIGURE 2-7.

A second
MS-DOS
Executive
window.

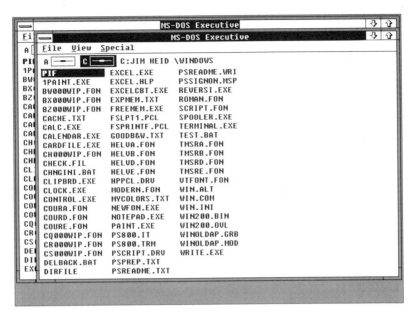

FIGURE 2-8.

Viewing two
directories
simultaneously.

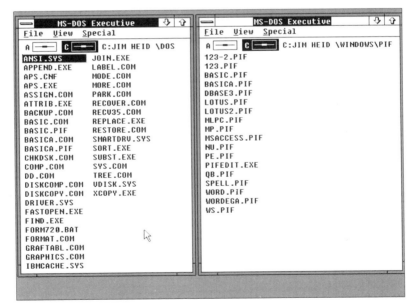

With the keyboard, press Ctrl along with the drive letter.) Viewing multiple directories is also useful for determining which of two files located in different directories is the most current. You can switch to the long view of each directory (choose Long from the View menu) and compare modification dates or select each file and choose the Get Info command.

Each instance of MS-DOS Executive uses 6 KB to 8 KB of memory, which is a small but not insignificant amount. When you're done with an instance, close it to reclaim its memory. Remember that if you attempt to close the last remaining instance of MS-DOS Executive, Windows displays the message *This will end your Windows session.*

TIP 7: Using the Copy Command

Between letting you use wildcards and letting you select multiple files, MS-DOS Executive provides enough copying options for any file-management chore. But two more copying concepts need to be examined. You can use the Copy command in different ways, depending on your location in the directory tree. Referring to Figure 2-9, assume you're copying a file named *LETTER* from the \WINDOWS\WINAPPS directory to \WORK\WRITE. Figure 2-10 shows how to do so from various locations in the directory tree.

The second copying option concerns copying all files in a directory. You can do so in two ways: by changing to that directory and using the *.* wildcards or by simply selecting the directory name. Figure 2-11 on the page after next illustrates both options.

FIGURE 2-9.

Location of the source and destination directories within the directory tree.

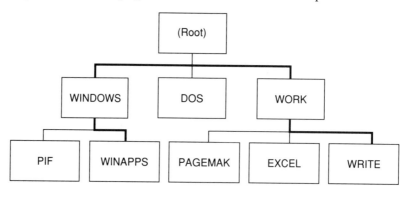

FIGURE 2-10.

Copying a file from various locations. (A) From within \WINDOWS-\WINAPPS, where LETTER was selected using MS-DOS Executive. (B) From within \WORK\WRITE. (C) From within \WINDOWS. (D) From the root directory (\).

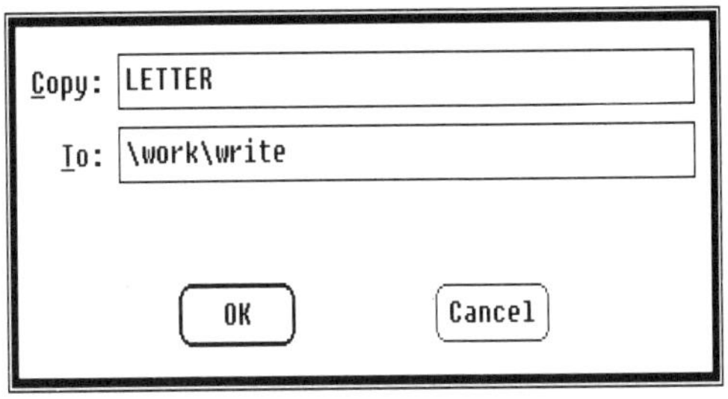

Copy: LETTER
To: \work\write

OK   Cancel

(A)

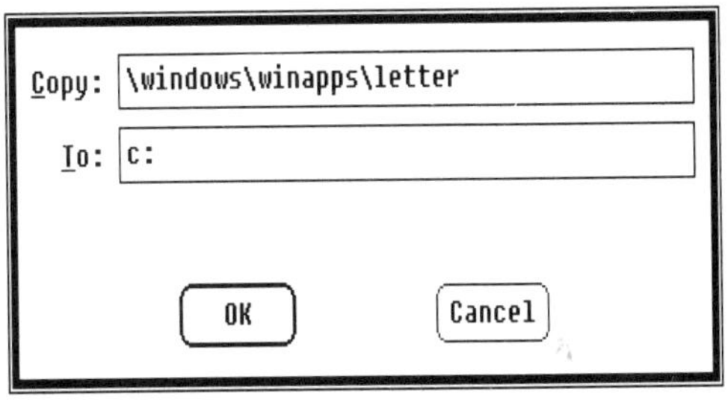

Copy: \windows\winapps\letter
To: c:

OK   Cancel

(B)

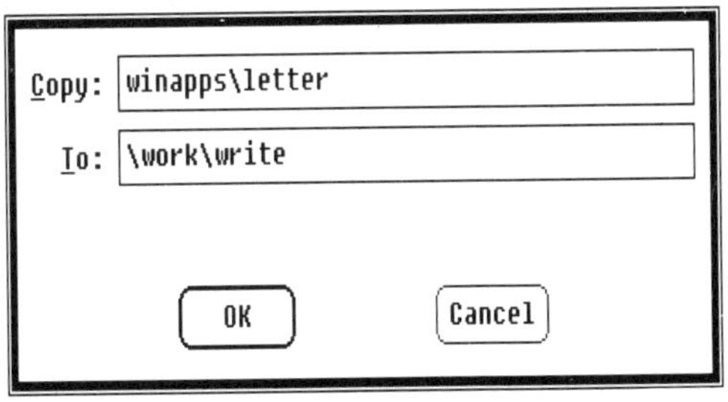

Copy: winapps\letter
To: \work\write

OK   Cancel

(C)

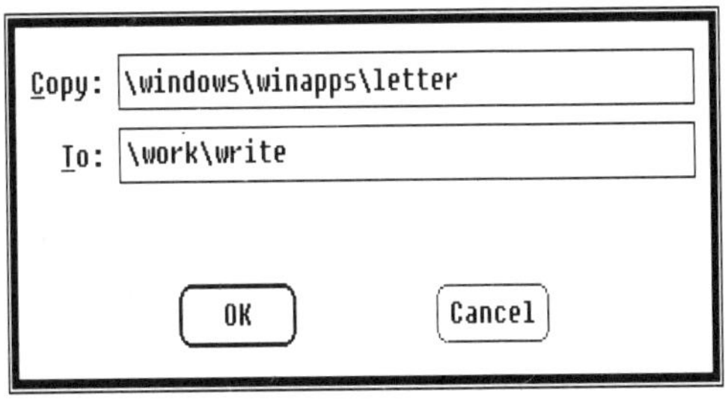

Copy: \windows\winapps\letter
To: \work\write

OK   Cancel

(D)

FIGURE 2-11.

Two ways to copy all files in a directory.

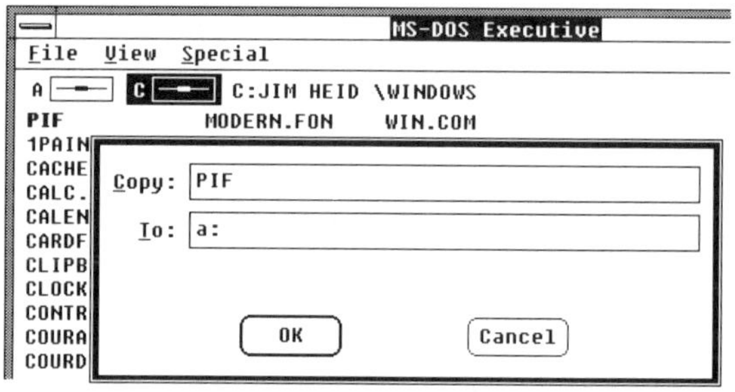

```
 ┌─┐                                MS-DOS Executive ├──┐
 │ │                              ──────────────────────┤
 └─┘                                                    
 File  View  Special                                    
 ┌────────────────────────────────────────────────────┐
 A │──│ C │══│ C:JIM HEID \WINDOWS                      
 PIF          MODERN.FON     WIN.COM                     
 1PAIN┌──────────────────────────────────────────────┐
 CACHE│                                                │
 CALC.│  Copy: │PIF                                  │ │
 CALEN│                                                │
 CARDF│    To: │a:                                   │ │
 CLIPB│                                                │
 CLOCK│                                                │
 CONTR│          ┌──────────┐      ┌──────────┐        │
 COURA│          │    OK    │      │  Cancel  │        │
 COURD│          └──────────┘      └──────────┘        │
      └──────────────────────────────────────────────┘
```

(A)

```
 ┌─┐                                MS-DOS Executive ├──┐
 │ │                              ──────────────────────┤
 └─┘                                                    
 File  View  Special                                    
 ┌────────────────────────────────────────────────────┐
 A │──│ C │══│ C:JIM HEID \WINDOWS\PIF                  
 123-2.PIF                                              
 123.P┌───────────────────────────────────────────────┐
 BASIC│                                                 │
 BASIC│  Copy: │*.*                                  │  │
 DBASE│                                                 │
 LOTUS│    To: │a:                                   │  │
 LOTUS│                                                 │
 MLPC.│                                                 │
 MP.PI│          ┌──────────┐      ┌──────────┐         │
 MSACC│          │    OK    │      │  Cancel  │         │
 NU.PI│          └──────────┘      └──────────┘         │
      └───────────────────────────────────────────────┘
```

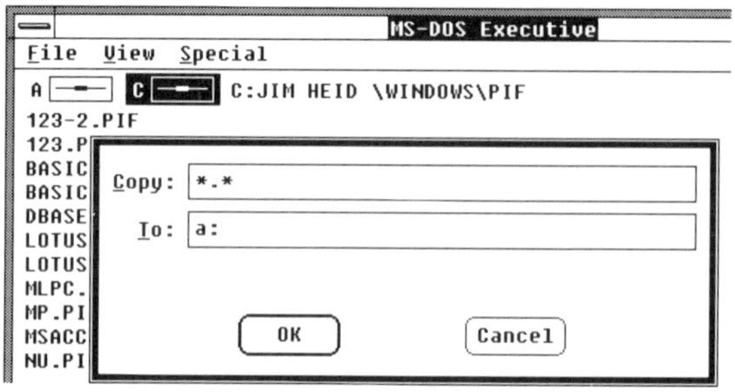

(B)

TIP 8: Accessing a File with the Keyboard by Typing Its First Character

You probably already know that you can highlight a file in MS-DOS Executive by typing its first character. You can use this MS-DOS Executive feature to quickly open a frequently used document by renaming the document and adding a number between 1 and 9 to the beginning of its name. (Of course, the file's original name must be less than eight characters long.) For example, if you often open a Microsoft Excel document named BIZPLAN.XLS, rename it by adding a number to the beginning of its name, as in 1BIZPLAN.XLS. After renaming the file, you can open it by typing the number *1* and pressing Enter.

This technique allows you two-keystroke access to applications, too. For example, if you frequently use Write and Paint, rename them, adding a unique number to each of their names, as in 4WRITE.EXE and 5PAINT.EXE. But there's a catch: The [extensions] section of Windows' WIN.INI configuration file expects an application's name to be in a specific form and uses that name to start an application when you choose one of its documents. If you rename an application and then attempt to run it by choosing one of its documents, Windows isn't able to find the application and displays an error message stating that it can't run the document you chose. The solution is to edit the [extensions] section of WIN.INI and update the application's filename. (Chapter 8 contains more information on the [extensions] section of WIN.INI.)

KEYBOARD OR MOUSE?

W indows offers you a choice of using the keyboard or mouse for any task. In this chapter, you'll learn guidelines for deciding whether the keyboard, the mouse, or a combination of both is most efficient for a particular task. The tips presented in this chapter reflect my preferences. As an experienced Windows user, you probably have your own. You might prefer to keep your hands glued to the keyboard, or you might prefer to run your mouse ragged. Nonetheless, try the tips presented in this chapter; you might find some that feel more comfortable than your current ways of working.

Keyboard Basics

The keyboard is best for choosing commands when you are engaged in a typing-intensive application, when you want to switch from one application to another, or when you are moving the cursor short distances.

Choosing Commands with the Keyboard

Windows lets you choose any menu command or any dialog box option by using the keyboard (although only a masochist or a rabid mouse-hater would attempt to do so).

To choose any command with the keyboard, you can use one of two methods: the Alt key and direction keys or the Alt key and a direct-access key. (Some commands offer a third method: shortcut keys, also called accelerator keys.)

The Alt and direction key method is the slowest, but the most mistake-proof. So, it is the method best suited to inexperienced Windows users.

1. Press and release the Alt key to tell Windows that you want to choose a command. Windows highlights the application's leftmost menu, which is the File menu in most applications. If the command you want isn't on the leftmost menu, press the Left or Right direction key until the menu you want is highlighted. If you overshoot the menu, use the Left direction key to move back to the menu you want.

2. Press the Down direction key to display a menu. To display a different menu, press the Left or Right direction key.

3. Press the Down direction key to move the highlight down the list of commands to the command you want. If you overshoot the command, use the Up direction key to move back to the command you want.

4. When the command is highlighted, press the Enter key.

A faster way to choose a command is by using the direct-access method. The direct-access key is the letter key that corresponds to the letter that's underlined in the menu or command name on the screen. This method for choosing a menu command is a three-step process:

1. Press and release Alt to tell Windows you want to choose a command. Windows highlights the application's leftmost menu, which is the File menu in most applications.

2. Press the desired menu's direct-access key to open the menu. If you press the wrong direct-access key and open the wrong menu, you can press Esc and start over or you can use the Left or Right direction key to move to the correct menu.

3. Press the desired command's direct-access key.

Let's use the Save command as an example. You're busily typing in Windows Write and wisely decide to commit your efforts to disk. Don't touch that mouse—press Alt, and then F, and then S instead. Alt and F summon the File menu; then S chooses the Save command. If you've never saved the document, a dialog box appears asking for a filename. Type one and press Enter.

The fastest way to choose a command is to use its shortcut key, provided that it has one. Using a shortcut key usually involves pressing a modifier key (Shift, Ctrl, or Alt) along with a second key. For example, the shortcut-key sequence for the Control menu's Minimize command is Alt+F9. In all applications written for Windows 2.0, the shortcut-key sequence for the Edit menu's Cut command is Shift+Del.

Because an application's developers decide which commands (if any) have shortcut keys, the specific key sequences often vary between applications. Fortunately, it's easy to determine the shortcut keys a program provides by simply pulling down its menus. Shortcut keys are listed to the right of their respective commands.

Selecting Dialog Box Options with the Keyboard

You can also use Windows 2.0's direct-access keys to choose options in a dialog box with the keyboard. To move to a set of options, press Alt along with the direct-access key for the option. If you've used Windows 1.0, you're familiar with using the Tab key to move from one set of dialog box options to the next. You can still use Tab to move between options, but it's obviously slower than using direct-access keys. Figure 3-1 shows the Communications Settings dialog box for Windows' Terminal. In Windows 1.0, changing the Handshake setting meant pressing Tab four times and then using the Left or Right direction key to choose the new setting. In Windows 2.0, pressing Alt+H immediately moves the highlight to the currently selected button within the list of Handshake option buttons.

To change an option, use the direction keys to move the selection to another button.

Clearly, a mouse remains the best way to tame a dialog box filled with options. With a mouse, you simply point to the desired option button and click.

FIGURE 3-1.

*Communications
Settings dialog
box.*

Direct access keys ——

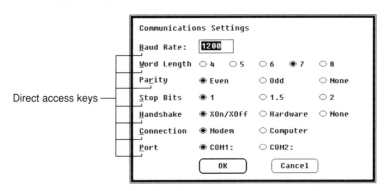

Moving Between Applications with the Keyboard

To switch between applications with the keyboard press Alt+Esc or Alt+Tab. Press Alt+Esc to activate the next open application.

Windows selects application windows or icons in the order you started them. You can also select them in the reverse order by pressing Alt+Shift+Esc. Unlike choosing a menu command, moving between windows requires you to hold down Alt while pressing Tab or Esc.

If you've used Windows 1.0, you're familiar with using Alt+Tab to switch between applications. This key combination still works in Windows 2.0, but it doesn't work the same as it did in Windows 1.0. When you use Alt+Tab to select an icon, the icon is restored to its previous size and position as soon as you release the Alt key. (If you started an application as an icon, it doesn't have a "previous" size or position. In this case, it assumes the size that it would take if you started it normally.) When you use Alt+Esc to select an icon, the icon isn't restored; instead, the application's name simply appears below the icon. To restore the icon, you must open the application's Control menu and choose Restore.

You can preview all the open windows on your desktop by holding down Alt and repeatedly pressing Tab. Windows activates each open window in turn, but it doesn't redraw the entire window—that is, it doesn't display portions of a window that were obscured by other windows. But if you repeatedly press Alt+Esc (or if you press Alt+Esc and then continue holding down Alt while you repeatedly press Esc), Windows always redraws each window. Using Alt+Tab to thumb through open windows can save a great deal of time if you work with graphics or desktop-publishing programs that take several seconds to redraw a complex image.

Mouse Basics

The mouse is best for drawing, for moving or resizing a window or other object, for minimizing and maximizing windows, for choosing commands when engaged in a mouse-intensive application, or for positioning a highlight or cursor at a specific location.

We've been hammering at the keyboard almost exclusively so far. Is a mouse really such a minor player in Windows? Hardly. Two of its specialties are resizing windows or spreadsheet columns and choosing options in a large dialog box. Another is moving windows: Clicking and dragging a window is easier than choosing Move from its Control menu, tapping direction keys, and then pressing Enter. And the most obvious place for mouse supremacy is in a desktop-publishing or graphics program. Drawing with the keyboard in Microsoft Windows Paint or Micrografx Designer requires the patience and dexterity of a brain surgeon. Aldus PageMaker makes no pretense of being keyboard controllable; you can choose PageMaker commands and dialog box options with the keyboard, but you can't position text and graphics or work with ruler guides.

Writers often debate the value of a mouse in a word-processing program, such as Microsoft Windows Write. Those in the keyboard camp claim it's distracting to leave the keyboard to move the cursor, while those in the mouse's corner say the mouse is best for quickly scrolling or repositioning the insertion point. Both groups are correct. The keyboard's direction keys are best for moving the cursor during the writing phase, when you generally need to move only a few words or lines away to rework a phrase. The mouse, however, excels during the editing phase, when you're jumping about in a document and need to quickly select text and move the cursor over large distances.

TIP 1: Typing While Windows Is Working

When you type while Windows is performing another task (such as opening an application), your keystrokes are stored in the event queue discussed in Chapter 1. As soon as an application opens, it checks the event queue for messages, finds your keystrokes waiting, and interprets them. If you type the proper keystrokes while the application loads, your command is executed at the soonest possible instant.

To try it yourself, open Write from the MS-DOS Executive window. While it's loading, press Alt, C, and then F—the direct-access key sequence for the Fonts dialog box. As soon as Write opens, it interprets your keystrokes and displays the dialog box, ready for you to choose a font for the new document. To try another example, quit Write: Press Esc to cancel the Fonts dialog box and then press Alt, F, and then X to exit. Now start Write again and, while it's loading, press Alt, D, and then R—the key sequence for the Document menu's Ruler On command.

This technique is especially useful for PageMaker users. Press Alt, F, and then N while PageMaker is loading to issue the New command and summon the Page Setup dialog box, or press Alt, F, and then T to choose the Target Printer command. Or if you're opening the Notepad desktop application to edit a file that has an extension other than TXT, press Alt, F, and then O while Notepad is loading; then type the filename. (Remember to type the full pathname if you're editing a file in a different directory, such as AUTOEXEC.BAT or CONFIG.SYS.)

TIP 2: Clicking While Windows Is Working

Windows also stores mouse clicks in its event queue. But it's a bit difficult to guess where an application's commands and menus will appear on the screen. Still, clicking ahead of Windows has some value— if you know where to click. If, for example, an application window is open and covering the MS-DOS Executive window, you can close the application and end your Windows session by double-clicking the application's Control-menu icon twice. The first double-click closes the application (which asks you to save changes, if necessary), and the second double-click brings up the MS-DOS Executive message *This will end your Windows session.* From there, a quick tap on the Spacebar takes you to the MS-DOS prompt.

TIP 3: Using the Mouse to Resize and Move Windows

If you have a mouse, use it for resizing and moving windows. These tasks require too much direction key tapping to be efficiently performed from the keyboard. You can maximize a window in two ways: by clicking its Maximize box, or by double-clicking within its title bar. When you double-click within the title bar of a window that's already maximized, the window is restored to its previous position.

TIP 4: Using the Keyboard to Maximize, Minimize, and Close Windows

The keyboard is effective for minimizing and maximizing windows, for restoring them to their previous size, and for closing them. Every Windows application has a Control menu, the icon of which appears in the upper left corner of the application's window. (If you run a standard application in a window, it also has a Control menu.) The

Control menu is the gateway to manipulating windows—resizing them, zooming (or maximizing) them to fill the screen, shrinking (or minimizing) them into icons, and closing them.

If the function keys on your keyboard are arranged in two vertical rows on the left side, you can minimize or maximize a window in a flash by pressing Alt with your index finger and F9 or F10 with your little finger and ring finger, respectively. On a keyboard with the function keys arranged horizontally across the top, however, you may find it more convenient to use the direct-access key sequence: Alt, space, and then N to minimize or Alt, space, and then M to maximize.

Incidentally, the Maximize and Minimize commands toggle back and forth. For example, choosing the Maximize command fills the screen when the window is smaller and restores the window to its previous size if it *is* maximized. The Minimize command toggles in a different way, switching between an icon and the previous size of the application's window. As mentioned earlier, if you started the application as an icon, the icon has no previous size. In this case, choosing Minimize causes the icon to assume the size it would take if you started it normally.

To quit an application and save changes to an already named document, use the direct-access key sequence for the Close command: Alt, space, C, and then space. That final tap of the Spacebar performs the job of answering "Yes" to the application's Save Changes dialog box. If you haven't saved the document, a dialog box asking for a filename appears after you press the Spacebar for the second time. Type one and then press Enter.

Issuing this sequence from the MS-DOS Executive window also gets you out of Windows in a flash. The second press of the Spacebar chooses OK to the message *This will end your Windows session.* And if any named, but unsaved, documents are open in other applications, you can continue to press the Spacebar to save them. Or you can press N to discard your changes.

TIP 5: Using the Alt Key

If your keyboard is an IBM enhanced 101-key keyboard or is designed like one—it has an Alt key on either side of its Spacebar—you can use both hands to choose commands even more quickly than you can with one hand. For example, to save a document, press the right Alt key with your right hand and tap F and S with your left. Or, press the left Alt key with your little finger and press F and S with your index finger and ring finger, respectively. You can use the F10 key instead of Alt, although Alt is more convenient, since it's closer to the keys you'll press next.

TIP 6: Combining the Keyboard and the Mouse to Choose Commands

Two input devices are better than one. The improved menu interface in Windows 2.0 lets the keyboard and mouse team up to choose commands. The trick is to use the mouse to open a menu and then press the desired command's direct-access key. For example, to choose the Change command in Write, click on the Search menu's title in the menu bar and then press the C key. To change fonts, click on the Character menu and then press F. In any application with a Save command in its File menu, click the File menu and then press S to save a document.

This technique works because a Windows 2.0 menu remains open after you click its title. Once a menu is open, you can use a direct-access key to choose a command within it. By pressing a direct-access key immediately after clicking a menu title, you can issue commands in less time than it would take to move the mouse to the desired command. And this technique works equally well for left-handed or right-handed mousers.

For a variation on this theme, try using the Enter key to choose the first command in any menu. When you click on a menu, Windows not only opens the menu, it selects the first command. Then press Enter to choose the command. In most Windows applications, the first command in a menu is the one you're most likely to choose. That makes the Click-Enter sequence a useful tool in any application.

TIP 7: Combining the Keyboard and the Mouse in Other Ways

You can combine mouse and keyboard in many ways.

Fans of Reversi, the game that comes with Windows, can move to a square by pointing to it with the mouse and then pressing Enter.

To quit an application, double-click its Control-menu box and then press Y to save any changes or press N to discard them.

To end a Windows session, double-click the MS-DOS Executive's Control-menu box and then press the Spacebar. (As an alternative to double-clicking the Control-menu box, you can click on it once and press the C key.)

To quickly close an application that's running as an icon, click the icon and press C. If you want to close several icons, simply repeat this sequence, working your way across the icon area as if it were a shooting gallery. As Figure 3-2 shows, if any applications contain un-saved documents, the dialog boxes containing the message *Save current changes?* remain on screen as you close other icons. When you've fin-ished closing icons, respond to the queries as necessary.

Figure 3-2.

Closing multiple icons.

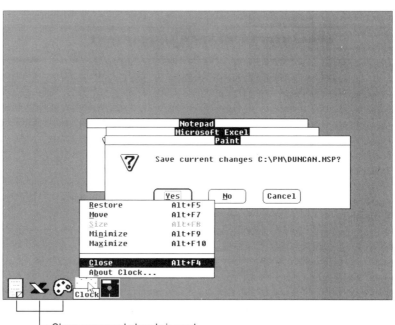

Close command already issued for these applications.

THE MS-DOS CONNECTION

Windows' MS-DOS Executive greatly simplifies disk and file management by eliminating the codes and ciphers of MS-DOS. But some tasks exceed the capabilities of MS-DOS Executive or can be performed only from the MS-DOS command prompt. By combining the power of the prompt with the elegance of Windows, you can have the best of both worlds. This chapter discusses the Windows/MS-DOS link.

Many computer neophytes have torn out their hair in frustration over the command-oriented operating style of MS-DOS, particularly when they get a series of messages that read *Bad command or file name*. But command-oriented operating systems have advantages, one of which is the batch file—a text file containing lists of commands. When you run a batch file, you force MS-DOS to execute each command in turn, as if each command were being typed from the keyboard. A batch file is a powerful tool for automating frequently performed tasks that require more than one MS-DOS command. In this chapter, we'll examine how to use batch files to start Windows in different ways and to automate repetitive tasks.

We'll also explore how to type MS-DOS commands directly within Windows by running COMMAND.COM, the MS-DOS command processor, in a window.

TIP 1: Using a Batch File to Start Windows

If you're not already using a batch file, you probably start Windows by typing the following:

```
cd \windows
win
```

By placing those commands in a batch file (a text file with the extension BAT), you can start Windows simply by typing the batch file's name. To try it, start Windows and then Notepad. (Because Notepad creates text files, it's an ideal tool for creating and editing batch files.) When Notepad's window appears, type the preceding commands, pressing Enter after each line. (If you use Windows/386, replace *win* with *win386*.) Then choose Save from the File menu, type *\w.bat*, and press Enter. Don't forget the backslash; it tells Notepad to save the file in your hard disk's root directory. The BAT extension tells MS-DOS that the file is a batch file. After you save the file, exit

Chapter 4: The MS-DOS Connection

Notepad and then Windows. When the MS-DOS prompt reappears, switch to the root directory by typing *cd* \ and pressing Enter.

Now try the batch file. Type *w* and press Enter. The commands you typed appear on the screen as MS-DOS executes them and starts Windows. From now on, you can start Windows in a flash simply by typing *w* and pressing Enter.

TIP 2: Adding a Replaceable Parameter to a Batch File

You may recall from Chapter 2 that you can start Windows and an application by typing the application's name after typing *win*. By adding two special codes to the W.BAT batch file discussed in Tip 1 of this chapter, you can retain that capability. Start Notepad and open W.BAT. (The fastest way to open the file is to choose Notepad's Open command with the keyboard by pressing Alt, and then F, and then O. Then type *w.bat* and press Enter.) When the file opens, position the blinking cursor after the *n* in *win*, type a space followed by *%1*, another space, and then *%2*. Your screen now looks like the one in Figure 4-1. Verify that it does, save the file, and exit from both Notepad and Windows.

When the MS-DOS prompt reappears, switch back to the root directory (type *cd* \ and press Enter) and then type *w write practice* and press Enter. The batch file adds the text *write practice* to the *win* command, as if you had typed *win write practice*. The secret behind this trick is a batch-file concept called the replaceable parameter. In essence, the %1 and %2 codes are placeholders; each represents a potential parameter. When you type a space followed by additional text after the batch file's name, MS-DOS replaces the codes with what you typed. If you don't supply two parameters—if, for example, you simply type *w write*—MS-DOS ignores the second placeholder. And remember that the first parameter can be the name of a Windows application or that of a standard application, such as Microsoft Word.

FIGURE 4-1.

Modified W.BAT file.

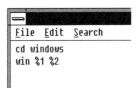

TIP 3: Using the MS-DOS Path Command

Because some of the batch-file examples in the rest of this chapter rely on the MS-DOS command Path, let's take a brief look at it. (Readers familiar with the Path command can skip to the next tip.) The Path command creates a search path that MS-DOS uses to look for programs and batch files that it doesn't find in the current directory. To create a search path, you type a Path command at the MS-DOS prompt, as in:

```
C>path c:\;c:\windows;c:\dos;c:\windows\winapps
```

The semicolon (;) acts as a separator between directory paths. This example tells MS-DOS, "If you don't find a program in the current directory, look for it in the root directory of drive C, in C:\WINDOWS, in C:\DOS, and then in C:\WINDOWS\WINAPPS." If it doesn't find the program in any of the directories named in the Path command, MS-DOS displays the message *Bad command or file name*. MS-DOS doesn't require that you type a drive specifier before each Path entry, but including one eliminates any ambiguity. Avoiding ambiguity is especially important if you use a network, RAM disk, or a partitioned hard disk. In such cases, you might use applications stored on numerous logical drives. Including drive specifiers in your Path command lets MS-DOS and Windows find them.

Two scenarios should clarify this process. Scenario One: You issued the Path command just described and switched to the C:\DOS subdirectory to view a directory listing. Having done that, you start Windows. While still within the C:\DOS directory, you type *win* and press Enter. MS-DOS first looks in the current directory (C:\DOS) for the file. After striking out there, it follows the path you supplied, looking first in the root directory of drive C and then in C:\WINDOWS, where it finds and runs WIN.COM. Question: When the MS-DOS Executive window appears, which directory is listed as the current one? Answer: The C:\DOS directory. Why? Because C:\DOS was the current directory when you typed *win*, and neither you nor the search path did anything to change that.

Scenario Two: You store your Windows applications, including Microsoft Excel, in the directory C:\WINDOWS\WINAPPS. You're in a different directory—say C:\123, which wasn't named in the Path command—and you want to start Windows and Microsoft Excel. You type *win excel* and press Enter. MS-DOS first checks the current directory for

WIN. Failing to find it, it starts traversing the search path, first checking the root directory of drive C and then C:\WINDOWS, where it finds
and runs WIN.COM, thereby starting Windows. Windows checks to see
if you added a parameter to the Windows start-up command. Finding
one (*excel*), it looks for EXCEL, first in the current directory. Using the
search path, it searches in order the root directory of drive C,
C:\WINDOWS, C:\DOS, and C:\WINDOWS\WINAPPS, where it finally
finds and runs EXCEL.EXE.

These scenarios illustrate the benefit of the Path command: It
lets you start a program located in a directory other than the current
one. As the second scenario shows, a search path is especially useful
for those times when you want to start Windows and an application.
WIN.COM and the application you're starting can each be in its
own directory, as long as both directories are named in the Path
command.

If Windows doesn't find EXCEL.EXE in one of the directories,
it displays a message instructing you to insert a disk containing
EXCEL.EXE in drive A. If that happens, simply click Cancel or press
Esc to make the MS-DOS Executive window reappear. From there, you
can change to the directory containing Microsoft Excel and start it
"by hand."

TIP 4: Using an AUTOEXEC.BAT File

The Path command may be useful, but typing a long list of file directories every time you start your computer may not be your idea of a
good time. Fortunately, you don't have to. You can place a Path command in a batch file so that you can issue it by simply typing the batch
file's name. Better still, place the command in a batch file named
AUTOEXEC.BAT. When MS-DOS starts, it looks for a file by that name
in the root directory; if it finds one, it executes the commands it finds
there, in order.

If you already use an AUTOEXEC.BAT file, you can add a Path
command to it. If you don't have an AUTOEXEC.BAT file, you can
create one in Notepad.

To use Windows to find out whether you already have an
AUTOEXEC.BAT file, be sure the MS-DOS Executive window is active
and then press the Backspace key until the root directory is displayed.
If you have an AUTOEXEC.BAT file, its name appears in the list of files,
shortly after the last directory name.

To create or add to your AUTOEXEC.BAT file, start Notepad and type the commands in Figure 4-2, pressing Enter at the end of each line. If your computer contains a battery-operated clock/calendar (as do IBM's PS/2 machines), you can omit the Time and Date commands. If you already use an AUTOEXEC.BAT file, open it. Then add the Path command in Figure 4-2 to the end of the file. If your AUTOEXEC.BAT file already contains a Path command (some applications place one there when you install them), simply add the text \;C:\WINDOWS to the end of the statement. (Be sure you include the semicolon and the backslashes.)

FIGURE 4-2.

An AUTOEXEC.BAT file.

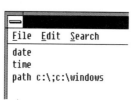

```
 File  Edit  Search
date
time
path c:\;c:\windows
```

After you complete the new file or modify the existing one, save it. Then exit both Notepad and Windows. When the MS-DOS prompt appears, restart your computer by pressing Ctrl+Alt+Del. In a few moments, you see the commands in the AUTOEXEC.BAT file appear. After they've finished executing, type *path* and press Enter. This illustrates another use of the Path command. When you type it by itself (with no directory names), MS-DOS displays the current search paths. If none exist, MS-DOS reports "No path."

However, you see a list of paths, with the \WINDOWS directory among them. Type *win* and press Enter. Windows starts, and the MS-DOS Executive window shows that the root directory is the current directory. Thanks to the Path command, you can start Windows from the root directory from now on. Of course, you can still start it from within \WINDOWS too. Or you can use the W.BAT batch file presented in Tip 1 of this chapter. If you always start Windows after booting up, add the commands from W.BAT to the end of your AUTOEXEC.BAT file. From then on, Windows will start when you start your system. (To exit a batch file before MS-DOS has executed all its commands, press and hold Ctrl+C while the batch file is executing and then type *y* when MS-DOS asks, *Terminate batch job?*)

TIP 5: Using a Batch File to Start Microsoft Excel

When you use the Path command, you open the doors to other useful batch files, such as the one shown in Figure 4-3. When executed from the MS-DOS prompt, this batch file, which I call WXL.BAT, changes to a subdirectory named C:\EXCELDAT (where, let's assume, you store your Microsoft Excel documents) and then starts both Windows and Microsoft Excel. If you type a document name after *wxl*, MS-DOS passes it along, causing Microsoft Excel to open the document.

FIGURE 4-3.

WXL.BAT file.

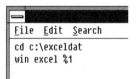

```
File  Edit  Search
cd c:\exceldat
win excel %1
```

TIP 6: Creating a Home for Batch Files

Batch files are so useful that you're likely to create many of them. Instead of allowing them to clutter your root directory, create a directory named BATCH and store them there. Then add a reference to the BATCH directory to your Path command, as in *c:\batch*.

To create the batch-file directory using MS-DOS Executive, choose Create Directory from the Special menu and then type *\batch* and press Enter. Next, switch to your root directory if necessary, and copy the batch files by choosing Copy from the File menu and typing *∗.bat* in the Copy text box and *batch* in the To text box. Finally, delete all the batch files from the root directory *except* AUTOEXEC.BAT, which must reside in the root directory. (The asterisk is a wildcard character that stands for any number of any legal characters, in any combination. Using the asterisk for the filename also copied AUTOEXEC.BAT to the C:\BATCH subdirectory. If you don't want the extra copy of AUTOEXEC.BAT, switch to C:\BATCH and delete the copy there.)

TIP 7: Running a Batch File Within Windows

Batch files are versatile tools for starting Windows in various ways, but that isn't their only use. You can also run a batch file within Windows by using the same techniques you use to start an application.

One batch file I often run within Windows appears in Figure 4-4. This file supplies the arguments that the MS-DOS Format utility needs to format a 720 KB 3½-inch disk. When you run Windows on an IBM PS/2 (except Model 30), the Format Data Disk command on the Special menu in MS-DOS Executive creates a 1.4 MB data disk. To create a 720 KB data disk—a disk in the format that lets you exchange data with laptop computers equipped with 720 KB floppy drives—you must delve into the MS-DOS manual to obtain the needed switches for the Format utility. To avoid having to memorize and type *format a: /n:9 /t:80* each time I want a 720 KB disk, I created the one-line batch file shown in Figure 4-4 and named it FORM720.BAT.

FIGURE 4-4.

FORM720.BAT batch file.

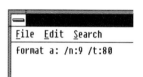

To use this batch file, you must also create a Program Information File (PIF) for the Format utility. Use the Windows PIFEDIT application (in the WINDOWS subdirectory) to create the file, giving it the parameters shown in Figure 4-5. Save the PIF as FORMAT.PIF within the PIF subdirectory. (PIFs and PIFEDIT are discussed in detail in Chapter 9.) To create a 720 KB data disk, simply double-click on the batch file's name when you are ready to format a 720 KB disk.

FIGURE 4-5.

PIF entries for the MS-DOS Format utility.

Program Information Editor	⇩ ⇧
File	F1=Help

Program Name: FORMAT.COM

Program Title: Format

Program Parameters:

Initial Directory: \DOS

Memory Requirements: KB Required 52   KB Desired 52

Directly Modifies   ☒ Screen   ☐ COM1   ☐ Memory

☐ Keyboard   ☐ COM2

Program Switch   ⦿ Prevent   ○ Text   ○ Graphics/Multiple Text

Screen Exchange   ⦿ None   ○ Text   ○ Graphics/Text

Close Window on exit   ☒

TIP 8: ## Using a Batch File
to Switch Between Two WIN.INI Files

Figure 4-6 shows a batch file that lets you switch between two WIN.INI configuration files, one of which is named WIN.ALT. (*ALT* stands for alternate.) To create WIN.ALT, open WIN.INI using Notepad and make any desired changes. (One suggestion appears in the next paragraph.) Next, choose the Save As command from the File menu, type *win.alt*, and then press Enter. The batch file renames the current WIN.INI file TEMP, and then renames the alternate WIN.INI file (currently named WIN.ALT) WIN.INI. Finally, it renames the TEMP file WIN.ALT. Each time you execute the batch file, it toggles between the two filenames; WIN.ALT becomes WIN.INI and vice versa.

FIGURE 4-6.

A batch file for changing WIN.INI files.

```
File  Edit  Search
ren win.ini temp
ren win.alt win.ini
ren temp win.alt
```

You might want to switch between two WIN.INI files if you prefer different screen-color combinations for certain applications. For example, I used a combination of colors that simulates a black-and-white Windows installation when creating the figures for this book, but I prefer a color display for day-to-day Windows use. The batch file lets me switch between the two WIN.INI files in a flash. You'll find other reasons for using and switching between multiple WIN.INI files in Chapter 8.

One more note: You can run this batch file from within Windows, but you must leave and restart Windows to put the settings in either WIN.INI file into effect.

TIP 9: ## Running COMMAND.COM in a Window

When you run a batch file within Windows, Windows runs the MS-DOS command processor, COMMAND.COM. The command processor is the portion of MS-DOS that lets it interpret and respond to the commands you type at the MS-DOS prompt. Think of COMMAND.COM as a primitive version of MS-DOS Executive.

You can type MS-DOS commands directly within Windows by running COMMAND.COM. To do so, be sure the MS-DOS Executive window is active and then press Backspace until the root directory is the current one. Locate COMMAND.COM and run it. A new window opens, containing, of all things, an MS-DOS prompt, as shown in Figure 4-7. At this point, you can issue MS-DOS commands such as Directory (*dir*) and Copy, or you can run an application. In fact, because Windows is already running, you can type the name of a Windows application without receiving the MS-DOS message *This program requires Microsoft Windows.*

To quit COMMAND.COM and close its window, type *exit* at the prompt and then choose the Close command from the Control menu.

FIGURE 4-7.
COMMAND.COM
running in
Windows.

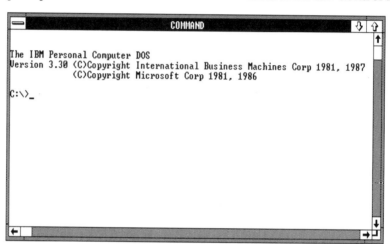

COMMAND.COM has talents MS-DOS Executive lacks. For instance, you can view the contents of *any* file by using the Type command. The Type command is most useful for viewing ASCII text files (such as WIN.INI and batch files), but you can also use it to view the contents of Microsoft Windows Write documents and even applications. Files that aren't pure ASCII, however, produce a lot of gibberish on the display and may even inspire your computer to beep a few times. Notepad is a better way to examine text files, because it lets you edit them and scroll through lengthy ones. But if COMMAND.COM's window is already open and you simply need a quick refresher as to what some mysteriously named batch file does, use the Type command.

By running COMMAND.COM within Windows, you can access MS-DOS' library of external commands and utilities without having to exit to the MS-DOS prompt. A few of the utilities you might use within Windows include the following ones.

Attrib. This utility modifies the file attributes that MS-DOS gives to a file. You can create a read-only file—one that's locked against modification—by typing *attrib +r filename*, substituting *filename* for the name of the file to be locked. To unlock the file, type *attrib −r filename*.

Xcopy. The Xcopy utility selectively copies groups of files and subdirectories. Xcopy provides versatile copying options that MS-DOS' and Windows' Copy commands lack. For instance, to copy all files in the root directory of drive C that were created on or after April 21, 1988 to a disk in drive A, type *xcopy c:\ a:\ /d:04-21-88*. To copy the files in your Windows directory as well as in the subdirectories beneath it to a disk in drive A, type *xcopy c:\windows a: /s*. To specify that MS-DOS prompts you before copying each file, add the parameter */p* to the end of the Xcopy command.

Recover. This utility salvages a file or disk containing defective sectors. For example, if you consistently receive a system error while trying to open a file, that file may contain defective sectors. To recover all the undamaged data in the file, type *recover filename*, where *filename* is the name of the file you want to recover. The Recover utility stores the salvaged data in a file named REC*nnnn*.REC, where *nnnn* is a number starting with 0001.

Backup. Use the Backup utility for making backup copies of the files on your hard disk.

Restore. Use the Restore utility for restoring the backed-up files to the hard disk.

Remember that these utilities must be on your hard disk and accessible to MS-DOS. (In other words, they must either be in the current directory or pointed to by your Path command.) And don't forget that you can access these utilities through batch files, using replaceable parameters to supply their arguments. For complete descriptions of these utilities and more examples of their use, refer to your MS-DOS manual or to *Running MS-DOS* by Van Wolverton (Microsoft Press).

Using Redirection and
Piping in a COMMAND.COM Window

Running COMMAND.COM within Windows also gives you access to the redirection capabilities of MS-DOS. Redirection lets you temporarily erect detour signs for MS-DOS, telling it to accept input from a source other than the keyboard or to route output to a destination other than the screen. For example, start COMMAND.COM if you haven't already, and then type *dir > dirfile* and press Enter. Your disk drive activates briefly, and then the MS-DOS prompt reappears. When it does, type *type dirfile* and press Enter. A directory listing scrolls onto the screen. You redirected the output of the DIR command to a file named DIRFILE. If you have a printer attached to your system, switch it on. When it's warmed up and ready, type *type dirfile > prn* and press Enter. A directory listing rolls out of your printer. This time, you redirected the output of the TYPE command to the printer.

A variation on redirection is piping, which involves establishing pipes, or connections, between two programs. If you want to see how it works, be sure the MS-DOS utilities MORE.COM and SORT.COM are on your hard disk and are accessible from the current directory (that is, they are in the current directory or in a directory named in the Path command). Then type *type \windows\win.ini ¦ sort ¦ more* and press Enter. The contents of your WIN.INI file appear on your screen, sorted in ASCII alphabetical order. Every 24 lines, the text —*More*— appears, and the display pauses until you press any character key. (You may see a screenful of blank lines first, since the Sort utility places blank lines before any lines containing text.)

In this example, you established pipes between the Type command and the SORT.COM and MORE.COM utilities. MS-DOS channelled the output of the Type command to Sort, which sorted it and then routed its output to More, which displayed it in 24-line chunks. (Don't worry, your WIN.INI file wasn't altered; MS-DOS sorted the *output* of the Type command, not the file itself.) SORT.COM and MORE.COM are called filters because they manipulate incoming characters, then channel the results to the screen—or to another filter.

MS-DOS includes another filter, FIND.COM, that does what its name implies—it searches incoming data for text you specify. When it finds the text in a given line, Find channels that line to the screen.

For example, to display a directory listing of all the subdirectories on your hard disk, switch to the root directory, and type *dir | find "<"* and press Enter. To locate all files modified on October 8, 1987, type *dir | find "10-08-87"* and press Enter. To view that list in alphabetical order, type *dir | find "10-08-87" | sort* and press Enter.

A more useful application of MS-DOS' redirection and filter features is this one-line batch file:

```
type %1 | find "%2" > %3
```

This file lets you search any file for a given text string and then saves any occurrences it finds in a new file. To create the batch file, use Notepad to type the commands and then save the file as SEARCH.BAT.

SEARCH.BAT uses replaceable parameters that act as placeholders for the three pieces of information the batch file needs: the name of the file you want to search, the text you're looking for, and the name of the file in which the found text will be stored. It also uses pipes to channel the output of the Type command into the Find filter, and redirection to route the output of the Find filter to a text file instead of to the screen.

To use the batch file, type at the COMMAND.COM prompt

```
search filename string output
```

For example, if you want to search a file named PROPOSAL.WRI for all references to someone named Eric and save those references in a file called ERIC.TXT, type

```
search proposal.wri Eric eric.txt
```

Note that the search text can't contain any spaces, and you must capitalize correctly in order for capitalized text to be found.

If you simply want to see the found references on screen instead of saving them to a file, type *con* instead of a filename. Doing so tells MS-DOS to route Find's output to the console—in other words, the screen. Remember that you can run this (or any other) batch file by using MS-DOS Executive's Run command. To do so, select the batch file, choose Run from the File menu, type the batch file's parameters (but not its name), and then press Enter. (Your MS-DOS manual contains more details on redirection and piping.)

TIP 10: **Copying Data**
from a COMMAND.COM Window

You can copy text that appears in COMMAND.COM's window by
selecting it and choosing Copy from the Control menu, as shown in
Figure 4-8.

FIGURE 4-8.

Copying text in the
COMMAND.COM
window.

TIP 11: **Pasting Data from the**
Clipboard into a COMMAND.COM Window

When the clipboard contains text, you can paste its contents into a
COMMAND.COM window. When you do, COMMAND.COM treats the
text as if it were coming from the keyboard. You can use this technique to reissue a command without having to retype it. Simply copy
the command by selecting it and choosing Copy, and then choose
Paste to insert it where you want it.

TIP 12: **Changing the Current Directory in a COMMAND.COM Window**

When you use the Change Directory (CHDIR or CD) command to change the current directory, the MS-DOS Executive window doesn't reflect the change. You must use the MS-DOS Executive's Change Directory command or the mouse shortcuts discussed in Chapter 2 to change the directory display.

TIP 13: **Staying Within the Maximum Number of Lines in a COMMAND.COM Window**

Because it formats output for a standard text display, COMMAND.COM can display a maximum of 25 lines at one time, even though the window may be more than 25 lines deep. That's why text scrolls off the screen even though there appears to be room for more in the window.

TIP 14: **Avoiding the MS-DOS Check Disk Command**

Although you can run most MS-DOS utilities from within Windows, heed Microsoft's warning: Avoid running Check Disk (*chkdsk*) with the /F parameter. (The /F parameter tells Check Disk to fix errors it finds in the disk's directory.) If any temporary files created by another running application exist, Check Disk falsely assumes errors in the directory and closes the temporary files. When you switch back to the other application, the system can crash or lose data. Use the About command in the MS-DOS Executive window to learn how much free disk space and memory remain. The About command is more accurate than Check Disk in reporting on free memory.

CHAPTER 5

THE DATA EXCHANGE

Integrated applications—programs that attempt to meet most users' needs by combining several popular applications modules (usually word processing, data management, spreadsheet analysis, communications, and business graphics)—have two main advantages: they offer a common interface among all the modules, which allows you to switch from one task to another without having to learn new commands, and they allow easy exchange of data between any two modules.

But the modules usually lack the power you find in stand-alone programs. So, if you want the convenience of a consistent user interface and of data exchange between applications, as well as the power of stand-alone programs, you need an operating environment that lets you create your own integrated system of separate, full-featured applications and lets you exchange data between them.

Microsoft Windows provides this vital foundation. Windows offers an especially flexible set of data-interchange options. This chapter explores them, and examines the issues involved in transferring data between programs and between computers.

The Clipboard

The most visible player in Windows' data-exchange team is the clipboard. The clipboard is a temporary holding place that stores text or graphics that you cut or copy for pasting elsewhere in the current document, into another document, or into another application. The clipboard holds one piece of information at a time; when you cut or copy something, it replaces any information already on the clipboard. (Some applications, however, let you restore the previous contents by choosing Undo.) Virtually all Windows applications support the clipboard by providing an Edit menu with Cut, Copy, and Paste commands. Windows also provides limited clipboard support for standard applications.

You can view the contents of the clipboard at any time by running the Clipboard application. Clipboard isn't the clipboard itself; you don't need to run it to use the clipboard. It's a clipboard viewer, a program that simply displays the contents of the clipboard. Clipboard uses Windows' messaging system (described in Chapter 1) to update its display when the contents of the clipboard change. When an application places something on the clipboard, it sends out a message saying, in effect, "Hey everybody, I've changed the contents of the clipboard." Applications that can display the clipboard's contents respond to the message by displaying the new contents.

The clipboard can store information in numerous formats, with each format tailored to a particular kind of data. When you cut or copy data to the clipboard, the "donating" application tells the clipboard which formats it can use to supply the data. (It's common for a donating application to place data on the clipboard in more than one format; doing so increases the odds that a receiving application will be able to accept the data.) When you switch to a different application and choose Paste, the receiving application selects a format and requests the data from the clipboard. Generally, a receiving application will select the format that best represents the data's original appearance and formatting. In order to accept the information, the receiving application must be able to interpret at least one of the formats in which it's stored.

Clipboard Formats

The Clipboard supports five standard data formats. When you run the Clipboard program to view the clipboard's contents, the formats of the data currently on the clipboard appear above the contents, as shown in Figure 5-1. The five standard formats are:

Text. This format stores ASCII text, with no font, style, or size attributes. Because virtually all applications can work with text, this format often acts as the common denominator for data transfers; that is, if a receiving application doesn't support a format that lets all aspects of the data be transferred, it can select the text format and accept the text characters. A variation on the text format is the OEM text format, which stores text copied from a standard application and uses the characters from your computer's native character set. When you copy text from a standard application and then paste the text into

FIGURE 5-1.

The Clipboard application window.

Data

Data formats

another standard application, Windows pastes the text in OEM text format. Like the text format, OEM text contains no formatting attributes. Chapter 9 discusses OEM text and describes how to use the clipboard with standard applications.

Bitmap. The bitmap format is for storing a graphic image copied from a bitmapped graphics program such as Microsoft Windows Paint. Bitmapped graphics are composed of a series of dots, representing the pixels of the display. Each dot corresponds to a bit in memory. If a particular dot appears black, its bit usually corresponds to a value of one on a bitmap, or table of values, in memory. If a dot appears white, its bit usually corresponds to a value of zero. Bitmapped graphics are restricted to a specific number of dots per inch because each dot is represented by a bit in memory.

Picture. The picture format, also called metafile picture, is a graphic image copied from a graphics program, such as Micrografx Designer, Micrografx Draw, or Micrografx Graph, or from Microsoft Excel. Pictures are represented not by a series of dots (although that's how they appear on your screen), but by a series of drawing commands for GDI, Windows' Graphic Device Interface. When you cut or copy a picture to the clipboard, Windows stores the GDI commands required to recreate it in a metafile. When you view the clipboard using Clipboard or when you paste the picture into another application, Windows plays back the commands in the metafile to recreate the picture. Pictures have significant advantages over bitmaps: Because they're stored as metafiles, they are resolution independent—that is, they are not locked into a specific number of dots per inch. This lets pictures take advantage of all the resolution your display or printer can provide, and it lets you easily resize, or scale, images without distortion. A picture is often called an object-oriented graphic because it's stored as a series of distinct objects (lines, rectangles, arcs, and so on) rather than as a map of bits.

SYLK. Short for SYmbolic LinK, this is an ASCII format developed by Microsoft that is commonly used to store spreadsheet and other row-and-column-oriented data.

DIF. Short for Data Interchange Format, this spreadsheet-data format was developed by VisiCorp and is currently controlled by the Lotus Development Corporation. (SYLK and DIF are described in more detail in Appendix B.)

Special Clipboard Formats

In addition to using the standard clipboard formats, a Windows application can define its own clipboard format. Microsoft Excel, for example, uses numerous custom clipboard formats, including:

Rich text. This format is similar to the standard text format, except that formatting attributes such as font, style, and size are retained. The rich-text format lets you transfer formatted text between applications, provided that the receiving application supports the format. For example, Microsoft Excel can transfer data to the clipboard in the rich-text format, but Microsoft Windows Write cannot interpret the format. So, if you copy text from Microsoft Excel to Write, the text appears unformatted. Write can't donate, or export, text in the rich-text format, either.

BIFF. Short for BInary File Format, this format lets you maintain all formatting information when you cut and paste information between Microsoft Excel worksheets. The SYLK and DIF spreadsheet formats lack the ability to describe the many attributes a Microsoft Excel worksheet can have, such as multiple fonts and sizes, variable-size columns and rows, cell borders, custom data formats, and so on.

CSV. Short for Comma Separated Variable format, this format is intended primarily for representing spreadsheet or database information. In the CSV format, each cell (or field, for a database) is separated, or delimited, by a comma, and each row (or record, for a database) is delimited by a carriage-return code. When a given field contains embedded commas—a large number, perhaps, or a full name in last-name-first order—you enclose it within quote marks, as in *"10,000,000"* or *"Polk, Helen"*. Many computer languages, including Microsoft BASIC, create data files in the CSV format.

WK1. The WK1 format stores data on the clipboard in the same way that it's stored in worksheet files created by Lotus 1-2-3 Release 2.

Link. The Link format contains information used for establishing links between applications using Windows' Dynamic Data Exchange (DDE) capabilities.

Aldus Corporation's PageMaker is another application that uses its own format. PageMaker's custom format is named, appropriately enough, Internal PageMaker Format. PageMaker stores cut or copied bitmapped graphics, object-oriented graphics, and text in the appropriate Windows format (Bitmap, Picture, or Text, respectively) as well as in its own internal format. (PageMaker's manuals refer to bit-mapped graphics as "paint-type" graphics and to object-oriented graphics as "draw-type" graphics.) If you cut or copy a mixture of elements—a graphic *and* some text or a bitmapped and an object-oriented graphic—PageMaker stores the elements in its internal format only, because another application would not be able to separate the two distinct data types.

Write also uses its own format, called WRITE Formatted Text. This format can store the formatting attributes of text you copy or cut from Write, as well as bitmapped graphics you paste into Write from other applications.

The ways you can use the clipboard are as varied as the Windows applications that support it.

TIP 1: Moving Graphics from Paint to Write

To add illustrations to a report, for example, you can draw a graphic in Paint, copy the graphic to the clipboard, and then paste it into a Write document. To copy a graphic in Paint, use the selection rectangle tool to enclose the graphic in a selection marquee. Don't select much extra space around the graphic; make the rectangle only slightly larger than the graphic itself. To copy an irregularly shaped portion of the graphic, use the selection net tool instead of the selection rectangle tool, as shown in Figure 5-2.

After you select the area you want to transfer, choose Copy from the Edit menu. Next, start or switch to Write and choose Paste. If the graphic is too large or too small, you can resize it. Select it and choose Size Picture from the Edit menu, and then—without pressing the mouse button—move the pointer to the graphic's lower-right corner. When it reaches the corner, move the pointer until the dotted frame is the desired size. Write shows the resizing percentage in the lower-left corner of its window (where the page number usually appears); to avoid giving the graphic a stretched or squeezed look, keep the X and Y values the same. Note also that if you enlarge a bitmapped graphic containing text, the text may take on a chunky appearance. You'll get the best results if you draw the graphic in the size it will appear in the Write document.

FIGURE 5-2.

Selecting an irregular area in Paint. (A) Selecting the shape with the selection net tool. (B) The resulting selection copied to the clipboard.

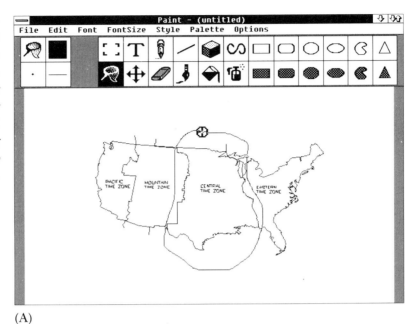

(A)

(B)

TIP 2: Moving Graphics from Other Programs into Write

You can apply the same copy-and-paste process described in Tip 1 to object-oriented graphics created in a drawing program, such as Micrografx Draw or Micrografx Designer, and to charts created with programs such as Micrografx Graph or Microsoft Excel.

With the Micrografx products, drawings or charts are usually composed of many separate objects; therefore, it's important to be sure you select the entire drawing or chart. To do so, choose Block Select from the Edit menu. Next, enclose the entire drawing or chart in the selection marquee and choose Copy. (If the graphic or drawing is too large to fit within the window, choose View Current Page from the View menu before choosing Block Select.)

If you're using Microsoft Excel, be sure the chart's window is active, and then hold down the Shift key while opening the Edit menu. Choose the Copy Picture command, select both As Shown on Screen buttons, and choose OK.

When you copy a chart by using the Copy Picture command, Microsoft Excel places it on the clipboard in Picture format only. You can copy a chart in another way: by choosing Select Chart from the Chart menu and then choosing Copy from the Edit menu. This approach places the chart on the clipboard in several formats, including Link. Using this approach, you can paste a chart into an application that supports DDE, and establish a link between that application and Microsoft Excel. This capability will become more important as more applications support DDE.

If you use Micrografx Draw or Micrografx Graph with a printer (such as the Hewlett-Packard LaserJet) that doesn't allow continuously scalable fonts, avoid resizing drawings or charts containing printer fonts such as 12-point Helv or Tms Rmn. If you do resize such a graphic, Write (or, for that matter, any other program that accepts graphics) tries to change the size of the text accordingly, but you usually end up with text that's too large or too small for the graphic, as shown in Figure 5-3. If you anticipate resizing a drawing or chart, use a stroke font such as Modern, Roman, or Script. Stroke fonts don't print as attractively on laser printers as do true typographic fonts, but Windows can resize the text to fit the graphic. Of course, the best approach is to draw the graphic or create the chart in the size it will appear in the final document.

TIP 3: Pasting Text into a Graphics Application

Although it's more common to paste graphics into a word-processing document, you can also paste text into a graphics application. You might, for example, want to create a graphic containing a great deal of text. No graphics application has the range of text-editing features

FIGURE 5-3.

A pitfall of resizing graphics with non-scalable fonts. (A) Original size. (B) Reduced in Windows.

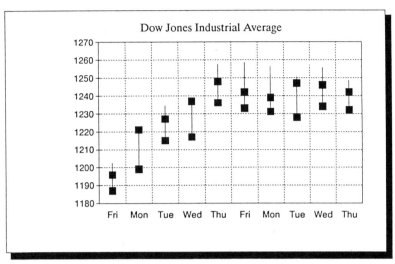

(A)

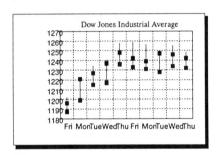

(B)

that Notepad or Write provides. So, instead of struggling with the primitive text-editing features of a graphics program, type the text in Notepad or Write, copy it to the clipboard, and then paste it into the graphics application. From there, you can format the text into the desired font and style.

When you paste text into Micrografx Draw, each line becomes a separate text object. To change the appearance of all the text, choose Block Select from the Edit menu, and select all the text objects by enclosing them in the selection marquee. To change the appearance of only one line, select it by clicking on it, as shown in Figure 5-4 on page 77.

When you paste text into Paint, the text appears in the System font, surrounded by a selection rectangle, as shown in Figure 5-5 on page 77. A point not mentioned in the Paint manual is that you can change the appearance of the text if you choose a command from the

Character, Size, or Style menus *before* doing anything else—that is, while the text is still enclosed by the selection rectangle. As soon as you deselect the text (which occurs when you activate any other tool, select something else, or switch to a different application window), the text becomes part of the picture and can't be reformatted.

TIP 4: Using the Clipboard and Communications

The clipboard teams up well with Terminal or with a full-scale communications program such as Palantir inTalk, letting you copy incoming characters to the clipboard for pasting into another application. (Chapter 11 describes inTalk and its applications in further detail.) The inTalk program offers especially versatile copying options. Its Copy Table command converts two or more consecutive spaces into a tab character, which serves as a cell or field delimiter in Microsoft Excel and most other spreadsheet programs. With information in this format, you can paste the data into a worksheet, as shown in Figure 5-6 on page 78, or into a word processor. Pasting the data into a word processor is useful when you're creating a report containing data downloaded from an on-line service such as Dow Jones News/Retrieval.

The inTalk application also has a Copy Bitmap command that lets you copy the entire communications window to the clipboard as a bitmap. This command is useful in conjunction with inTalk's CompuServe/VIDTEX-emulation option, which lets you receive weather maps and other graphics from the CompuServe Information Service, as shown in Figure 5-7 on page 79. Like Terminal, inTalk provides a conventional copy command that simply places the selected text on the clipboard.

Terminal's and inTalk's Paste commands also have communications applications. Electronic-mail users can compose communiqués off-line using Notepad or Write, copy the text, start or switch to Terminal or inTalk, and then paste it to the remote system. This approach can reduce your on-line charges dramatically.

FIGURE 5-4.

Selecting one or all text objects in Micrografx Draw.
(A) Selecting all text objects.
(B) Selecting one text object.

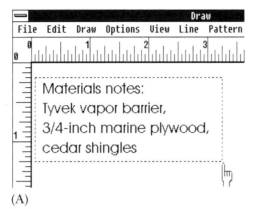

(A)

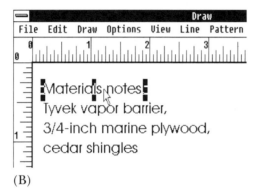

(B)

FIGURE 5-5.

Text pasted in Paint and still enclosed by the selection rectangle.

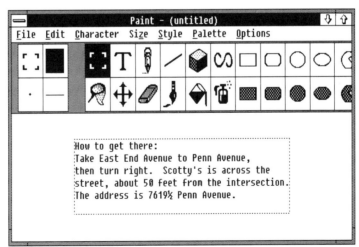

FIGURE 5-6.

*Transferring a
table from inTalk
to Microsoft
Excel.
(A) The Copy
Table command
replaces two or
more spaces with
a tab character.
(B) The tab
character places
each value in its
own cell.*

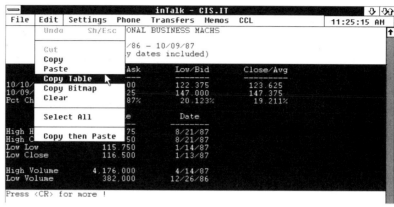

(A)

(B)

FIGURE 5-7.

Copying a bitmap in inTalk.

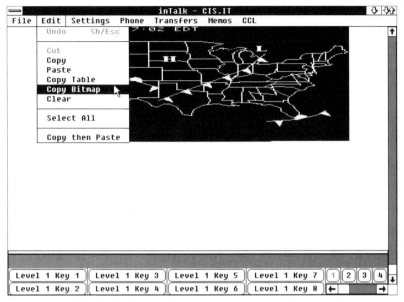

TIP 5: Using the Clipboard and Calculator

A simple but handy use of the clipboard is to copy or paste values from or to Calculator. Choosing Calculator's Copy command places the current value on the clipboard, ready for pasting into another application. Choosing Calculator's Paste command sends the contents of the clipboard to Calculator. If the clipboard contains an equation that Calculator can interpret, you'll see its buttons blink and the values flash across its display as if you were typing them from the keyboard. Note that Calculator ignores some characters, such as parentheses. If you're pasting a complex formula containing parentheses, you might not get the correct results, since Calculator won't use the parentheses to control the order in which it calculates the values in the formula.

TIP 6: Using the Clipboard and PageMaker

Because Aldus PageMaker uses its own clipboard format, you cannot paste the following combinations of PageMaker elements into other applications:

- One or more bitmapped graphics and one or more object-oriented graphics

- More than one bitmapped graphic or more than one object-oriented graphic

- One or more graphics and one or more text blocks

These combinations of elements are stored in PageMaker's internal format because no standard Windows clipboard format represents combinations of data. To move numerous disparate elements into another application, cut or copy them one at a time. Of course, if a Windows application is developed that can interpret PageMaker's internal format, this restriction will not apply.

Pasting into PageMaker is more straightforward. You can paste text or graphics into a PageMaker publication, adding them to an existing text block (by clicking to create an insertion point before pasting) or creating a new text block (by choosing Paste when no insertion point exists). You can paste bitmapped or object-oriented graphics into PageMaker publications, although PageMaker version 1.0a cannot accept color bitmaps, such as those created by ZSoft Corporation's PC Paintbrush.

TIP 7: Using the Clipboard and Microsoft Excel

Microsoft Excel teems with clipboard options, many of which are unique. We've already examined the process of copying a chart to the clipboard. We haven't, however, looked at the process of pasting a chart format into Microsoft Excel. You can change the appearance of one chart to match that of another by selecting the desired chart (choose Select Chart from the Chart menu), copying the chart to the clipboard (choose Copy from the Edit menu), and then activating the second chart's window and choosing Paste Special from the Edit menu. (The Full Menus command on the Chart menu must be active to get the Paste Special command.) When the Paste Special dialog box appears, choose the Formats option and choose OK. Microsoft Excel replaces the format of the active chart with that of the chart you copied. (To paste the data series as well as the format, select the All option. This option gives the same result as choosing Paste, rather than Paste Special. To paste the data series but not the format, use the Formulas option.)

Within worksheets and macro sheets, you can cut or copy cells by selecting them and then choosing the Cut or Copy commands. Where worksheets are concerned, Microsoft Excel's Cut command doesn't work the same as the Cut commands of other applications. When you choose Cut, instead of removing the contents of the selected cells, Microsoft Excel surrounds them with a moving marquee. To paste the cell's contents elsewhere, select another cell or range of cells and choose Paste. When you do, Microsoft Excel moves what you cut to the new cells, as in Figure 5-8 on the following page. Choosing Cut, then, is the first step in moving the contents of a cell or cells to a different worksheet or to different cells in the same worksheet. (If you decide to leave the cells where they are, cancel the marquee by pressing the Esc key.) If you want to delete the contents of one or more cells, use the Delete command instead of Cut.

When you move spreadsheet cells using Cut, beware of the pitfall illustrated in Figure 5-9 on page 83. In Figure 5-9, the shape of the destination range of cells differs from the shape of the cut selection, causing Microsoft Excel to display the message *Cut and Paste areas are different shapes*. The solution is to be sure that the destination range's shape matches that of the cut cells or to simply select one cell before choosing Paste, as shown in Figure 5-10 on page 84. When you take the latter approach, Microsoft Excel pastes the upper-left cell of the cells on the clipboard into the current cell, and fills the rest of the range downward and to the right.

The Paste Special command lets you selectively paste the cut or copied cells, specifying which parts of the cells—their formulas, values, formats, notes, or all four—should be pasted. You can also specify how Microsoft Excel combines the values of the cells on the clipboard with those of the destination cells by using the options of the dialog box shown in Figure 5-11 on page 85. The Paste Special command is available on the Edit menu when Full Menus is chosen.

FIGURE 5-8.

Moving a cell using Microsoft Excel's Cut and Paste commands. To move one cell: (A) Select the cell to be cut and choose the Cut command. (B) Select the destination cell and press Enter or choose Paste. (C) Microsoft Excel moves the cell's contents.

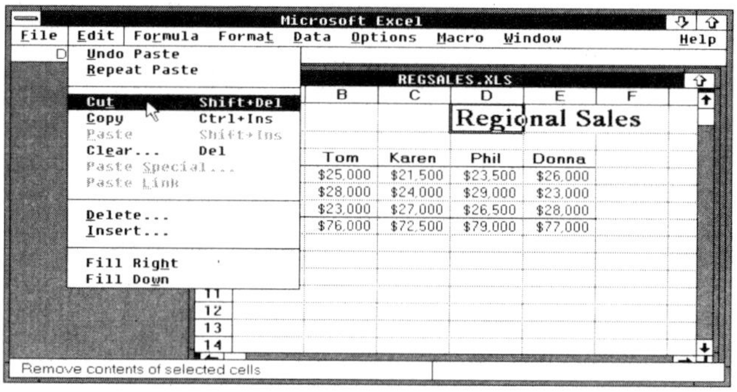

(A)

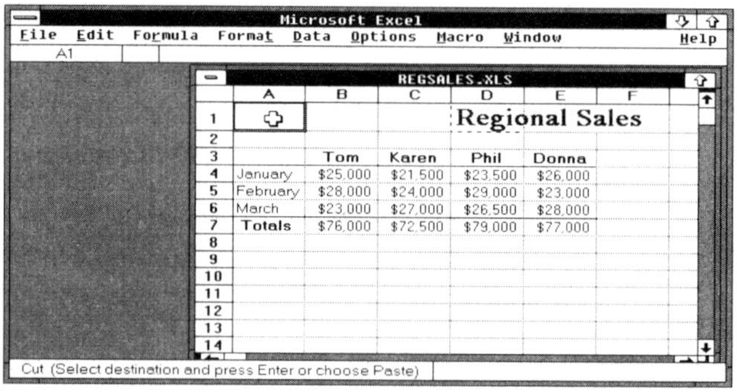

(B)

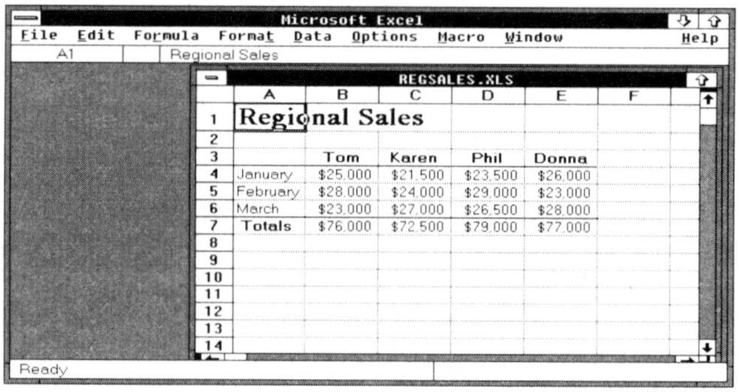

(C)

FIGURE 5-9.

Pitfall of different shaped cut and paste areas. How not to move a range of cells: (A) Select the cells and choose the Cut command. (B) The shape of the destination range differs from the shape of the cut cells. (C) Microsoft Excel displays an error message when you choose Paste.

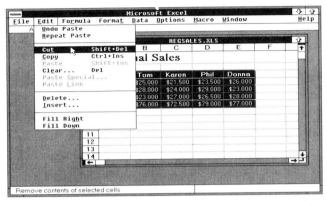

(A)

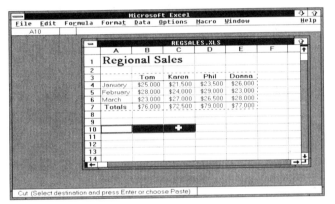

(B)

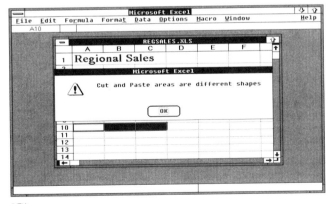

(C)

FIGURE 5-10.

*Pasting a range
of cells with a
single cell
selected.
How to move a
range of cells:
(A) Select a
single cell or a
range of cells
with the same
shape as the
cut cells.
(B) Microsoft
Excel moves the
cells when you
choose Paste.*

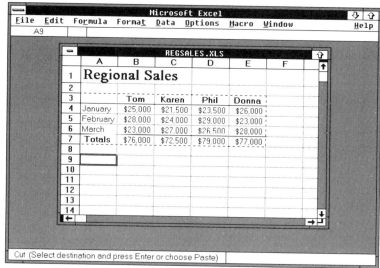

(A)

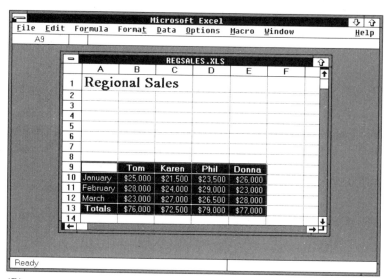

(B)

When you cut or copy cells and then switch to a chart window, the workings of the Paste and Paste Special commands change. When you choose Paste in the Chart window, Microsoft Excel creates data series based on the cells on the clipboard and then pastes them into the chart window. If the chart window is empty, it creates a new chart. If the window contains a chart already, Microsoft Excel adds the new data series to the chart. In either case, the program creates new data series using the same techniques it uses when you create a new chart by choosing New from the File menu. You can change this default series-creation scheme by choosing Paste Special and selecting the options you want from the dialog box shown in Figure 5-12.

You can also paste charts into documents created in other applications using the technique described earlier in this chapter, and you can copy and paste worksheet data. For example, to turn a range of cells into a table in a Write document, select the cells, choose Copy, and start or switch to Write. Position the insertion point at the beginning of a line and choose Paste. The data appears, with each cell's data separated by a tab character. To align the columns, select the table, choose Ruler On from the Document menu, and adjust tab settings as needed. This process is shown in Figure 5-13 on the next page.

You can also reverse these steps to move data from a Write table into a Microsoft Excel worksheet: Select the data in Write, choose Copy, start or switch to Microsoft Excel, select a cell or range of cells, and choose Paste. The tab character between each column separates each cell, and the carriage return at the end of each line tells Microsoft Excel to advance to the next row.

FIGURE 5-11.

*Paste Special
(worksheet)
dialog box.*

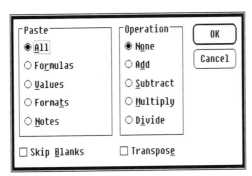

FIGURE 5-12.

*Paste Special
(chart) dialog
box.*

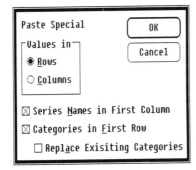

If you use Microsoft Word or another non-Windows word processor, you can use similar steps to create tables from worksheet data or to move tables into worksheets. Standard applications, however, require a slightly different approach to cutting and pasting. Those differences are discussed in Chapter 11.

FIGURE 5-13.

Creating a table in Write from Microsoft Excel data. (A) Select the data and choose the Copy command. (B) Paste the data into Write and adjust tabs and formatting as needed.

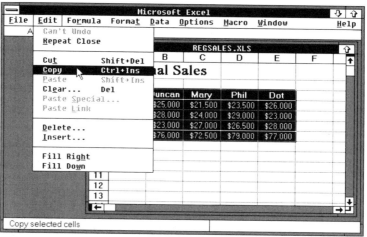

(A)

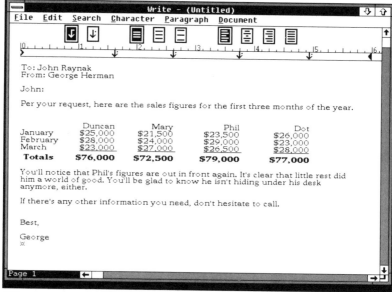

(B)

TIP 8: Creating a Scrapbook

The Apple Macintosh includes a small program (in Mac parlance, a desk accessory) called the Scrapbook that lets you store information from the Mac's Clipboard. Each time you paste text or graphics into the Scrapbook, a new "page" is created. You can use a scroll bar to leaf through the Scrapbook's pages, copying or cutting pages back to the clipboard for reuse.

Windows doesn't offer a Scrapbook, but you can create a close approximation by using the Cardfile application to store text and graphics pasted from the clipboard, as shown in Figure 5-14. Cardfile isn't a perfect scrapbook: It limits the amount you can store on a single card to 440 characters, it can't hold a full-page bitmapped graphic, and it converts object-oriented graphics to bitmaps. But unlike the Macintosh Scrapbook, your Windows scrapbook lets you index and sort your scrapbook entries, lets you search for particular entries, and lets you create multiple scrapbooks by simply starting new Cardfile documents.

FIGURE 5-14.

Cardfile used as a scrapbook.

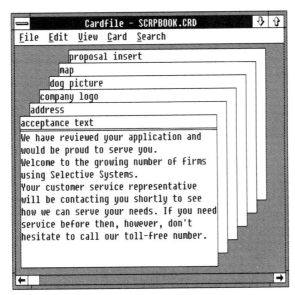

TIP 9:   Using Windows' Dynamic Data Exchange

There's no question that the clipboard is a wonderful way to swap data between programs. But the clipboard is a static data-transfer mechanism. If you prepare a daily sales report containing charts created by Microsoft Excel, you must create and then copy and paste new charts each time the sales figures change. If you use Micrografx Graph to create a daily chart that uses on-line stock market data to show how your favorite stocks are performing, you must daily move the data between your communications program and your chart application. The clipboard falls flat when it comes to data-transfer applications that involve constantly changing data.

But Windows provides a data-exchange mechanism that makes the clipboard look old-fashioned. It's the Dynamic Data Exchange, or DDE for short, mentioned in Chapter 1. DDE uses Windows' messaging system—the same system Windows uses to recognize and respond to keyboard and mouse events—to create what is called a "hot link" between applications. When you combine DDE-supporting applications, you can create dynamic documents, the contents of which are updated as data changes. For example, using DDE and applications that support it, you can link:

- A communications program and Microsoft Excel. The communications program can download stock market data from an on-line service, then shuttle the data into Microsoft Excel worksheets and charts.

- Microsoft Excel and a word processor. To carry the preceding example one step further, you can link a Microsoft Excel chart to a word-processing document. As the stock quotes change, the chart is updated in both Microsoft Excel and in the word-processing document.

- A microcomputer and scientific equipment. A seismologist might use DDE to send information received in real time from seismographic equipment to an application that plots the incoming data on the screen, replacing mechanical seismographs. The application might, in turn, use DDE to send the data to a Microsoft Excel worksheet running a macro that compares the current data to previous data, searching for patterns in the earth's movement.

In DDE terms, an application that sends data to another application is called a server; an application that receives data is a client. Although the specifics depend on the application, you generally establish a link between a server and a client by choosing a Link command or, in Microsoft Excel's case, using a macro.

These three examples barely scratch the surface of DDE's capabilities. DDE is limited primarily by the availability of applications that support it. (And by the hardware on which you use it: Shuttling data between multiple applications in real time requires a generous amount of memory and a swift microprocessor.)

TIP 10: Exchanging Data by Using Disk Files

A more common and more basic form of data sharing than the clipboard or DDE is the disk file. Disk files are the best way to exchange data when you need to use documents created by a different application (for example, a convert to Microsoft Excel may need to use old Lotus 1-2-3 worksheets) or when you need to exchange more information than will fit in the clipboard (for example, including a scanned image or other large graphic in a desktop publication).

The only requirement is that the destination application is able to read the format in which the data is saved. Microsoft Excel, for example, shares several common file formats with Lotus 1-2-3: the standard WKS format, Data Interchange Format (DIF), and tab-delimited ASCII. Microsoft Excel is especially adept at file swapping; it can open or save files in the formats just mentioned, as well as in dBASE II and dBASE III formats and in comma-delimited ASCII format. In Microsoft Excel's Save As dialog box, the latter three formats are called DBF 2, DBF 3, and CSV, respectively.

To open a document in any of these formats in Microsoft Excel, choose Open from the File menu. If you know the name of the file you want to open, simply type it in the File Name text box and press Enter. Otherwise, type *.* in the File Name text box and press Enter. This step tells Microsoft Excel to display a list of all files in the current directory, instead of only the ones with extensions beginning with XL. Finally, locate and select the file and then choose OK. That's all there is to it: Microsoft Excel recognizes the file's format and opens it. When you open a dBASE II or dBASE III file, Microsoft Excel uses the file's field names as column headings.

To save a document in a format other than Microsoft Excel's, choose the Save As command and choose the Options button. Microsoft Excel's Save dialog box expands to reveal the list of file formats shown in Figure 5-15. Select the desired format. When you do, notice how the filename extension changes accordingly. (If you plan to use a worksheet with version 1.0 of Micrografx Graph, save it as a DIF file. Graph is unable to read the SYLK files Microsoft Excel creates. Moreover, Graph expects a SYLK file to end with the SYL extension, but Microsoft Excel gives SYLK files the extension SLK.) Remember that only the Microsoft Excel XLS format is able to represent all the formatting attributes possible in Microsoft Excel worksheets. Use a different file format only when you need to open a worksheet with a different program.

Swapping files with other Windows applications is a similar process. To save a file in a different format, choose the application's Save As command and then select the desired format. When you select a different format, the application will change the filename extension to reflect the new format.

To open a file in a format other than the application's standard format, you usually need to type the appropriate filename extension in the application's Open dialog box. (Remember, you can type the *.* wildcard combination in the Open dialog box to see a list of all the files in the current directory.) If the application is unable to open a given file, it displays an error message. Figure 5-16 shows the file formats supported by numerous popular Windows applications. A description of today's most popular file formats appears in Appendix B.

FIGURE 5-15.

Microsoft Excel-supported file formats.

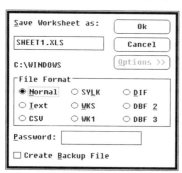

FIGURE 5-16.

File formats and applications that support them.

	Microsoft Excel 2.0	Aldus PageMaker 3.0	Microsoft Windows Write 2.0	Micrografx Draw 1.04	Micrografx Designer 1.0	Micrografx Graph 1.0	ZSoft Paintbrush 1.0	Palantir Filer 3.01	Blyth Omni Quartz 1.0
Spreadsheet and database formats									
Microsoft Excel (XLS)	R/W	—	—	—	—	—	—	—	—
Lotus 1-2-3 (WK1)	R/W	—	—	—	—	—	—	—	R/W
Data Interchange Format (DIF)	R/W	—	R*	—	—	R	—	—	R/W
dBASE III (DBF)	R/W	—	—	—	—	—	—	R/W	R/W
Comma Separated Values (CSV)	R/W	—	R	—	—	—	—	R/W	R/W
Symbolic Link (SYLK)	R/W	R*	—	—	R/W	—	—	—	—
Word processing and text formats									
Rich-text format (RTF)	—	R	—	—	—	—	—	—	—
Microsoft Word 4.0 format (DOC)	—	R/W	R/W	—	—	—	—	—	—
Document Content Architecture (DCA)	—	R/W	—	—	—	—	—	—	—
Microsoft Windows Write (WRI)	—	R	R/W	—	—	—	—	—	—
Text-only ASCII (TXT)	R/W	R/W	R/W	—	—	R	—	R/W	R/W
Graphics formats									
Microsoft Windows Paint (MSP)	—	R	—	—	—	—	R	—	—
Windows GDI metafile (WMF)	—	R	—	—	—	—	—	—	—
Micrografx Draw (PIC)	—	R	—	R/W	R/W	R/W	—	—	—
Micrografx Designer (DRW)	—	—	—	—	R/W	—	—	—	—
Tagged-image file format (TIF)	—	R	—	—	—	—	—	—	—
Encapsulated PostScript (EPS)	—	R	—	—	—	—	—	—	—
PC Paintbrush (PCX)	—	R	—	—	—	—	R/W	—	—
Macintosh MacPaint (PNT)	—	R	—	—	—	—	—	—	—

* Microsoft Windows Write opens DIF and SYLK files as text files only; it does not interpret their formatting commands.

R = Reads
W = Writes

TIP 11: Exchanging Data with Other Computers

Several options exist for exchanging files with other computers. If the computers are in different offices or buildings, you can transfer the files by using a modem and a communications application such as Palantir inTalk. If the computers are physically close together, you can use a null modem cable and a communications program.

Transferring files by using a communications program and a modem works well once you iron out the wrinkles. The following scenario is an example of how a file-transfer session should transpire. In it, the person receiving the file ("Person One") is using Palantir inTalk; Person Two is using a different program (and could even be using a different brand of computer).

It's often said that one successful data call requires four voice calls. You can lower that ratio, eliminating those "What went wrong that time?" phone calls, by planning ahead. Determine in advance who will call whom and what baud rate and protocol settings you will use. Use the following script as a guide.

Person One (file receiver)	*Person Two (file sender)*
(Answering phone) Hello?	
	Hi!
Ready to transfer?	
	Yes. Let's use 1200-baud, 8 data bits, 1 stop bit, no parity, and Xmodem protocol. Will you call me, or shall I call you?
You call me. We'll type briefly on screen first to be sure our settings match. Then wait a few seconds, and start transmitting.	
	OK. Set your communications program for auto answer. I'll call in about two minutes.

Both parties hang up and adjust their communications settings. Person One chooses Communications from the Settings Menu and sets the agreed-upon baud rate, data bits, and parity settings, as shown in Figure 5-17. It may be necessary for both persons to choose On for the Local Echo option so that each can see what he or she types. Next, Person One chooses Binary Transfers from inTalk's Settings menu and selects the Xmodem option. (Xmodem is a common file-transfer protocol, a set of communications rules that uses an error-checking system to ensure that data isn't garbled during the transfer.) Person Two performs the equivalent steps on his or her program. Finally, Person One sets inTalk to the answer mode by choosing Wait For Call from the Phone menu. Person Two chooses his or her program's dial command and types Person One's phone number.

When Person One's phone rings, his or her modem answers and sends a carrier tone. When a connection is established, the two people should exchange brief, typed pleasantries to verify the connection:

Person One	*Person Two*
(Typing) Are you there?	
	I'm here and ready.
OK. I'll switch into receive mode now. Give me a few seconds, and then start sending.	
	OK.

At this point, Person One chooses Receive Binary File from the Transfers menu, types a filename for the incoming file, and presses Enter. Person Two chooses the command that begins a binary file transmission and specifies the file to be sent. After a brief handshaking period, both programs begin communicating: the sending program transmits the file in chunks called blocks, with a checksum at the end of each block that allows inTalk to verify that the data was received accurately.

FIGURE 5-17.

Settings for inTalk for modem-to-modem file transfers.

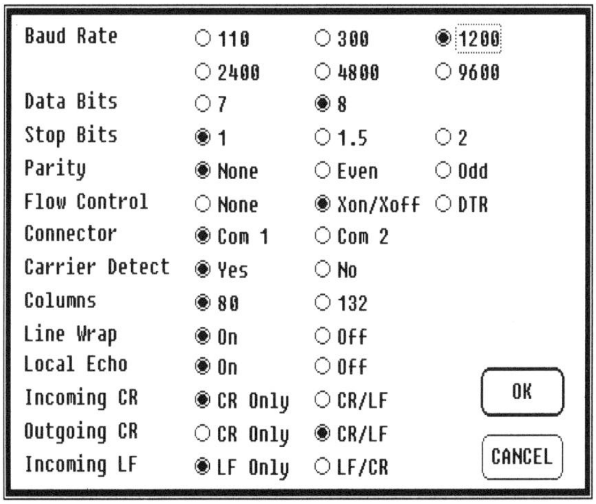

Baud Rate	○ 110	○ 300	⦿ 1200
	○ 2400	○ 4800	○ 9600
Data Bits	○ 7	⦿ 8	
Stop Bits	⦿ 1	○ 1.5	○ 2
Parity	⦿ None	○ Even	○ Odd
Flow Control	○ None	⦿ Xon/Xoff	○ DTR
Connector	⦿ Com 1	○ Com 2	
Carrier Detect	⦿ Yes	○ No	
Columns	⦿ 80	○ 132	
Line Wrap	⦿ On	○ Off	
Local Echo	⦿ On	○ Off	
Incoming CR	⦿ CR Only	○ CR/LF	
Outgoing CR	○ CR Only	⦿ CR/LF	
Incoming LF	⦿ LF Only	○ LF/CR	

OK

CANCEL

When inTalk receives a block, it, too, calculates a checksum, and compares it to the one it received. If the two values match, inTalk knows that the block was received accurately, and requests the next block. If the checksums differ, inTalk knows that the block was garbled, and requests that it be sent again.

In the previous example, both parties use the Xmodem protocol to exchange a binary file. However, if the file being transferred is an ASCII text file (such as a batch file or WIN.INI file), both parties could throw caution to the wind by exchanging the file without an error-checking protocol. In that case, Person One chooses the command that begins a text file transfer, and Person Two chooses inTalk's Receive Text File command. A text transfer is risky because no error checking is performed, but it may be the only way to exchange a file with someone whose communications program doesn't support binary file transfers.

If your machines are in the same room, you can establish a direct serial link between them called a null modem to transfer files without a modem. To do this, you need a compatible cable connecting each computer's serial port and a communications program running on each machine. If the option is available on your communications program, you should also select the switch signifying direct connection between computers. To set this option in Windows Terminal, choose Communications from the Configure menu, and choose the Computer option button. Using a null modem to transfer files between computers is a bit easier because you can perform the entire job by yourself, adjusting each computer's communications program as needed. And because null modems don't use noisy phone lines, you can use much higher transmission speeds. I routinely transfer files between a Macintosh and an IBM PS/2 Model 50 at 9600 baud, using Software Ventures' MicroPhone on the Mac and inTalk on the PS/2. Aside from the slower modem speed and the lack of voice contact by phone calls, the steps are virtually the same. Before you initiate the transfer, type a few characters on each machine to verify that they appear on the other.

CHAPTER 6

PRINTING

I n this chapter, we examine how Windows accesses printers, how its Spooler program works, and how you can add and remove printer drivers. And because Windows works well with printers that use Adobe Systems' PostScript page-description language, we'll take a close look at how you can use a PostScript printer with Windows. You'll even learn how to tap the power of PostScript without having to own a PostScript printer by modifying Windows to create special print files that you can send to a desktop-publishing service for output on a PostScript printer or a phototypesetter.

Chapter 1 described how Windows' Graphic Device Interface (GDI) lets it create displays on screens of varying resolution. To recap briefly, GDI acts as a middleman between Windows applications and your display hardware. Windows applications create screen displays using GDI commands that are device independent—not tied to a specific screen resolution. Windows then passes these GDI commands to a device driver, which translates them into commands that your display hardware understands.

Windows uses similar techniques to access printers. When you choose an application's Print command, the application uses GDI commands to create a description of a page's appearance. Many of these commands are the same ones that produce display output; others are printing oriented, performing such tasks as enabling draft printing mode or kerning—the adjustment of space between specific pairs of letters. GDI then passes these device-independent commands to the printer driver, which translates them into the control codes that your printer requires. For a Windows application, printing a page isn't too different from creating a screen display. Indeed, it's this similarity that allows Windows to provide its WYSIWYG ("what you see is what you get") operating style.

Where does the Spooler program fit in? It accepts the stream of device-specific information coming from the device driver and spools it—stores it on disk in a temporary file. Because a disk drive (especially a hard disk or RAM disk) can accept data far faster than a printer, you can get back to work sooner. The names of Spooler's temporary files begin with the characters ~SPL and end with the extension TMP. (Should you see one of these files during a Windows session, don't delete it. If you do, Spooler displays an error message. However, if a spool file remains after a Windows session or if your system malfunctions while Spooler is active, you can delete it to reclaim the disk space it used.)

After it's accepted all the data, Spooler begins despooling the temporary file, sending data to the printer in periodic bursts while you perform other tasks. And because Windows allows more than one application to print simultaneously, Spooler maintains the separation between each application's output, keeping track of which application printed which document and storing each document in the queue in the order it was received. Figure 6-1 shows how Windows prints.

FIGURE 6-1.

How Windows prints.

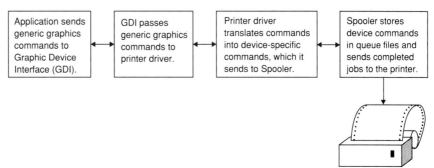

| Application sends generic graphics commands to Graphic Device Interface (GDI). | GDI passes generic graphics commands to printer driver. | Printer driver translates commands into device-specific commands, which it sends to Spooler. | Spooler stores device commands in queue files and sends completed jobs to the printer. |

TIP 1: Using Spooler to Pause Printing

For most printing tasks, Spooler works so unobtrusively that you don't even know it's there. But knowing a few fine points can help you get more out of it. One particularly useful feature is the Queue menu's Pause command, which lets you temporarily halt the transmission of data to the printer. You can use Pause to build up a large queue of documents for printing at a convenient moment or to change printer font cartridges or paper. To pause a printing job, start Spooler, select the name of the printer the documents will be printed on (if you have more than one printer installed), and choose Pause. Once you've paused despooling, the text *[Paused]* appears before the printer's name in the Spooler window, as in Figure 6-2 on the following page. Don't close Spooler at this point; instead, minimize it. All subsequent print jobs will be held in the queue until you choose the printer's name again and choose Resume from the Queue menu. When you do, Spooler will shuttle each spooled document to the printer, in the order it was received. If you try to close Spooler before all its queued documents have been printed, it asks if you want to terminate the unprinted jobs. Choose OK to do so; otherwise, choose Cancel.

FIGURE 6-2.

Spooler window showing paused printing with a queue of documents.

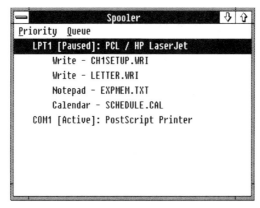

TIP 2: Deleting Print Jobs Waiting in Spooler

Another useful Spooler feature is the ability to delete a print job before it reaches the printer. Assume, for example, that you paused despooling to build up a queue of documents and then found a blunder in a document that you already spooled. Simply select the document's name in the Spooler window with direction keys or the mouse, choose Terminate from the Queue menu, and then choose OK when asked to verify the termination. You aren't deleting the original document, only its spool file, which contains the contents of the document as well as the printer commands needed to commit it to paper.

TIP 3: Setting the Spooler Priority

Spooler's other menu, Priority, lets you choose how quickly print jobs are despooled. In the Low setting, Spooler gets less processor time for despooling. In High, it gets more time, which allows faster despooling, but tends to slow other running applications. If you're in a hurry or you're printing a large queue of documents when you're away from your computer, use the High setting. Otherwise, use Low.

TIP 4: Adding, Removing, and Choosing Printers

You already know that a printer driver is the key to accessing a specific printer's features. How does Windows know which printer driver or drivers you need? You tell it when you run the Setup program. When you select your printer and specify the port it's attached to, Setup copies the printer driver to the directory that will contain Windows and makes notations in the fledgling WIN.INI configuration file that tell Windows which port the printer uses.

To add or remove a printer driver after you've installed Windows or to change the port setting, you use the Control Panel application. Chapters 8 and 9 explore Control Panel in detail; for now, we'll concentrate only on its printer-related features. For the following exercises, you'll need your Windows Utilities 1 Disk. When you have the disk handy, start Control Panel from the MS-DOS Executive window. After a few moments, Control Panel appears, as shown in Figure 6-3.

In the following example, you're going to see how to add a printer driver, and then you're going to learn how to tell Windows which port it's attached to. If you want to follow along on your own computer, you need not actually have the printer or the port you'll specify; you'll be deleting the printer driver immediately after the exercise. When you choose Add New Printer from the Installation menu, a dialog box appears instructing you to insert a disk containing printer drivers into drive A. A text box lets you specify a different drive and directory, but you don't need to. Insert the Utilities 1 Disk in drive A and choose OK. Control Panel scans the disk for printer drivers. When it finds a driver, it reads part of it to obtain the name of the printer or printers that the driver is for. Control Panel repeats this search-and-locate process until it has scanned all the printer drivers on the disk. Then it displays a list of the printer names, as shown in Figure 6-4 on the following page. (Some drivers work with more than one model of printer. For example, the driver IBMGRX.DVR is not only for IBM graphics printers, but also for compatible printers, such as the Okidata 92/192 and 93/193 models. It isn't obvious from the driver's filename that the driver may be for more than one printer, so

FIGURE 6-3.

Control Panel.

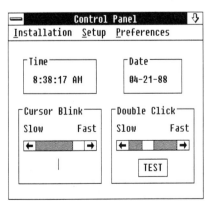

FIGURE 6-4.

List of printer names.

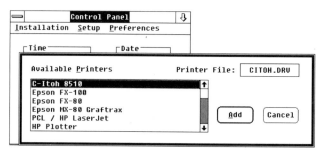

Windows displays the names of printers in the list box and the name of the printer driver for the selected printer in the text box in the upper right corner of the dialog box.)

In the list box, locate the entry NEC P2/P3, and then double-click on it; doing so selects the driver and carries out the command in one step. (If you have an NEC Pinwriter and you've already installed its driver, choose a different printer.) Windows asks if you really want to copy the printer driver to your Windows directory. Choose Yes to copy the driver.

You've copied the driver, but you haven't told Windows which port the NEC Pinwriter is connected to. To do so, choose Connections from Control Panel's Setup menu. A dialog box appears listing all the printers you've installed as well as the ports that Windows 2.0 supports, although your computer may not have all of them.

The four-character abbreviations are called device names. The COM1 and COM2 entries are for serial ports, used by modems and some printers. The LPT entries are for parallel ports, which most printers use. The EPT entry is for use with the enhanced parallel port built into the printer controller board that accompanies IBM's Personal PagePrinter, a PostScript laser printer. In addition to transferring data faster than a standard parallel port, the EPT port is able to transfer data bidirectionally, which makes possible the high degree of two-way communications that PostScript printers require.

For this exercise, let's assume your Pinwriter is connected to LPT2, your computer's second parallel port. To tell Windows that, be sure the Pinwriter's name is selected in the left list box and then select LPT2 in the right list box. When you select LPT2, the Pinwriter's entry changes to *NEC P2/P3 on LPT2*. If it doesn't, verify that you selected the proper printer and port combination. When you're sure it's correct, choose OK to confirm the settings in the dialog box and carry out the command.

Having installed the driver and specified the new printer's connections, you're ready to print, right? Not quite. When you've installed more than one printer, you must tell Windows which one to use. To do that, choose Printer from the Setup menu. As Figure 6-5 shows, a dialog box appears, listing available printers. Be sure the Pinwriter's entry is selected; then choose OK. Another dialog box appears for specifying paper format, orientation, and other options. You don't need to adjust anything here because you aren't going to be printing anything, so simply choose OK. When you do, your disk drive activates for a few seconds as Control Panel makes notations in the WIN.INI file to reflect your choices.

To sum up, adding a new printer is a three-step job:

1. Use the Installation menu's Add New Printer command to copy the printer driver from your Windows Utilities 1 Disk to the drive and directory containing your copy of Windows.

2. Use the Setup menu's Connections command to tell Control Panel which port the printer uses.

3. Use the Setup menu's Printer command to choose the current printer and specify printing options.

By the way, depending on the software you're using, you may not need to go through the third step. The File menu in many Windows applications includes a command, usually called Change Printer or Target Printer, that lets you choose a printer and specify print options. With applications that don't include Change Printer commands (such

FIGURE 6-5.

List of available printers in Control Panel.

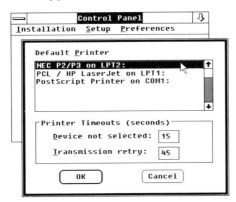

as Notepad), you must use Control Panel to change printers. Regard-less of which printer-selection method you use, one rule holds true: Avoid changing printers after you begin work on a document, espe-cially one containing a variety of type styles. That way, you won't have to reformat your document because of differences between one printer's capabilities and another's.

To delete the printer driver you installed earlier, start Control Panel and choose Delete Printer from the Installation menu. Select the driver for the NEC Pinwriter (or whichever driver you installed), choose Delete, and choose Yes when asked if you want to delete the driver from your Windows directory. Finally, close Control Panel.

TIP 5: Using a PostScript Printer

Getting Windows to converse with most printers is a straightforward process: Attach the printer, install its driver, and specify its connection port and print options. But printers that use the PostScript page-description language require a few more steps. The following section describes how to attach a PostScript printer to an MS-DOS computer and covers some of the special printing techniques available with Post-Script printers.

The PostScript Printer's Serial Interface

To understand how Windows communicates with PostScript printers, you need to understand how PostScript printers communicate with computers. Understanding the interface options available to you will help you decide which is best for your needs. PostScript printers usually offer two serial interfaces: RS-232C and AppleTalk. Although parallel communication dominates the printer world, PostScript print-ers generally use serial interfaces because PostScript printers require two-way communication capabilities that parallel interfaces don't offer. A PostScript printer often must send sophisticated messages to the computer to which it's connected, telling it that you want it to download a font, that a bad PostScript command was received, or that another error occurred. Parallel printers can report out-of-paper er-rors, but that's usually the extent of their communication with the computer. Some PostScript printers, such as Texas Instruments' OmniLaser series, contain a Centronics parallel interface, in addition to a serial interface. This additional, parallel interface is primarily intended for use with the printers' Diablo 630 emulation mode, which lets the printer imitate that venerable daisy-wheel printer, letting you print from older applications that don't support PostScript. If you have one of these dual-interface printers and you use both applications that support PostScript and those that don't, you should connect to the serial interface for PostScript printing and to the parallel interface for non-PostScript printing. You could use the printer's parallel port to receive PostScript. But if you did, you would also need to connect the printer's serial port so that it could send status messages to the computer, and neither Windows nor most other current software supports this convoluted dual-port connection method.

Connecting a PostScript Printer

Even though the most common way to unite a PostScript printer and an MS-DOS computer is through a serial interface, few printers include instructions on wiring a cable for the task. Perhaps it's because most PostScript printers are used with Macintoshes. Or perhaps it's because no definitive scheme for cabling an MS-DOS computer to a PostScript printer exists that is guaranteed to work with every serial board and every printer.

Figure 6-6 shows a wiring diagram for the cable I use. I've used it successfully with several computers, from a Tandy 1000 to an IBM PS/2 Model 50, and with two PostScript printers: an Apple LaserWriter Plus and a QMS-PS 800+. If wiring a cable isn't your idea of fun, you can use a serial cable for connecting an MS-DOS computer to a Hewlett-Packard LaserJet (Hewlett-Packard part number 17255D, available from Hewlett-Packard dealers). If you have an IBM PC/AT, which has a serial port that uses a DB-9 connector instead of the more common DB-25, you also need a 9-pin-to-25-pin adapter. Needless to say, you also need a free serial port; if you use a modem or serial mouse, you may need to add a second port.

FIGURE 6-6.
Wiring diagram for RS-232C cable to connect an MS-DOS computer to a PostScript printer.

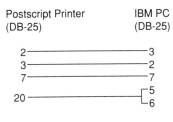

Postscript Printer (DB-25)   IBM PC (DB-25)

As an alternative to using an RS-232C serial link, you might consider adding an AppleTalk expansion board to your computer and using a software utility called WinPrint from Tangent Technologies. WinPrint allows Windows applications to print to a PostScript printer using AppleTalk. Because AppleTalk transfers data at speeds faster than 9600 baud, your printing times will decrease, but there's a price to pay: You must forego the use of Windows' spooler. If you use MS-DOS computers and Macs, however, the sacrifice will be worthwhile for convenience, since you won't have to fuss with switching your PostScript printer between its AppleTalk and 9600-baud modes.

And because an AppleTalk board lets your machine connect to an AppleTalk network, you can exchange files with Macintosh users by using networking software such as Tangent Technologies' TangentShare, which lets a PC join an AppleShare network. (AppleShare is the Apple software that turns a hard-disk-equipped Macintosh into a network file server.) Tangent Technologies' AppleTalk board for IBM PCs and IBM PC/XTs is PCMacBridge ATB/II. The IBM PS/2 Models 50, 60, and 80 version is PCMacBridge ATB/MCA. Apple Computer also manufactures an AppleTalk board for IBM PCs and IBM PC/XTs, as does Tops, makers of the Tops local-area network software for MS-DOS computers and Macs.

Configuring the Printer Port

The MS-DOS-computer-to-PostScript bridge isn't complete until you configure the printer and your computer's serial port to speak the same serial language. First, be sure the printer's port switch is set for 9600-baud serial PostScript operation. With a LaserWriter or LaserWriter Plus, set the four-position switch to the 9600 position. On a QMS-PS 800 and QMS-PS 800+, turn the thumb switch until the number 1 is visible. With a Texas Instruments OmniLaser 2108, use the front-panel keyboard to activate 9600-baud operation. Check your work by switching on the printer and waiting for its startup page; most PostScript printers indicate their current operating mode there.

Setting Serial Communications Handshaking

From here, things can get complicated. The complicating factor is a communications concept called handshaking. When a receiving serial device, such as a printer, fills with data or is busy with another task, it can send signals to the transmitting device (the computer), telling it to temporarily stop sending data. When it's ready to receive data again, it sends another signal telling the transmitting device to resume. This "Wait a moment" and "OK, go ahead" dialog is handshaking.

Two handshaking methods exist: hardware handshaking and software handshaking. With hardware handshaking, the printer says "Wait a moment" by changing the voltage on one of the serial wires; the computer senses the change and stops transmitting until the voltage changes again. With software handshaking, the printer sends control codes to the computer telling it to pause or resume. Most Post-Script printers can handshake either way, although early models of Apple's LaserWriter are limited to software handshaking. They respond to the industry standard Control-S and Control-Q codes—the same control codes you would use to pause and resume, respectively, a scrolling directory display in MS-DOS.

Which handshaking method should you use? The serial ports in most MS-DOS computers use hardware handshaking, so start there. Be sure your printer's mode switch is set for 9600-baud communications; then start Windows' Control Panel, choose the Communications Port command from the Setup menu, and complete the Communications Settings dialog box as shown in Figure 6-7. (If your printer is attached to COM2, choose that port instead of COM1.) Be sure your settings match those of Figure 6-7, then choose OK and close Control Panel. (You choose these settings because they're Adobe's default settings for communications through an RS-232C serial port, the type that most MS-DOS computers use.)

Next, you must configure your printer for hardware handshaking. Doing so involves sending a short PostScript program, located on

FIGURE 6-7.

Communications settings for a PostScript printer.

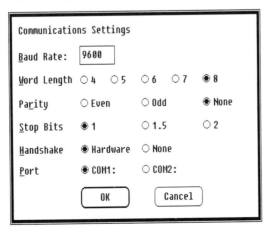

your Windows Utilities 2 Disk, to the printer. This program activates the printer's hardware-handshaking setting. The current handshaking setting is stored in the printer's permanent memory, so you need to perform this step only once.

Be sure your printer is on and ready, and then insert your Utilities 2 Disk in drive A. Next, switch to MS-DOS Executive and display the directory of the disk in drive A. Locate the file named HARDWARE.TXT, and then select it. (If you have trouble locating it, use the View menu's Partial command to include the wildcard *.txt* to narrow down the list of files.) With the file selected, choose Copy from the File menu, type *com1* in the To text box (or *com2* if you're using that port), and choose OK. (Don't type a colon after the device name; although it works in MS-DOS, it doesn't in MS-DOS Executive.) Your printer's activity light should blink briefly while the file is sent over the serial cable. While the Utilities 2 Disk is still in drive A, copy the files PSPREP.TXT and READMEPS.TXT to the Windows directory of your hard disk; you'll use them later.

If you didn't specify a PostScript printer when you set up your Windows installation, your next step is to copy the PostScript printer driver, PSCRIPT.DRV, to your hard disk. Use Control Panel's Installation menu as described in Tip 4 to do it. The driver itself is also stored on the Utilities 2 Disk, so leave it in drive A. After you copy the driver, use the Setup menu's Connections command to specify which port the printer uses, and use the Printer command to make the PostScript printer the current printer. Close Control Panel when you've finished.

Testing the Serial Link

With all that behind you, you're ready to try printing. Start Notepad, and open the READMEPS.TXT file you copied from the Utilities 2 Disk. Be sure your printer is on and ready, and then choose Print from the File menu and stand back. You'll see the Spooler icon appear (unless the Notepad window is maximized), and in a few moments, your printer's activity light should begin blinking. Shortly after that, the hard copy should appear in the printer's output tray.

If it doesn't, it wouldn't be the first time serial communications inspired frustration. Check your work. Start by verifying that the printer's mode switch is set for 9600 baud PostScript operation; the other settings place the printer in 1200 baud PostScript mode or configure it for AppleTalk or Diablo 630 emulation mode. Next, restart Control Panel and use the Setup menu to double-check your communications, connections, and printer settings. Be sure the printer driver PSCRIPT.DRV is in your Windows directory.

If all settings are correct, try the software handshaking route. In Control Panel, choose Communications Port from the Setup menu, and, in the Handshake section, choose the None button. (That may seem as if you're disabling handshaking. Don't worry; the PostScript print driver will know to use software handshaking.) Then choose OK and close Control Panel. Next, return to the MS-DOS Executive window, be sure the Utilities 2 Disk is in drive A, and then copy the file SOFTWARE.TXT to the printer using the techniques described earlier. Finally, try printing the READMEPS.TXT file again.

If you still have no success, you may have a problem with your computer's serial port. If it has more than one serial port, try the other one. If you're able to borrow a multifunction expansion board with its own serial port, do so and try it. If you made your own cable, be sure you wired it correctly and that there are no loose or cold solder joints on either connector. If you suspect your cable, try it with another printer. And don't neglect the obvious: be sure that the printer is warmed up and contains paper.

Printing to Disk

By making a minor modification to Windows, you can send the output of Spooler to a disk file instead of to the printer. For most printers, that's of little value, but it has great potential for PostScript printer users. You can "print" a PageMaker publication—or any document created by a Windows application—to disk, and then take the disk or transmit the disk file over a modem to any typesetting service bureau that uses PostScript typesetting equipment (such as Allied Linotype's Linotronic series). This procedure lets you tap the typographic talents of PostScript without having to own a PostScript printer. If you have your own PostScript printer, you can print proofs on it to check for errors before going to the expense of transmitting your final documents to a typesetter. And because the print file contains all the information the printer needs to create the document, the service bureau need not have Windows or the application you used. (It must, however, have all the fonts called for in the document. A print file does not contain PostScript fonts, only the commands that access them.)

Coercing Windows to print to a disk file requires making a minor modification to WIN.INI, the Windows configuration file discussed in Chapter 1. The many facets of WIN.INI are the subjects of Chapter 7 and 8; we'll look only at its print-to-disk modification here. WIN.INI is a text file that you can edit with the Notepad desktop application. To do so, simply open WIN.INI from the MS-DOS Executive window. Windows starts Notepad and loads the WIN.INI file, as shown in Figure 6-8.

To locate the portion of WIN.INI where you'll make the modification, choose Find from Notepad's Search menu, type *ports* and press Enter. Next, scroll down a dozen or so lines, until the blinking cursor is at the end of the line beginning with *EPT* and then press Enter. Now carefully type *printfil.prn* followed by an equal sign. When your screen looks like the one in Figure 6-9, save the changes and close Notepad.

Because Windows reads the WIN.INI file every time it starts up, you must end your session and restart Windows in order for Windows to recognize the modification. Do it now. Your next step is to tell Windows that your PostScript printer is "attached" to the print file. Open Control Panel and choose Connections from the Setup menu. Select the name of your PostScript printer in the left list box, and then scroll the right list box until you see the entry for printfil.prn. Select it, and as Figure 6-10 shows, the left scroll box changes to reflect the new "connection." Choose OK to confirm the dialog box, and then close Control Panel.

FIGURE 6-8.

Open WIN.INI.

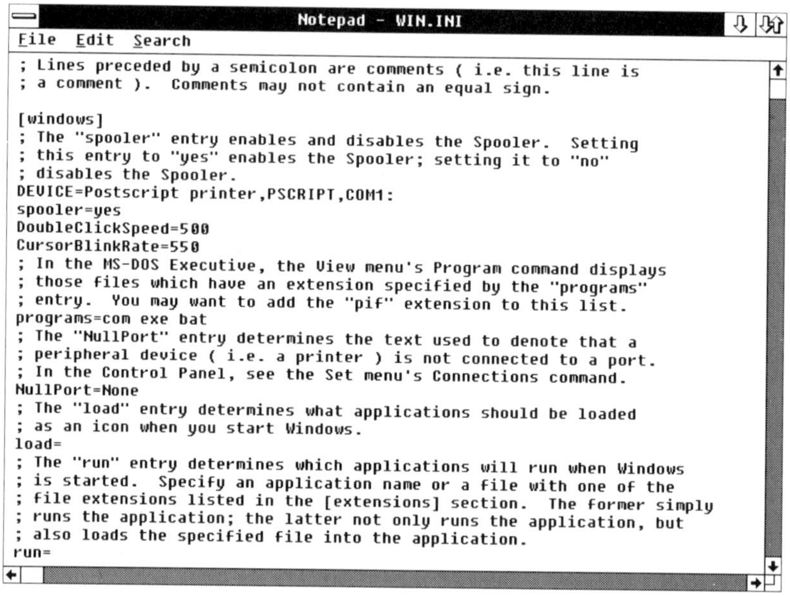

```
===                        Notepad - WIN.INI                        ⇩ ⇧⇩
 File   Edit   Search
 ────────────────────────────────────────────────────────────────────── ⬆
 ; Lines preceded by a semicolon are comments ( i.e. this line is
 ; a comment ).  Comments may not contain an equal sign.

 [windows]
 ; The "spooler" entry enables and disables the Spooler.  Setting
 ; this entry to "yes" enables the Spooler; setting it to "no"
 ; disables the Spooler.
 DEVICE=Postscript printer,PSCRIPT,COM1:
 spooler=yes
 DoubleClickSpeed=500
 CursorBlinkRate=550
 ; In the MS-DOS Executive, the View menu's Program command displays
 ; those files which have an extension specified by the "programs"
 ; entry.  You may want to add the "pif" extension to this list.
 programs=com exe bat
 ; The "NullPort" entry determines the text used to denote that a
 ; peripheral device ( i.e. a printer ) is not connected to a port.
 ; In the Control Panel, see the Set menu's Connections command.
 NullPort=None
 ; The "load" entry determines what applications should be loaded
 ; as an icon when you start Windows.
 load=
 ; The "run" entry determines which applications will run when Windows
 ; is started.  Specify an application name or a file with one of the
 ; file extensions listed in the [extensions] section.  The former simply
 ; runs the application; the latter not only runs the application, but
 ; also loads the specified file into the application.
 run=                                                                     ⬇
 ←                                                                      → 
```

FIGURE 6-9.

Print file addition to WIN.INI.

```
┌──────────────────────────────────────────────────────────────────┐
│ ▭              Notepad - WIN.INI                          ⇩ ⇪│
├──────────────────────────────────────────────────────────────────┤
│ File   Edit   Search                                               │
│ subst.exe=20                                                     ▲│
│ win.com=1                                                        ░│
│                                                                  ░│
│ [intl]                                                           ░│
│ dialog=yes                                                       ░│
│                                                                  ░│
│ [ports]                                                          ░│
│ ; A line with [filename].PRN followed by an equal sign causes    ░│
│ ; [filename] to appear in the Control Panel's Connections dialog.░│
│ ; A printer connected to [filename] directs its output into this file.░│
│ LPT1:=                                                           ░│
│ LPT2:=                                                           ░│
│ LPT3:=                                                           ░│
│ COM1:=9600,n,8,1                                                 ░│
│ COM2:=9600,n,8,1                                                 ░│
│ EPT:=                                                            ░│
│ printfil.prn=                                                    ░│
│                                                                  ░│
│ [devices]                                                        ░│
│ PCL / HP LaserJet=HPPCL,LPT1:                                    ░│
│ Postscript printer=PSCRIPT,COM1:                                 ░│
│                                                                  ░│
│ [fonts]                                                          ░│
│ Helv 8,10,12,14,18,24 (Set #6)=HELVE                             ░│
│ Courier 8,10,12 (Set #6)=COURE                                   ░│
│ Tms Rmn 8,10,12,14,18,24 (Set #6)=TMSRE                          ░│
│ Roman (Set #1)=ROMAN                                             ░│
│ Script (Set #1)=SCRIPT                                           ▼│
│ ←                                                                →│
└──────────────────────────────────────────────────────────────────┘
```

Next, start Write and type a few words. Then choose Print from the File menu, and choose OK. The Spooler icon appears briefly as Write sends data to Spooler, which, in turn, sends it to the print file.

To verify that the print file actually contains something, you're going to open it with Write. Examining a print file is also an excellent way to learn how Windows talks to a given printer. When the Spooler icon disappears, choose Open from the File menu, and then choose No when asked to save what you typed. In the Open File Name text box, type *printfil.prn* and press Enter. When you're asked if you want to convert the file to Write format, choose No Conversion. After a few moments, your screen should resemble the one in Figure 6-11 on the following page.

FIGURE 6-10.

Print file selected in Control Panel.

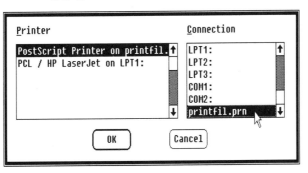

FIGURE 6-11.

Open newly created print file.

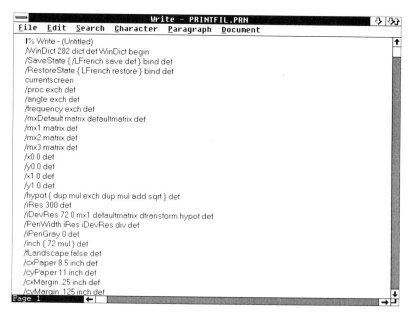

```
Write - PRINTFIL.PRN
File  Edit  Search  Character  Paragraph  Document

!% Write - (Untitled)
/WinDict 282 dict def WinDict begin
/SaveState { /LFrench save def } bind def
/RestoreState { LFrench restore } bind def
currentscreen
/proc exch def
/angle exch def
/frequency exch def
/mxDefault matrix defaultmatrix def
/mx1 matrix def
/mx2 matrix def
/mx3 matrix def
/x0 0 def
/y0 0 def
/x1 0 def
/y1 0 def
/hypot { dup mul exch dup mul add sqrt } def
/iRes 300 def
/iDevRes 72 0 mx1 defaultmatrix dtransform hypot def
/PenWidth iRes iDevRes div def
/iPenGray 0 def
/inch { 72 mul } def
/fLandscape false def
/cxPaper 8.5 inch def
/cyPaper 11 inch def
/cxMargin .25 inch def
/cyMargin .125 inch def
Page 1
```

Those cryptic codes comprise Windows' PostScript dictionary, a set of extensions and enhancements to the PostScript language that lets it work better with Windows. One part of the dictionary remaps the character codes for certain special characters, such as accents and typographic quotes, from the ANSI standard that Windows uses to the Adobe PostScript standard. Another part of the dictionary adds Post-Script functions for printing strikethrough and underlined text. Other dictionary definitions add graphics commands that let Post-Script and Windows' GDI coexist.

If you scroll to the end of the file, you can see, sandwiched between the first set of lines reading *SaveState* and *RestoreState*, a description for the page you printed. Somewhere in the middle, you should see the text you typed, enclosed within parentheses.

"Wait a minute," you might be saying. "You mean that entire dictionary and all those PostScript commands are necessary to print those few measly words?" No. The PostScript printer driver isn't smart enough to know which PostScript extensions will be necessary for a given print job, so it transmits the entire 12,000-byte dictionary each time you print a document. And that takes time—about 30 seconds at 9600 baud. Indeed, if you're printing a two-page or three-page document, transmitting the dictionary will be the most time-consuming portion of the print job. (There is an alternative: If you know you're going to be printing a large number of documents, you can transmit the dictionary to the printer manually when you first switch it on. You'll learn how shortly.)

Sending the Print File to a Local Printer

In this exercise, you're going to send the print file you created to a PostScript printer attached to your MS-DOS computer. If it was off, switch on your printer and wait for it to print its startup page, and then close Write and return to the MS-DOS Executive window. Select the file named PRINTFIL.PRN, and then choose Copy from the File menu. In the To box, type *com1* and press Enter. Your printer's activity light flashes and, after a minute or so, a printout of your words appears in the output tray. That's all there is to transmitting a print file over a direct cable connection.

Sending the Print File to a Remote Computer

With a telecommunications program and a modem, you can transmit PostScript print files over the phone lines to another computer—for example, to one at a distant typesetting service or to one connected to a PostScript printer located beyond the reach of printer cables.

If you are transmitting a file to a typesetting bureau, you would not be sending it directly to its PostScript typesetter. More likely, you would be transmitting it to the service's computer, where it would be stored until the service was ready to print it. In such cases, follow the bureau's communications instructions. They'll be similar to the steps described below, although you will probably transmit the print file using an error-checking protocol such as Xmodem to avoid garbled data due to noisy phone lines.

If you are transmitting a file to an MS-DOS computer in another location, agree on communication parameters and instruct the person with whom you're communicating to save incoming data in a text file. The person at the other end of the line can then copy this PostScript file to the PostScript printer at a convenient time.

Because a PostScript print file is only a series of ASCII text characters, the procedure for transmitting a file to an Apple Macintosh is the same: Agree on communication parameters and instruct the Macintosh owner to save incoming data in a text file. The Macintosh owner can then use a PostScript downloading program to print the file on a PostScript printer connected to AppleTalk or to one of the Mac's serial ports. Two fine downloading programs are SendPS by Adobe Systems and CricketDraw by Cricket Software. Adobe's Font Downloader for the Mac can also download PostScript files.

The following example uses Windows inTalk, a capable communications program from Palantir Software. I use inTalk because it's a Windows application, but you could also use Microsoft Access, Hayes Smartcom II, or any other communications program that can transmit disk files. Windows Terminal cannot.

Set your communications parameters as follows: 1200 baud, 8 data bits, 1 stop bit, no parity, and handshaking (inTalk calls it Xon/Xoff flow control). Then instruct the receiving computer user to do the same. If your modems have the capability, you may want to increase the speed to 2400 baud after you have established a strong connection. If you have trouble, use the Xmodem protocol, which provides extra error detection and correction. Figure 6-12 shows the inTalk settings I use for transmitting over telephone lines.

When the receiving computer user is ready to receive your Post-Script file, choose Send Text File from the Transfers menu, then type *printfil.prn* in the Filename box and press Enter. In a few moments the file is safely stored on the receiving user's computer.

One more word about print files: Each time you route a document to a print file, Windows replaces the previous contents of the print file with a new version of the file. If you want to create print files for several documents, use MS-DOS Executive's Rename command to rename the print file after "printing" each document.

FIGURE 6-12.

Palantir inTalk Communications Settings.

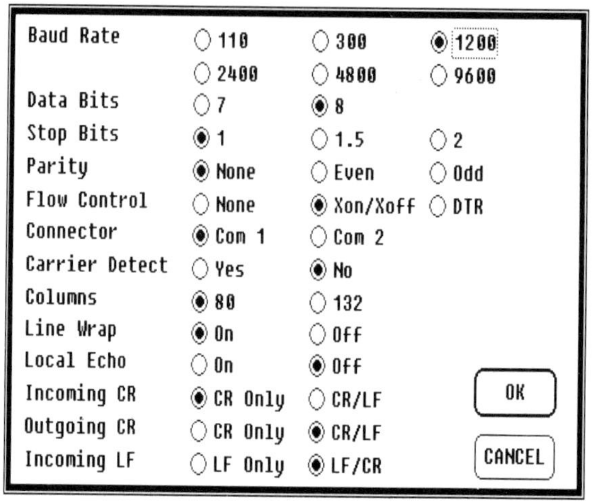

Baud Rate	○ 110	○ 300	◉ 1200
	○ 2400	○ 4800	○ 9600
Data Bits	○ 7	◉ 8	
Stop Bits	◉ 1	○ 1.5	○ 2
Parity	◉ None	○ Even	○ Odd
Flow Control	○ None	◉ Xon/Xoff	○ DTR
Connector	◉ Com 1	○ Com 2	
Carrier Detect	○ Yes	◉ No	
Columns	◉ 80	○ 132	
Line Wrap	◉ On	○ Off	
Local Echo	○ On	◉ Off	
Incoming CR	◉ CR Only	○ CR/LF	OK
Outgoing CR	○ CR Only	◉ CR/LF	
Incoming LF	○ LF Only	◉ LF/CR	CANCEL

Downloading the PostScript Dictionary

When you know you're going to be printing a large number of short
documents, you may want to download the Windows PostScript dictionary to the printer when you first switch it on. Doing so eliminates
the need for Windows to transmit the dictionary with every print job
and reduces by roughly a half minute the time it takes to print each
job. If saving 30 seconds on every print job isn't important to you, you
can skip this section.

The PostScript dictionary that you'll download is stored in a file
called PSPREP.TXT on your Utilities 2 Disk. Earlier in this chapter, I
asked that you copy that file to your hard disk's Windows directory. If
you skipped that step, do it now.

You transmit the PostScript dictionary using the same technique
you used to transmit the print file. Be sure your printer is on and
ready, and then select PSPREP.TXT in the MS-DOS Executive window
and choose Copy from the File menu. In the To box, type *com1* and
press Enter. Your printer's activity light blinks, and after a minute or
two, a page appears saying "PSPREP.TXT loaded." The dictionary remains in the printer's memory until you turn the printer off. You can
also transmit the dictionary automatically each time you restart your
computer by adding the following line to your AUTOEXEC.BAT file:

```
copy c:\windows\psprep.txt com1:
```

In order for this technique to work, however, you must be sure that
your printer is on and ready when you start your computer. Otherwise,
the printer will not receive the dictionary. If you forget to turn your
printer on before booting up, you don't have to restart your computer.
Simply turn on your printer, wait until it's warmed up and ready, and
then either type the above command at the MS-DOS prompt, or follow
the instructions above to transmit the dictionary using MS-DOS Executive's Copy command.

To tell Windows not to send the dictionary, you must add a line
to the WIN.INI configuration file. Open WIN.INI, and then use the
Find command to locate the line that reads *[PostScript,COM1]* (or
COM2, if you're using that port). Just below that line, add a new line
reading: *Header Downloaded=yes.* The lines should resemble Figure 6-13
on the following page. When they do, save the changed WIN.INI and
close Notepad. Remember, however, that you must quit and restart
Windows for it to recognize the changes you made.

FIGURE 6-13.

Header
Downloaded line
added to
WIN.INI.

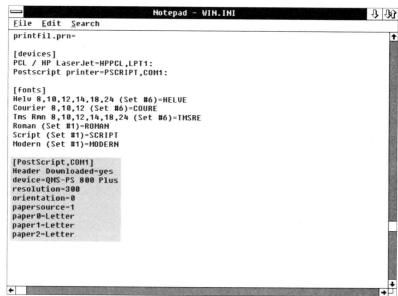

You might be wondering what the difference is between PSPREP.TXT and the PSCRIPT.DRV printer driver. PSPREP.TXT is not a printer driver; it's simply a series of PostScript routines that extend PostScript to work with Windows. PSCRIPT.DRV contains the identical routines, as well as the software that lets it translate a document into PostScript commands. When Windows sees the *Header Downloaded=yes* line in the WIN.INI file, it knows not to download the dictionary from the driver with each print job.

A final, important point about the PostScript dictionary: If you're creating print files for transmission to a service bureau, *do not* add the *Header Downloaded* line to WIN.INI. If you add this line, your print files will not contain the vital PostScript enhancements that the dictionary provides.

Using the PostScript Printer Interactively

You can interact directly with a PostScript printer, typing commands and viewing responses, by placing the printer in interactive mode. To do so, you need to be connected to a PostScript printer and to have a communications package running. Set your communications parameters as follows: 9600 baud, 8 data bits, 1 stop bit, no parity, and hardware handshaking (DTR in inTalk). Set the communications port to COM1 and connect the PostScript printer to COM1. As mentioned earlier, change the PostScript printer's mode switch from AppleTalk to 9600 baud PostScript mode. To enter interactive mode, be sure your communications program's window is active, and then type *executive* and press Enter. You won't see the word as you type it. After pressing Enter, you should see the following message (your version number may differ):

PostScript(r) Version 44.0
Copyright (c) 1986 Adobe Systems Incorporated.
PS>

You are now in interactive mode—anything you type goes directly to the PostScript interpreter. For example, you can type *showpage* and press Enter to tell your printer to eject a sheet of paper. Or you can type *FontDirectory { pop == } forall* and press Enter to see a list of your printer's resident typefaces scroll onto the screen. Type the short PostScript program in Figure 6-14, to tell your printer to produce a large uppercase C filled with the word PostScript, as shown in Figure 6-15 on the following page. To leave interactive mode, type *quit* and press Enter.

PostScript's interactive mode is an excellent way to experiment with the language.

FIGURE 6-14.

PostScript special-effect program.

```
%!
200 350 translate
/Roman /Times-Roman findfont 6 scalefont def
/Bold /Times-Bold findfont 200 scalefont def

/strg (POSTSCRIPT-POSTSCRIPT-POSTSCRIPT-POSTSCRIPT-POSTSCRIPT-
POSTSCRIPT-POSTSCRIPT) def

/crlf
{ currentpoint 6 sub
    exch pop 0 exch moveto } def

/prtstring { strg show crlf} def

/Background
{ 25 { prtstring } repeat } def

gsave
    newpath 0 0 moveto
    8 setflat
    Bold setfont (C) true charpath clip

    0 133 moveto
    Roman setfont Background
grestore

showpage
```

FIGURE 6-15.

*Output of
PostScript
special-effect
program.*

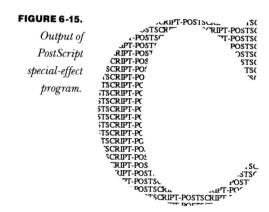

Where to Find
More Information About PostScript

You can learn more about PostScript from Adobe's *PostScript Language Tutorial and Cookbook* and *PostScript Language Reference Manual*, both published by Addison-Wesley. Another excellent source of information is Adobe's *Colophon* newsletter, available free of charge by writing, on your company letterhead, to Adobe Systems, 1585 Charleston Road, P.O. Box 7900, Mountain View, CA 94039.

CHAPTER 7

FONTS

Windows' ability to display and print text in different fonts, sizes, and styles has helped it become a key component for desktop publishing on MS-DOS computers. But you might wonder if fonts are worth the trouble of installing and using. They are. In this chapter, we look at installing and using screen and printer fonts. If you're unfamiliar with such typographic terms as "point," "serif," and "sans serif," you might want to read the section of this chapter titled "Tip 7: Typography Terminology."

Installing fonts requires becoming familiar with Control Panel and the WIN.INI file. You worked with many of Control Panel's printer-related commands in Chapter 6. The WIN.INI configuration file, which is read by Windows each time you start Windows, gives you access to other customization options, such as Windows' ability to use downloadable laser printer fonts. If you read the PostScript printer tip in Chapter 6, you encountered WIN.INI when you added the line *HeaderDownloaded=yes*.

Control Panel and WIN.INI may appear to be two entirely different ways to personalize Windows, but they're actually closely related. When you change any Control Panel setting except the time and date, Control Panel saves your changes in WIN.INI. Control Panel, then, is mostly a friendly facade for WIN.INI. Indeed, you can bypass Control Panel by using MS-DOS Executive to add or remove printer drivers or fonts and Notepad to edit WIN.INI. That isn't always a good idea, however; unlike you and me, Control Panel doesn't make typing errors.

Raster Versus Stroke Fonts

When you run the Setup program to install Windows, Setup copies certain font files to your hard disk based on the graphics adapter you select. These files, which end with the extension FON, contain the data that enables Windows' Graphic Device Interface to create characters in different type styles and sizes. Windows uses two types of fonts: raster and stroke. Raster fonts are intended for use with output devices—video screens and printers—that produce images using a series of fine parallel lines. In the microcomputer world, most video screens and laser printers are raster devices. (Raster comes from the Latin word for "rake"—imagine lines being raked across a screen or a page.) In a video monitor, the lines are drawn on a phosphor-coated video tube by a pinpoint beam of electrons. In a laser printer, the lines are drawn on a light-sensitive drum that attracts powdered toner and transfers it to paper. In both cases, the computer or the laser printer's controller circuitry flashes the beam on and off, and in doing so, lets it create dots on the screen (pixels) or on paper.

Raster font files contain the data that tells Windows which dots should be activated to create a given character in a given size. Because the arrangement of activated dots is different in each point size, raster font files contain separate data for each size. For example, Windows' Helv font, which is similar to the more widely known Helvetica, contains data describing 8-point, 10-point, 12-point, 14-point, 18-point, and 24-point characters. If you choose a size other than one of these six, Windows must scale an existing size to approximate it. The scaling process often results in jagged-edged characters.

The raster fonts on Windows fonts disks are organized into sets, with each set intended for a specific resolution. You can determine a given font file's set by finding its name in the Add Font dialog box, which appears when you choose Add New Font from Control Panel's Installation menu. If you want to try it, dig out your Fonts Disk 1, place it in drive A, start Control Panel, and choose Add New Font. When the dialog box appears asking which drive and directory contains the font files, press Enter. Control Panel scans the disk for font files. When it finds one, it reads part of it to determine the font's name and set. Finally, the Add Font dialog box appears, as shown in Figure 7-1.

The left side of the dialog box shows the information about each font file, and the upper-right corner shows each file's name. If you select (but don't double-click) each file in turn while watching the Font File text box, you might notice something odd. Sets are numbered 1 through 6, but in font files, a set is indicated by a letter from A to E. (Yes, that's only five letters; stroke fonts, which are in set 1, don't have letters.) That little inconsistency can be confusing as you start to

FIGURE 7-1.

Add Font dialog box.

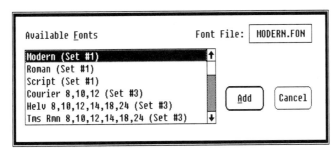

delve into WIN.INI, so keep it in mind. We won't be adding any fonts now, so choose Cancel to close the Add New Font dialog box.

Stroke fonts, also called vector fonts, don't contain data for specific sizes. Instead, they contain general descriptions of a font's appearance. For example, in a raster font, an uppercase T might be described as a stem 20 dots high topped with a crossbar 15 dots wide. In a stroke font, however, a T might be described as a stem topped with a crossbar that's 20 percent shorter. (Of course, the underlying technicalities are more complex than this; we're discussing only basics.) As a result, you can scale stroke fonts to any size without distortion; a separate description for each size isn't required. (Notice the parallel here between bitmapped and object-oriented graphics?) The biggest drawback of stroke fonts is that they take longer to appear on screen because Windows must perform calculations in order to draw the characters in the required size.

Stroke fonts are intended primarily for use with plotters, the most popular non-raster output devices. Rather than creating characters by using a series of fine parallel lines, plotters draw characters by zipping special felt-tipped pens around on a sheet of paper. But stroke fonts aren't the exclusive province of plotters. As the previous chapter describes, they also have a place in graphics that you bring into Microsoft Windows Write or Aldus PageMaker for resizing and subsequent printing.

Screen Fonts Versus Printer Fonts

If you use a laser printer with Windows, it's important to know the difference between screen fonts and printer fonts. Screen fonts are approximations—reasonable facsimiles—of a true typographic font. They can't convey all the subtleties of a font because of the screen's limited resolution. But they can show the font's basic qualities.

Printer fonts are the font descriptions the printer uses to create a typeface. Windows can't display printer fonts on the screen; they exist in a format only the printer can interpret. Printer fonts are built into read-only memory chips in the printer or in a plug-in cartridge or are stored on a hard disk and downloaded to the printer before use. Fonts that are stored on disk and downloaded to the printer's memory are sometimes called soft fonts. Regardless of where the font is stored—in the printer or on your hard disk—one rule applies: You can't print in a typeface unless you have a printer font for that typeface.

In non-PostScript printers, such as the Hewlett-Packard LaserJet series, fonts are stored in bitmap form, with separate bitmap descriptions for each type size and orientation (portrait or landscape). Therefore, the printer fonts you have also determine the available type sizes. For example, Windows' Helv screen font includes 8-point, 10-point, 12-point, 14-point, 18-point, and 24-point Helv characters. If, however, you have Hewlett-Packard's F cartridge, you are able to print only 14-point Helv Bold. A wider selection of a better-looking Helv is available in a Hewlett-Packard soft font package that includes 8-point, 10-point, and 12-point sizes, and Helv Bold in 10-point, 12-point, 18-point, and 24-point sizes. Even with this package, however, you can't print text in all the sizes of Helv for which screen fonts exist.

PostScript printers don't have this limitation because, like Windows' stroke fonts, their fonts are stored as mathematic character descriptions called outlines, not as bitmaps for specific sizes, as shown in Figure 7-2. Just as an object-oriented graphic or a stroke font can be scaled to any size without distortion, a single PostScript font description can produce text in virtually any size, including nonstandard type sizes such as 31-point. If Windows can't find a screen font in a matching size, it uses the size closest to the one you chose.

Regardless of the printer you use, the Font menus and dialog boxes of most Windows applications display only those fonts or sizes that your printer provides. To see this for yourself, install more than one printer driver, start Write, and choose Fonts from the Character menu. Observe the fonts and sizes currently available. Then choose Cancel and use the File menu's Change Printer command to switch to the other printer driver. Finally, choose the Fonts command again. The dialog box lists different combinations of fonts and sizes.

FIGURE 7-2.

Bitmapped (left) versus outline (right) fonts.

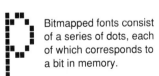 Bitmapped fonts consist of a series of dots, each of which corresponds to a bit in memory.

 Outline fonts consist of geometric curves and lines that can be scaled to any size without distortion.

TIP 1: Specifying Fonts in WIN.INI

Windows determines which fonts are in your installation when it reads the WIN.INI file during startup. The section of WIN.INI labeled *[fonts]* lists the available screen font files. Figure 7-3 shows the *[fonts]* section in a typical WIN.INI file. Each line is an entry for one font file; the text to the left of the equal sign lists the font's name, set number, and the point sizes provided. This descriptive text is the same as that which appears in the left side of Control Panel's Add New Font and Delete Font dialog boxes. To the right of the equal sign is the name of the font's FON file.

A printer description section of WIN.INI can also contain font information. A printer-description section starts with a listing of the printer type and connection port within brackets, as in:

[PostScript,COM1] for PostScript printers

or:

[HPPCL,LPT1] for LaserJets and other PCL printers.

Windows updates a printer-description section when you use the dialog box that appears when you choose the Printer command from Control Panel's Setup menu or when you choose an application's Change Printer command. (In some applications, that command may be called Target Printer or Current Printer.) This dialog box lets you specify such print options as page orientation, paper size, and graphics resolution. When you change a setting, you probably notice your hard disk chugging for a few moments; that's the sound of Windows opening WIN.INI, locating the appropriate section, and updating the information.

If you use downloadable printer fonts, your printer-description section contains entries listing the pathname and filename of each font's font-metrics file. A font-metrics file, which ends with the extension PFM, contains character-spacing information for a given font. The

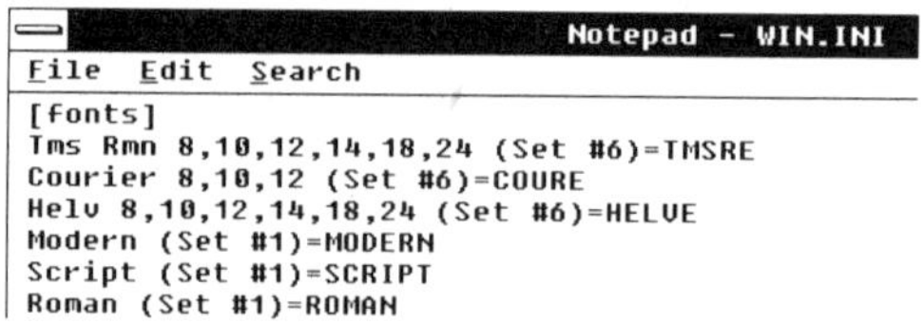

FIGURE 7-3.

The [fonts]
section of a
typical WIN.INI
file.

```
┌───┐                    Notepad - WIN.INI
│   │  File  Edit  Search
├───────────────────────────────────────────
│ [fonts]
│ Tms Rmn 8,10,12,14,18,24 (Set #6)=TMSRE
│ Courier 8,10,12 (Set #6)=COURE
│ Helv 8,10,12,14,18,24 (Set #6)=HELVE
│ Modern (Set #1)=MODERN
│ Script (Set #1)=SCRIPT
│ Roman (Set #1)=ROMAN
```

character-width information in the PFM files controls the way in which Windows positions text on the screen; it lets Windows accurately reflect on screen the character spacing of the printer font. Figure 7-4 shows the printer-description section for a PostScript printer, a QMS-PS800+, for which several downloadable Adobe Systems fonts have been installed. With some downloadable fonts, your printer-description section may also contain the pathname and filename of the printer font file itself.

FIGURE 7-4.

Printer description with soft-font entries.

```
┌─────────────────────────────────────────────────┐
│ ⊜                  Notepad - WIN.INI             │
├─────────────────────────────────────────────────┤
│ File  Edit  Search                               │
├─────────────────────────────────────────────────┤
│ [PostScript,COM1]                                │
│ device=QMS-PS 800 Plus                           │
│ resolution=300                                   │
│ orientation=0                                    │
│ papersource=1                                    │
│ paper0=Letter                                    │
│ paper1=Letter                                    │
│ paper2=Letter                                    │
│ softfonts=8                                      │
│ softfont1=C:\WINDOWS\OPBO_____.PFM               │
│ softfont2=C:\WINDOWS\OPB_____.PFM               │
│ softfont3=C:\WINDOWS\OPO_____.PFM               │
│ softfont4=C:\WINDOWS\OP_____.PFM               │
│ softfont5=C:\WINDOWS\GYBO_____.PFM               │
│ softfont6=C:\WINDOWS\GYB_____.PFM               │
│ softfont7=C:\WINDOWS\GYO_____.PFM               │
│ softfont8=C:\WINDOWS\GY_____.PFM               │
```

TIP 2: Using Downloadable Fonts

For some time after Windows' introduction, laser-printer users could have any screen font they wanted, as long as it was Courier, Helv, or TmsRmn. Windows applications could access the other fonts a printer might contain, but no screen fonts for them were available. Windows simply used TmsRmn to depict serif fonts, Helv to represent sans serif fonts, and Courier to represent monospace fonts.

Fortunately, this one-face-fits-all situation changed in late 1987, when two leaders in digital typography, Adobe Systems and Bitstream, released downloadable font packages for Windows. Adobe Systems' fonts are designed for use with PostScript printers; Bitstream's Fontware package works with PostScript printers and with Hewlett-Packard LaserJets and compatibles.

If you own a LaserWriter Plus or other PostScript printer containing 35 fonts, you might want to acquire the Adobe screen fonts that correspond to your printer's fonts. Adobe has placed the screen font files in the Adobe forum of the CompuServe Information Service, where they're available free, except for the connect time charges you incur when downloading them. Adobe also plans to release the screen font files as a separate product that you can purchase through dealers. As this book was being written, however, no price or availability date had been set. (For information on their availability, contact Adobe Systems at the address listed in Appendix A.)

Both the Adobe and Bitstream font packages use an installation program that lets you select which fonts you want to install. The program then copies the printer and corresponding screen fonts to your hard disk and modifies WIN.INI to reflect the new faces. After that, you can use the fonts normally, selecting them from your applications' Font menus or dialog boxes.

When you print a document containing downloadable Bitstream fonts on a Hewlett-Packard LaserJet Plus or Series II printer, Windows' LaserJet printer driver downloads the fonts and then removes them from the printer's memory at the end of the print job. If you use Bitstream's fonts with a PostScript printer, you must replace the standard Windows PostScript driver with one included with Fontware. That driver downloads Bitstream's fonts without your intervention. It cannot, however, download Adobe's PostScript fonts. If you use Adobe's fonts, you must download the fonts manually ahead of time. Manually downloaded fonts remain in the printer's memory after the print job. You can combine both Bitstream's and Adobe's PostScript fonts by first downloading the Adobe fonts manually and then printing the document as you normally would. The Bitstream PostScript driver downloads Bitstream's fonts for you.

TIP 3: Installing and Using the Adobe Type Library

The MS-DOS version of the Adobe Type Library opens Windows to Adobe's large library of high-quality PostScript typefaces. Each Adobe typeface package includes four printer fonts, matching screen fonts (in 10-point, 12-point, 14-point, 18-point, and 24-point sizes), and an excellent downloading and printer setup utility.

Adobe's installation program copies the fonts in a given package to a directory named PSFONTS, creating the directory for you if it doesn't exist. Next, the program asks if you want to copy Adobe Font Downloader to your hard disk. Answer ''Yes''; besides being able to download fonts, Adobe Font Downloader provides useful commands for viewing or printing a listing of the fonts in your printer, checking the printer's free memory, changing its communications settings, and more. And you can run it in a window by creating the PIF (Program Information File) shown in Figure 7-5. (PIFs are discussed in detail in Chapter 9.)

After copying Adobe Font Downloader, the installer asks if you want to proceed with the Windows installation process. Answer "Yes." You're then asked which screen fonts you want to copy into your Windows directory. Generally, you'll want to copy all four of the package's screen fonts. But if hard-disk space is sparse, you can copy only the fonts you need. (You can add the others later using Control Panel.) Finally, the installer modifies the WIN.INI file, adding the new screen font entries to the *[fonts]* section and the new printer font entries to the printer-description section. As a safety measure, the installer creates a backup copy of WIN.INI, naming it WIN.SAF, before modifying the file.

You can use the newly installed fonts as soon as your printer is warmed up. Figure 7-6 on the next page shows several screen fonts and their printed counterparts.

As you work with downloadable fonts, remember that a finite number of them can fit in a printer's memory at once. Apple Computer's pioneering LaserWriter and LaserWriter Plus have room for approximately four downloadable fonts. Apple's LaserWriter IINT and NTX printers, introduced in January 1988, manage memory more efficiently and can hold six to eight downloadable fonts. The PS 800 printer family from QMS has this same advantage.

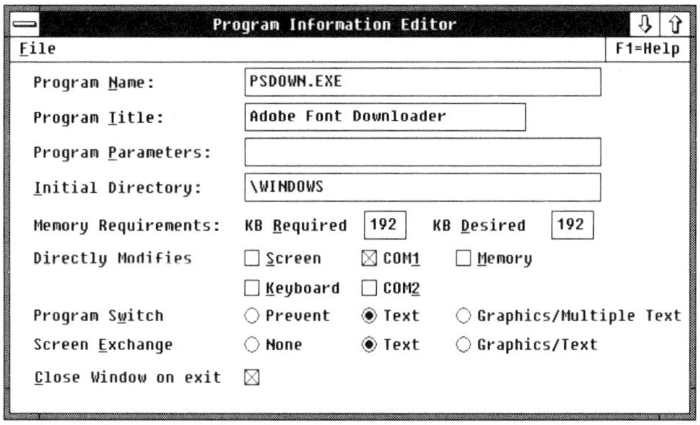

FIGURE 7-5.

PIF entries for Adobe Font Downloader.

Program Information Editor	⇩ ⇧
File	F1=Help

Program **N**ame: `PSDOWN.EXE`

Program **T**itle: `Adobe Font Downloader`

Program **P**arameters: `_____`

Initial Directory: `\WINDOWS`

Memory Requirements: KB **R**equired `192`   KB **D**esired `192`

Directly Modifies   ☐ **S**creen   ☒ CO**M1**   ☐ **M**emory
                    ☐ **K**eyboard   ☐ COM2

Program S**w**itch   ◯ Prevent   ⦿ Text   ◯ Graphics/Multiple Text

Screen E**x**change   ◯ None   ⦿ Text   ◯ Graphics/Text

Close Window on exit   ☒

(The PS 800 series includes the PS 800, PS 800+, PS 800 II, PS 810, and their PS Jet counterparts, which are distributed by QMS subsidiary The Laser Connection.) Moreover, many PostScript printers, including the LaserWriter IINT and NTX and the QMS-PS 810, accept memory expansion upgrades that boost their downloadable-font capacities. To verify that your printer can house the downloadable fonts needed for a given job, check Adobe Font Downloader's free-memory indicator, shown in Figure 7-7, and don't let it drop below 50 KB.

FIGURE 7-6.

Screen fonts (top) and printer output (bottom).

This is 18-point Palatino, a serif typeface.

This is 18-point Optima, a sans serif typeface.

This is 18-point Glypha, a serif typeface.

This is 18-point Palatino, a serif typeface.

This is 18-point Optima, a sans serif typeface.

This is 18-point Glypha, a serif typeface.

FIGURE 7-7.

Adobe Font Downloader running in a window.

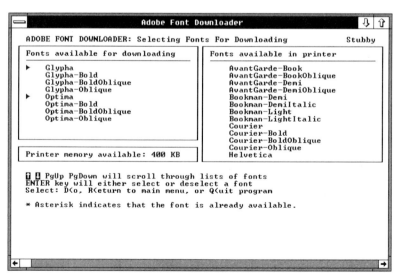

TIP 4: Installing and Using Bitstream Fontware

Several significant differences exist between the Adobe Type Library and Bitstream's Fontware:

Adobe's fonts are for PostScript printers only; Bitstream's fonts work on PostScript printers, Hewlett-Packard LaserJet Pluses, and numerous dot-matrix printers.

Each Adobe font package includes the installation program and font downloader; Bitstream's installation program—the Fontware Installation Kit—and the actual font files it uses are sold separately.

Adobe screen fonts come in 10-point, 12-point, 14-point, 18-point, and 20-point sizes; Fontware lets you specify the sizes you want.

Installing the printer and screen fonts for one Adobe font family takes a few minutes; installing one Bitstream font family can take nearly an hour.

Unlike Adobe's installation program, the Fontware Installation Kit resides on your hard disk.

Most of these differences exist because Bitstream distributes its fonts in its own proprietary outline format. The Fontware Installation Kit asks you questions about your printer and display and then creates screen and printer fonts from the original master outlines. This approach lets Bitstream fonts work on a dozen different printers and is the reason a Bitstream font-installation session takes so much time. Converting the Bitstream outlines into Hewlett-Packard bitmapped fonts or PostScript outline fonts requires enough calculations to make a microprocessor sweat. (You can speed up the process significantly by adding a math coprocessor such as an 8087 or 80287.) You must exit Windows to use the installation kit. Besides being unable to run in a window, the installation kit needs all the memory your system can offer to do its work.

The Fontware Installation Kit offers three main commands. One lets you view the Fontware Control Panel, which lists (and lets you change) your printer and display as well as the directories you've chosen for storing fonts. Another command lets you add and remove Fontware typefaces—the original Bitstream outlines from which you create fonts. The third command—Make Fonts—lets you make screen and printer fonts. Fontware displays a list of the master outlines you've installed. If you're making fonts for a Hewlett-Packard printer, you must specify each point size you want. (Remember that HP printer fonts are bitmaps; a separate bitmap description is required for each size and each orientation.) You don't need to specify sizes when making fonts for a PostScript printer (which, you'll recall, uses one outline description to create text in any size and orientation). After you specify sizes, you must create a corresponding screen font. You can copy all the sizes you specified for printer fonts, or you can enter other values. You might, for example, want to create extra-large fonts for use with a desktop-publishing program's enlarged viewing scale.

After you specify all the fonts and sizes you need, press the F10 key and wait while Fontware churns through the batch files and programs it uses to translate master outlines into screen and printer fonts. On an IBM PC/AT without a math coprocessor, a typical font-creation session can take 20 minutes. Giving Fontware a complex assignment—for example, creating half a dozen fonts in many different sizes—can earn you enough time for a long lunch. On an 80287-equipped PS/2 Model 50, the average is closer to eight minutes.

When you return from lunch and start Windows, you'll notice that Fontware modified your WIN.INI file to include the new fonts. Unlike Adobe's installer, Fontware precedes each entry in the *[fonts]* section with a comment describing the fonts and sizes it installed, as shown in Figure 7-8. That's fortunate because the font files themselves have cryptic names such as CQ000WIP.FON.

After you've made the screen and printer fonts, you may want to delete the original outline files to regain some of your dwindling hard-disk space. (The installation kit consumes nearly a megabyte of space, and you should plan to donate another half a megabyte to font

FIGURE 7-8.

Portion of WIN.INI modified by Fontware.

Entries made by Fontware installer

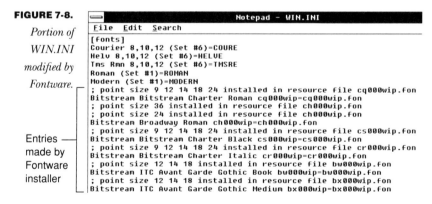

```
                          Notepad - WIN.INI
 File  Edit  Search
[fonts]
Courier 8,10,12 (Set #6)=COURE
Helv 8,10,12 (Set #6)=HELVE
Tms Rmn 8,10,12 (Set #6)=TMSRE
Roman (Set #1)=ROMAN
Modern (Set #1)=MODERN
; point size 9 12 14 18 24 installed in resource file cq000wip.fon
Bitstream Bitstream Charter Roman cq000wip=cq000wip.fon
; point size 36 installed in resource file ch000wip.fon
; point size 24 installed in resource file ch000wip.fon
Bitstream Broadway Roman ch000wip=ch000wip.fon
; point size 9 12 14 18 24 installed in resource file cs000wip.fon
Bitstream Bitstream Charter Black cs000wip=cs000wip.fon
; point size 9 12 14 18 24 installed in resource file cr000wip.fon
Bitstream Bitstream Charter Italic cr000wip=cr000wip.fon
; point size 12 14 18 installed in resource file bw000wip.fon
Bitstream ITC Avant Garde Gothic Book bw000wip=bw000wip.fon
; point size 12 14 18 installed in resource file bx000wip.fon
Bitstream ITC Avant Garde Gothic Medium bx000wip=bx000wip.fon
```

storage.) If you need the master outlines again—to make screen fonts in additional sizes, for example—you can always recopy them from their floppy disks.

TIP 5: Installing and Using Hewlett-Packard Soft Fonts

Both Adobe and Bitstream make the job of installing downloadable fonts a matter of answering a few questions. However, not all downloadable font products are as hospitable. Ones that aren't designed for use with Windows don't modify WIN.INI for you and often don't include printer-font-metrics (PFM) files. You can still use such products, however, if you're willing to do the work yourself.

This tip describes the steps for installing the Tms Rmn family from Hewlett-Packard's Tms Rmn/Helv soft-font set (HP 33412AB), designed for use on Hewlett-Packard LaserJet Plus and LaserJet Series II printers. The basic steps for installing other downloadable fonts for Hewlett-Packard printers are the same; however, the filenames and extensions *you* type will be different. For example, the filenames in Hewlett-Packard's Prestige Elite soft-font package have the extension R8P. For the names and extensions of the font files on your disks, see your soft-font documentation.

Copying the Font-Metrics File-Creation Utility

The Hewlett-Packard font kit does not include font-metrics files, so you need to create them. A utility named PCLPFM.EXE on the Windows Fonts 1 Disk creates font-metrics files by reading the printer-font files and extracting the character-width information they hold. You need to copy that program to your Windows subdirectory. Insert Fonts 1 Disk in drive A and, from the MS-DOS Executive window, click the drive A icon to display its directory. Locate and select PCLPFM.EXE, choose Copy from the File menu, type *c:\windows* in the To box, and then press Enter. From the MS-DOS prompt, type *copy a:pclpfm.exe c:\windows* and press Enter. If you plan to run the utility in a window, you should create a PIF for it.

Copying the Printer-Font Files

Before making the font-metrics files, you must copy the printer-font files to your hard disk. Change to the WINDOWS directory and then use the Create Directory command in MS-DOS Executive's Special menu to create a new directory within WINDOWS named PCLPFM. After you create the directory, switch to it. You see an empty directory window, as shown in Figure 7-9.

You're going to copy the printer-font files to this directory, so insert the appropriate fonts disk in drive A and then choose the drive A icon to display its directory. In this example, we're installing the Tms Rmn family for portrait (vertical) printing, which is located on disk 3 of 4 in the HP soft-font kit. The filenames for fonts you copy begin with TR (for Tms Rmn) and end with the extension SFP (for soft font in portrait orientation). The other characters indicate the font's size, style, and character set. For example, the filename TR10B#R8.SFP holds Tms Rmn 10-point Bold in the Hewlett-Packard Roman 8 character set.

The quickest way to copy all the fonts is to choose Copy from the File menu, type *tr*.sfp* in the From box, type *c:* in the To box, and press Enter. If you don't want to install all the printer fonts, select the ones you do want and then choose Copy. In either case, after the copy is complete, the MS-DOS Executive window shows the new font files in \WINDOWS\PCLPFM, as shown in Figure 7-10.

FIGURE 7-9.

After switching to
\WINDOWS
\PCLPFM.

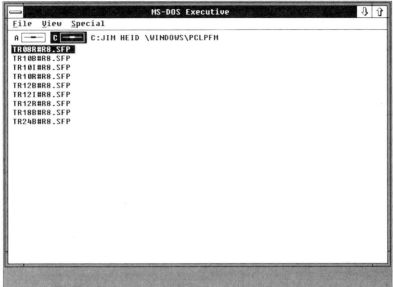

Creating the Font-Metrics Files

With the fonts and the PCLPFM.EXE program copied to your hard disk, you're ready to create the printer-font-metrics files. If you're running in Windows and are still within the PCLPFM directory, step up one level in the directory tree to your Windows directory. Next, start PCLPFM.EXE. If you're at the MS-DOS prompt, be sure you're in your Windows directory, type *pclpfm*, and press Enter.

When PCLPFM starts, it asks for the name of a font file. Type *pclpfm\tr*.sfp* (substitute the name of your own font files for *tr*.sfp* if they are different) and press Enter. The program looks in the PCLPFM directory for files meeting the criterion you supplied (*tr*.sfp*). The utility examines the first file it finds, extracts the character-width information, and builds a corresponding printer-font-metrics file, as shown in Figure 7-11 on the next page. This process is repeated for each font file.

When the last font-metrics file is created, PCLPFM redisplays the prompt *Download file name.* When you press Enter without typing anything, PCLPFM asks *Do you want an APPNDWIN.INI file? (Y or N)*; to answer "Yes," type *y* and press Enter. Doing so tells PCLPFM to create a file named APPNDWIN.INI containing the soft-font entries that WIN.INI needs so that it can recognize and download the fonts. If you

FIGURE 7-11.

*Using PCLPFM
to create a
printer-font-
metrics file.*

```
PCL Printer Font Metrics Creation Utility, Version 1.04b6
Copyright (C) Aldus Corporation, 1987.  All rights reserved.

Download file name >  TR08R#R8.SFP
( ←┘ [Enter] to exit )

PFM (output) file name > TR08R#RP.PFM


Checking TR08R#R8.SFP
```

were running PCLPFM in a window, you can close the window by choosing Close from the System menu. In the next (and final) step, you're going to insert the contents of APPNDWIN.INI into your WIN.INI file by using Notepad.

Modifying WIN.INI

By now, you've probably developed an appreciation for the installation programs that accompany Adobe and Bitstream downloadable fonts. But you're almost finished, so stay with it.

If you ran PCLPFM from the MS-DOS prompt, start Windows. Open APPNDWIN.INI (placed in your Windows directory). This also opens Notepad. In a few moments, Notepad's window appears, as shown in Figure 7-12.

You're going to add the information in APPNDWIN.INI to WIN.INI by copying it to the clipboard, opening WIN.INI, and pasting it at the appropriate place. To copy the contents of APPNDWIN.INI,

FIGURE 7-12.

*APPNDWIN.INI
in Notepad
window.*

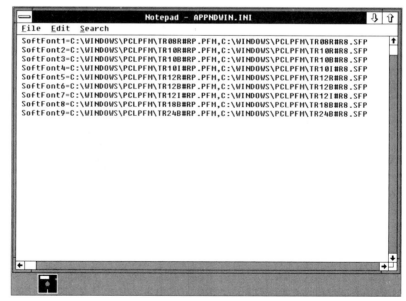

132

choose Select All from Notepad's Edit menu and then choose Copy from the Edit menu. Now that the printer-font-metrics file information from APPNDWIN.INI is safely in the clipboard, choose Open from the File menu, type *win.ini* in the Open File Name dialog box, and press Enter.

Recall that downloadable-printer-font entries reside in the section of WIN.INI that describes your printer setup. Locate that section by choosing Find from the Search menu. In the Search For box, type *[hppcl* and press Enter. Notepad highlights the text. Move the blinking insertion point to the beginning of the next line. Finally, choose Paste from the Edit menu. Notepad pastes the entries from APPNDWIN.INI, as shown in Figure 7-13.

Before choosing Save, examine the printer-description section to be sure it's correct. Then choose Save from the File menu, close Notepad, and exit Windows.

FIGURE 7-13.
APPNDWIN.INI entries pasted into WIN.INI.

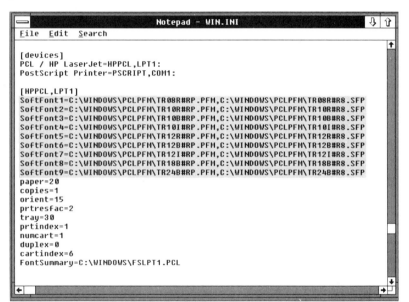

Using Downloadable Fonts

To try the newly installed fonts, restart Windows and start Write. Choose Change Printer from the File menu and verify that the Laser-Jet is selected as the current printer and that your other printer settings are correct. Next, choose Fonts from the Character menu and select Tms Rmn (or the font you installed) in the Fonts box. You can see the sizes you installed in the Sizes list box. Select a font size and press Enter.

Turn on your printer and type a sentence or two while it warms up. When it's ready, choose Print from the File menu, and press Enter to confirm the Print dialog box. During the spooling process, your hard disk churns away a bit more than usual—that's the sound of Windows spooling the printer-font file to disk. In a few moments, your hard copy appears, with the text in the soft font you specified.

You might want to try printing some text in each of the sizes and styles you installed. If the text appears in another font or doesn't appear at all, reopen WIN.INI and check to see that the soft-font entries are correct.

Once your downloadable fonts are working properly, make a floppy-disk backup copy of your WIN.INI file and of the printer-font-metrics files.

TIP 6: Converting Windows 1.0 Fonts to 2.0 Format

In Chapter 1, I mentioned that the internal structure of Windows screen fonts changed between versions 1.0 and 2.0. A utility on the Windows Fonts disk named NEWFON reads Windows 1.0 screen fonts and creates new, Windows 2.0-compatible screen fonts. If you bought an early version of Adobe's fonts or of Bitstream's Fontware (a version that includes or creates fonts for Windows 1.0), you can use NEWFON to convert the screen fonts to Windows 2.0 format. You can also use NEWFON to convert special fonts from such applications as PageMaker 1.0a. PageMaker uses several custom screen fonts that hold its Toolbox's icons, page-turning icons, and ruler numerals. If you run PageMaker 1.0a under Windows 2.0 without converting PageMaker's fonts, its Toolbox appears empty and its rulers valueless. (PageMaker 3.0 includes Windows 2.0-compatible screen fonts.)

To create Windows 2.0 screen fonts using NEWFON, first rename the screen-font files, changing each file's extension to OLD. Next, copy NEWFON to the directory containing the fonts and then exit Windows. Finally, convert each font file by typing *newfon oldname newname* and pressing Enter. For example, to convert the PageMaker 1.0a font file PMFONTA.OLD, type *newfon pmfonta.old pmfonta.fon.* As NEWFON runs, it displays the typeface name and point size of the font it's translating. After NEWFON creates the new font file, you can delete the old file. If you're converting more than one screen font, wait until you've converted them all before you delete all the old fonts: Type *del *.old* and press Enter at the MS-DOS prompt.

As an alternative to exiting Windows to run NEWFON, create a PIF for NEWFON to allow it to run in a window. You can even switch to another Windows application while NEWFON works in the background, which is especially useful when you're converting a large font file containing numerous sizes. To run NEWFON from Windows, select it or its PIF, choose Run from MS-DOS Executive's File menu, and type NEWFON's parameters (the old and new font filenames) after the program's name in the Run dialog box.

TIP 7: Typography Terminology

As in any specialized field, typography has its own terminology. The following is a glossary of some common typographic terms you may encounter when working with fonts in Windows.

Ascender. An ascender is the portion of a lowercase character that extends above its main body, as in the vertical stem of the character d.

Baseline. The baseline is an imaginary line upon which the characters in a line of type rest. Leading (pronounced *ledding*) is measured from baseline to baseline.

Descender. A descender is the portion of a lowercase character that extends below the baseline, as in y or g.

Font. A font is the implementation, for a specific device, of one typeface.

Kerning. Kerning is the process of decreasing space between two characters for improved readability, such as tucking a lowercase *o* under an uppercase *T*. A variation of kerning, called tracking, involves decreasing the amount of space between all characters by a specified percentage.

Leading. Pronounced *ledding*, leading is the amount of vertical space between lines of text.

Point. The smallest unit of measurement in typography, a point equals about $1/72$ of an inch.

Pica. A pica is a unit of measurement equal to 12 points. There are about 6 picas in one inch.

Sans serif. Sans serif means without serifs and refers to a character (or typeface) that lacks serifs. Figure 7-6 shows examples of sans serif typefaces.

Serif. A serif is an ornamental aspect of a character. A serif typeface is one whose characters contain serifs. Figure 7-6 shows examples of serif typefaces.

Typeface. A typeface is a unique design of uppercase and lowercase characters, numerals, and special symbols.

X-height. X-height is the height of a lowercase character in a given font.

CONTROL PANEL AND WIN.INI

C hapter 7 described how to install screen and printer fonts by using Control Panel and by editing the WIN.INI configuration file with Notepad. This chapter continues to explore the customization options of Control Panel and WIN.INI. We'll use Control Panel to adjust screen colors, mouse settings, and other preferences, and we'll use Notepad to access WIN.INI's customizing options, such as its ability to run applications when you start Windows. Remember that, with the exception of the time and date, any option that you can set with Control Panel you can also set by modifying WIN.INI. That's because Control Panel uses WIN.INI as a repository for key Windows information.

TIP 1: Changing the Display Color of Windows

Windows runs in living color on computers equipped with VGA video circuitry or an Enhanced Graphics Adapter (EGA) with more than 64 KB of memory. Using the Screen Colors command in Control Panel's Preferences menu, you can specify the color of virtually every element of Windows' interface.

When you choose Screen Colors, a dialog box appears containing a sample window, a list box naming the elements for which you can change the color, and three scroll bars labeled Hue, Bright, and Color, as shown in Figure 8-1. To change a given element's appearance, first select its name in the list box. When you do, the scroll boxes in each scroll bar jump to the position corresponding to that element's current settings. As you adjust the settings, the sample window's appearance changes accordingly. You can revert to the color settings you started with by using the Reset button, or you can make the current settings permanent by confirming the dialog box.

When you confirm the dialog box, your screen's colors change accordingly, and your hard disk churns as Control Panel commits your new colors to the [colors] section of WIN.INI, shown in Figure 8-2. The three numbers to the right of each Windows element in the [colors] section tell Windows how much red, green, and blue to mix to form the color you chose for that element. Like a color-mixing chart at a paint store, they allow Windows to recreate your preferred color settings at startup time. The higher the number, the greater the intensity of that color.

FIGURE 8-1.

Screen Colors dialog box.

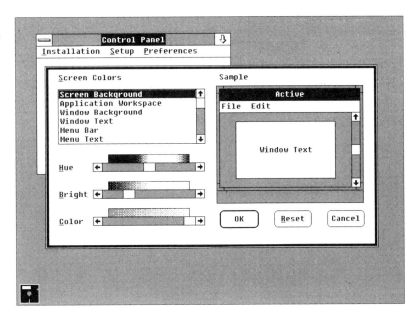

FIGURE 8-2.

The [colors] *section of WIN.INI.*

```
[extensions]
cal=calendar.exe ^.cal
crd=cardfile.exe ^.crd
trm=terminal.exe ^.trm
txt=notepad.exe ^.txt
ini=notepad.exe ^.ini
msp=paint.exe ^.msp
wri=write.exe ^.wri

[colors]
Background=0 128 128
AppWorkspace=0 128 255
Window=255 255 255
WindowText=0 0 0
Menu=255 255 255
MenuText=0 0 0
ActiveTitle=0 0 0
InactiveTitle=0 0 255
TitleText=255 255 255
ActiveBorder=127 127 127
InactiveBorder=127 127 127
WindowFrame=0 0 0
Scrollbar=0 128 128

[pif]
swapdisk=?
swapsize=0
assign.com=1
```

This process seems straightforward enough—until you begin adjusting color settings and find your adjustments don't always produce the results you expected. Questions arise. Aren't hue and color the same thing? Why does each have a separate scroll bar? If Windows mixes red, green, and blue to create colors, why aren't the scroll bars in the Screen Colors dialog box labeled Red, Green, and Blue?

Windows' Color System

Answering those questions requires some background on additive color—the system computers (and televisions) use to produce color. With additive color, colors are produced by light in three primary colors—red, green, and blue. (Note that these primary colors are not the same as the primary colors for pigment color—the color system used in mixing paint. The pigment primaries are red, *yellow*, and blue.) The surface of a color video screen is coated with triads of red, green, and blue phosphor, which glow when struck by electrons from three (one for each color) electron guns. Each dot, or pixel, in a video image is actually composed of a combination of red, green, and blue, but because the spots of color are too small to be seen individually at a normal viewing distance, the eyes blend them into a single color.

Besides the intensity of each primary color, three factors determine the pixel's appearance: hue, luminance, and saturation.

Hue. Hue is a primary color or a secondary color that is formed by mixing equal amounts of primary colors. (Yellow, for example, is a secondary additive color formed by mixing equal amounts of red and green.) In Control Panel, you adjust the hue using the Hue scroll bar. The available hues appear above the scroll bar. By adjusting the hue, you determine the relative intensity of the red, green, and blue spots that form a pixel.

Luminance. Also called lightness or value, luminance refers to the lightness or darkness of a color. (For example, you can create a light yellow by adding white to pure yellow. Of course, when you add white, you actually add equal amounts of red, green, and blue.) Control Panel's luminance scroll bar is called Bright. Above it, a bar depicts available luminance settings by showing a gradual shift from black (actually dark blue) to white.

Saturation. Also called intensity or chroma, saturation refers to a color's purity. A fully saturated color contains no gray, and thus appears quite vivid. Colors can be made less intense by adding gray. In the Screen Colors dialog box, the scroll bar for adjusting saturation is called Color. Above the scroll bar is a bar showing a gradual transition from gray to vibrant blue.

Experimenting with Windows' Colors

Theory is important, but experimentation is the best way to learn how hue, luminance, and saturation interact. Start Control Panel and then choose Screen Colors from the Preferences menu. To ensure that we're starting from the same point, move the Hue scroll box to its leftmost position in the scroll bar. Next, move the Color scroll box to its rightmost position. Finally, move the Bright scroll box to the center of its scroll bar. You'll know it's in the very center when the sample's screen background becomes a solid red color. When the scroll box is to the left or right of dead center, the red color is interspersed with black or white pixels.

First, explore the spectrum of fully saturated colors by using the Hue scroll bar's right scroll arrow. Watch the sample screen background as it displays a rainbow of solid colors, created by interspersing pixels of different colors. In the world of bitmapped displays, this technique of creating new colors by mixing pixels of different colors is called dithering.

Next, let's examine the effect of the Bright scroll bar, which controls the luminance of the color formed by the current Hue and Color settings. Move the Hue scroll box to its leftmost position to display the fully saturated red. Next, use the Bright scroll bar's left scroll arrow while watching the sample screen background. The red grows progressively darker as Windows adds black pixels, finally turning completely black. Next, use the right scroll arrow. As you'd expect, the color grows progressively lighter until it becomes white. Regardless of the scroll box's position, the color is always fully saturated; it simply assumes different degrees of lightness or darkness, as though it were attached to a dimmer switch.

Finally, let's look at the Color, or saturation, adjustment. Move the Bright scroll box back to the middle of its scroll bar to return to the solid red color on the sample screen. Next, decrease the color's saturation by using the left scroll arrow. Watch the sample screen to see Windows adding white (and occasionally a few black) pixels to decrease the color's saturation. When the scroll box is at its leftmost position, the color becomes completely gray.

Position the Color scroll box in the middle of the scroll bar. At this position red and gray are equally mixed.

Finally, experiment with the Hue settings. You see the same range of colors you did before, but because the colors share the screen with an equal amount of gray, they appear less intense.

A Systematic Approach to Color Experimentation

Now that you know how the Hue, Bright, and Color controls interact, you might want to try your hand at pixel mixing. You can simply drag each control's scroll box around until you stumble on a setting you like, but a better approach is to use a solid, fully saturated hue as a starting point.

1. In the list box, select the user interface element for which you want a different color. When you do, the scroll boxes jump to positions corresponding to the element's current color setting.

2. Drag the Bright scroll box to the middle of its scroll bar (medium brightness) and the Color scroll box to its rightmost position (fully saturated color).

3. Use the Hue scroll bar to locate the desired color.

4. Adjust the brightness or the saturation (or both) to attain the desired shade.

In your quest to find the ideal color scheme, remember one word: restraint. Color is a powerful player in visual communication; use it conservatively. A mélange of conflicting hues may show off that new color monitor nicely, but it won't provide a visually soothing work environment.

One approach is to use the same hue for all user interface elements, but to vary brightness and saturation. Figure 8-3 shows the *[colors]* settings I use in my WIN.INI file. They provide a basic blue decor that seems appropriate for my IBM PS/2—a dark-blue screen background, dark-blue and light-blue active and inactive title bars, respectively, and light-blue scroll bars. The dark background

FIGURE 8-3.

Basic blue color settings.

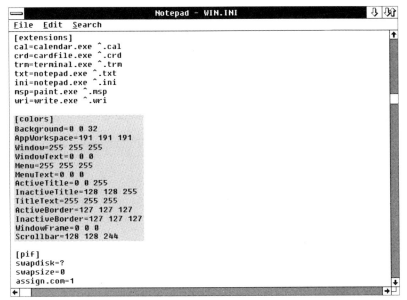

```
[extensions]
cal=calendar.exe ^.cal
crd=cardfile.exe ^.crd
trm=terminal.exe ^.trm
txt=notepad.exe ^.txt
ini=notepad.exe ^.ini
msp=paint.exe ^.msp
wri=write.exe ^.wri

[colors]
Background=0 0 32
AppWorkspace=191 191 191
Window=255 255 255
WindowText=0 0 0
Menu=255 255 255
MenuText=0 0 0
ActiveTitle=0 0 255
InactiveTitle=128 128 255
TitleText=255 255 255
ActiveBorder=127 127 127
InactiveBorder=127 127 127
WindowFrame=0 0 0
Scrollbar=128 128 244

[pif]
swapdisk=?
swapsize=0
assign.com=1
```

minimizes the screen burn-in that can occur over time when the screen's phosphor is constantly battered by all-white pixels. Whenever I take a break from the computer, I minimize all open applications, bathing the screen in the dark-blue hue.

Avoid colors or shades containing awkward splotches of black or white pixels; they're distracting, especially for the screen background color. Favor solid hues instead. Examples of each approach are shown in black and white in Figure 8-4 on the following page. And black-on-white text appears more familiar and is less fatiguing than colored text. (If you do adjust color settings for text, you'll notice that Windows doesn't provide the same range of brightness settings for text it does for other elements. Text can appear in solid colors only.)

As you experiment, remember that you can restore your previous color scheme by using the Reset button. As soon as you confirm the Screen Colors dialog box, however, Control Panel commits your changes to your WIN.INI file. You can return to the Screen Colors dialog box and adjust each color to get back to the default colors, but an easier way is to open WIN.INI using Notepad and delete the *[colors]* section. When you restart Windows, it uses the preset color scheme.

FIGURE 8-4.

Spotted,
distracting
shades (top)
versus solid,
restful ones
(bottom).

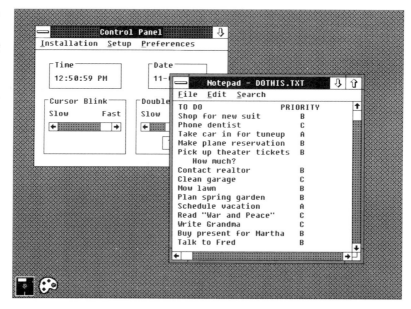

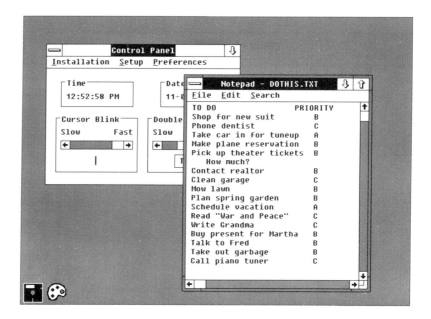

TIP 2: Setting WIN.INI to Display Black and White

For variety, you can simulate a black-and-white environment on an EGA or VGA system by using the *[colors]* settings shown in Figure 8-5. Doing so is useful when you're printing Windows screen dumps on a black-and-white printer.

FIGURE 8-5.

Settings in [colors] for simulating a black-and-white installation.

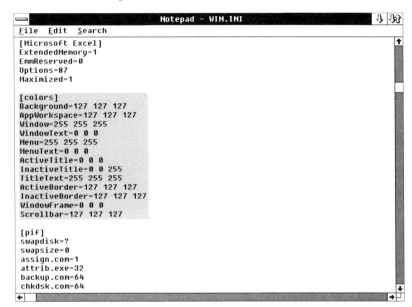

```
                        Notepad - WIN.INI
 File   Edit   Search
[Microsoft Excel]
ExtendedMemory=1
EmmReserved=0
Options=87
Maximized=1

[colors]
Background=127 127 127
AppWorkspace=127 127 127
Window=255 255 255
WindowText=0 0 0
Menu=255 255 255
MenuText=0 0 0
ActiveTitle=0 0 0
InactiveTitle=0 0 255
TitleText=255 255 255
ActiveBorder=127 127 127
InactiveBorder=127 127 127
WindowFrame=0 0 0
Scrollbar=127 127 127

[pif]
swapdisk=?
swapsize=0
assign.com=1
attrib.exe=32
backup.com=64
chkdsk.com=64
```

TIP 3: Setting the Width of Window Borders

The Border Width command on Control Panel's Preferences menu lets you specify, in pixels, the width of the border that surrounds all resizable application windows. The default width of most windows is 5. (Control Panel and Calculator have fixed-size windows and, therefore, have a border of 1.) If you have trouble positioning the mouse on window borders when resizing windows, increase the border width. Conversely, if you don't use a mouse, change the border width to 1 to eliminate the border. You will still be able to resize a window using the Control menu's Resize command. A border can be no smaller than one pixel wide and no larger than 50 pixels, a value that erects fortress walls around windows.

The border-width setting is stored in the *[windows]* section of WIN.INI, adjacent to the *BorderWidth* keyword.

TIP 4:   Turning the Warning Beep Off and On

The Warning Beep command on Control Panel's Preferences menu
determines whether Windows sounds a beep when you try to perform
an action that Windows doesn't allow, such as pressing the wrong key
or clicking within an application window when that application displays a dialog box. If you don't like the beep, choose the Warning
Beep command to remove the check mark from beside it and disable
the audible warning.

This setting is stored adjacent to the *Beep* keyword in the
[windows] section of WIN.INI.

TIP 5:   Setting Mouse Options

Two Control Panel areas let you change mouse options: the Mouse
command on the Preferences menu and the Double Click option in
the Control Panel window.

The Mouse command summons the Mouse Options dialog box,
which lets you swap the left and right mouse buttons and adjust the
pointer's speed. Normally, Windows considers the left mouse button
the primary button—the one used to resize and select objects and to
choose commands. The right button is the secondary button and can
be used by some applications for special tasks. (In PageMaker, for
example, clicking the secondary button changes the magnification
scale.) To switch the primary and secondary buttons, click the Swap
Left/Right Mouse Buttons check box. In WIN.INI, your swap prefer-
ence is denoted by the word *yes* or *no* adjacent to the *SwapMouseButtons*
keyword. (Note that the *SwapMouseButtons* keyword does not appear in
WIN.INI until the buttons have been swapped in Control Panel.)

The Double Click option in the Control Panel window lets you
change what Windows considers a double-click. The Double Click
option is represented in the *[windows]* section of the WIN.INI file by
the *DoubleClickSpeed* keyword and is recorded in milliseconds (thousandths of a second). A *DoubleClickSpeed* value of 500, for example, tells
Windows that two clicks occurring within a half second of each other
are a double-click. Two clicks occurring outside that range are simply
two individual clicks.

TIP 6: Changing Mouse-Acceleration Settings

The Mouse Acceleration option lets you govern how fast the pointer moves relative to the mouse speed. When the None button is selected, the pointer moves at a constant speed regardless of the mouse speed. With the Medium button selected, the pointer moves faster when the mouse moves faster. With the High button selected, the pointer blazes across the screen when the mouse speed is anything faster than a crawl. Once you choose the medium or high mouse-acceleration setting in Control Panel, the *xMouseThreshold*, *yMouseThreshold*, and *MouseSpeed* keywords appear in WIN.INI with numbers next to them.

As a technical aside, let's look at how the three factors interrelate. A mouse generates interrupts as it moves, and Windows responds to the interrupts by moving the pointer. The smallest degree of movement a mouse can register is called a unit. The *xMouseThreshold* and *yMouseThreshold* settings determine the maximum number of units the mouse can move between mouse interrupts before Windows changes the mouse pointer position on the screen. When the mouse's speed is below either threshold, the pointer moves one pixel for each unit of mouse movement. When the mouse's speed exceeds either threshold, the pointer's speed is equal to 2 raised to the power of the *MouseSpeed* setting. Thus, if the *MouseSpeed* setting is 2 and the mouse's speed exceeds either threshold, the pointer moves four pixels for each unit of mouse movement. Figure 8-6 shows each keyword's value in each setting, and how far a Microsoft mouse must move for the pointer to move from one end of the screen to the other when you move the mouse quickly.

By editing the *xMouseThreshold* and *yMouseThreshold* settings directly in WIN.INI and giving them different values, you can create some strange results. A high *xMouseThreshold* value combined with a low *yMouseThreshold* value produces a pointer that burns rubber moving from left to right, but is as slow as a snail moving up and down. And if you want to see a hyperactive mouse, try a *MouseSpeed* setting of about 5. But first make a backup copy of your WIN.INI file.

FIGURE 8-6.

Results of mouse speed settings.

Setting	xMouse-Threshold	yMouse-Threshold	MouseSpeed	Distance (in inches)
None	0	0	0	3
Medium	2	2	1	$1^1/_2$
High	5	5	2	$^7/_8$

TIP 7: Changing the Symbols and Formats for Currency, Time, Date, and Numbers

The final command in Control Panel's Preferences menu is Country Settings. Its dialog box lets you choose one of 16 countries for the symbols and formats Windows uses to represent currency, date and time values, and numbers. Your country setting is the *[intl]* section of WIN.INI. Each keyword in the section corresponds to an option in the Country Settings dialog box except the final line, which tells Windows whether to include the Country Settings command in the Preferences menu. If you change it to read *dialog=no*, Country Settings disappears from the menu. Unless you're a particularly nationalistic Windows user, however, there's no benefit to removing the command.

TIP 8: Changing the Cursor-Blink Rate

Control Panel lets you change the rate at which the cursor blinks with the Cursor Blink option. Use the scroll bar as marked to change the blink rate. The Cursor Blink setting is represented in the *[windows]* section of WIN.INI by the *CursorBlinkRate* keyword. The value for the entry is in milliseconds (thousandths of a second). A *CursorBlinkRate* of 1000 means the cursor alternates between being on for one second and off for one second. Its minimum and maximum values are 200 (the fastest blink) and 1200 (the slowest). However, you can exceed that range by bypassing Control Panel and dealing directly with WIN.INI. For example, if you change the blink rate to 1, you get a strobe-like cursor; if you change it to 5000, your cursor blinks almost as slowly as trees make rings.

TIP 9: Disabling and Enabling the Spooler

The *[windows]* section of WIN.INI contains several other entries that lack Control Panel façades and can be accessed only by directly editing WIN.INI with Notepad. The first such entry is the *spooler=yes* line. If you change this entry to *spooler=no*, Windows will not use the spooler as a printing intermediary. You might want to eliminate Windows' spooler and use the network's spooler if you're using Windows on a network (indeed, you may *have* to). Or you might want to disable the spooler if you're using Windows on a floppy-drive system, because using the spooler can easily exhaust your disk space. (Although, given Windows' lethargy on a floppy-drive system, your patience would probably go first.) You also might want to do without the spooler if you use a large SMARTDrive disk cache or a RAMDrive RAM disk. (SMARTDrive and RAMDrive are discussed in Chapter 10.) When despooling on a system that uses either a SMARTDrive or a RAMDrive, Windows retrieves the contents of a spooled print file from memory, rather than from disk. Because it takes far less time to retrieve data from memory than from disk, Windows can retrieve data faster and, thus, send more data to the printer in less time. The result is that the printer's internal memory might fill, causing text to be lost. The usual symptom of this ailment is a print job in which the first page prints perfectly, but subsequent pages end about halfway down.

TIP 10: Displaying PIFs with MS-DOS Executive's Programs Command

Below the *spooler, DoubleClickSpeed,* and *CursorBlinkRate* settings in WIN.INI are three comment lines describing the *programs* entry, as shown in Figure 8-7. This entry determines which files appear when you choose the Programs command from MS-DOS Executive's View

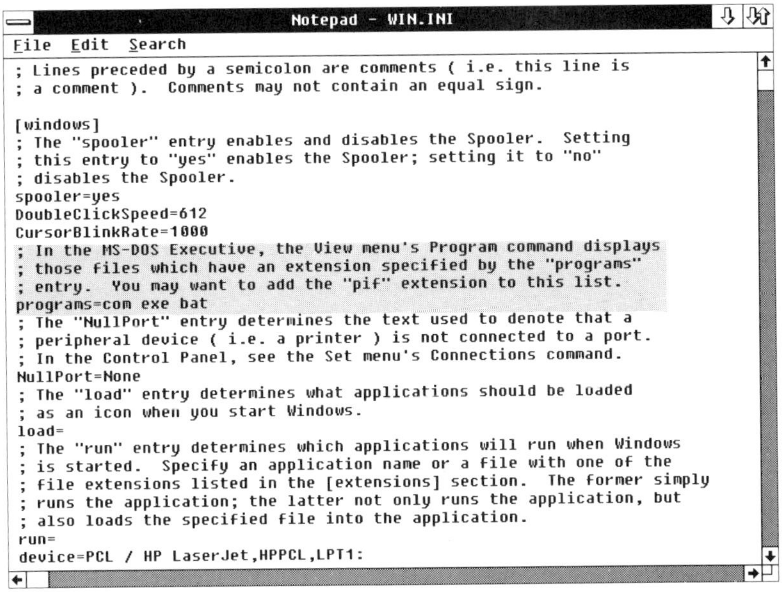

FIGURE 8-7.

The programs *entry in the* [windows] *section of* WIN.INI.

```
▭                        Notepad – WIN.INI                    ⇩ ⇕
 File  Edit  Search
; Lines preceded by a semicolon are comments ( i.e. this line is
; a comment ).  Comments may not contain an equal sign.

[windows]
; The "spooler" entry enables and disables the Spooler.  Setting
; this entry to "yes" enables the Spooler; setting it to "no"
; disables the Spooler.
spooler=yes
DoubleClickSpeed=612
CursorBlinkRate=1000
; In the MS-DOS Executive, the View menu's Program command displays
; those files which have an extension specified by the "programs"
; entry.  You may want to add the "pif" extension to this list.
programs=com exe bat
; The "NullPort" entry determines the text used to denote that a
; peripheral device ( i.e. a printer ) is not connected to a port.
; In the Control Panel, see the Set menu's Connections command.
NullPort=None
; The "load" entry determines what applications should be loaded
; as an icon when you start Windows.
load=
; The "run" entry determines which applications will run when Windows
; is started.  Specify an application name or a file with one of the
; file extensions listed in the [extensions] section.  The former simply
; runs the application; the latter not only runs the application, but
; also loads the specified file into the application.
run=
device=PCL / HP LaserJet,HPPCL,LPT1:
←                                                             →
```

menu. By default, the entry tells Windows to display any files with the extension COM, EXE, or BAT. You might want to add the PIF extension so that you can run a program by double-clicking on its PIF when you've chosen the Program view. To do so, type a space after the last entry and then type *pif* (but don't precede the extension with a period). Conversely, if you don't want to see batch files when viewing only programs, delete the BAT extension.

TIP 11: Specifying a Null Port Name

Below the *programs* entry is the *NullPort* entry. It simply provides Windows with a string—a word or series of words—for Control Panel, the spooler, or an application to use when a device is installed (that is, its device driver has been copied to your WINDOWS directory) but not connected to any port. Normally, the null port's name is None and appears after the list of ports in Control Panel's Connections dialog box. Selecting it causes its name to appear in the Printer list box, as in: *PCL/HP LaserJet on None.* For some variety, you can change the *NullPort* entry—perhaps to *Zilch* or *Squat*—to replace *None* as the name of the null port.

TIP 12: Specifying Programs and Files to be Loaded or Run on Startup

The *load* and *run* entries in WIN.INI let you specify that applications or batch files be loaded as icons or run as soon as Windows starts up. To use either entry, type the application's filename after the equal sign; you don't need to type its filename extension. You can, however, type a drive letter and directory name to load or run an application on a different drive or in a directory not named by your Path command. To load or run more than one program or batch file, separate filenames with a space. To run multiple instances of an application, specify its name twice. To load a document and run its application, simply specify the document's name. Figure 8-8 shows a WIN.INI file with a *load* entry that loads Clock and Calculator as icons and a *run* entry that runs Microsoft Excel and opens a worksheet called FORECAST.XLS.

FIGURE 8-8.

Sample load *and* run *entries in the* [windows] *section of* WIN.INI.

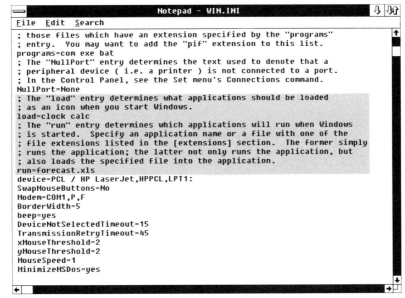

TIP 13: Changing the Default Printer in WIN.INI

The *device* entry of WIN.INI lists the default printer, the filename of its driver, and the port to which the printer is connected. The *device* entry gets its information from the commands in Control Panel's Setup menu. You can override this entry by using an application's Change Printer or Target Printer command (in Microsoft Excel, the Printer Setup command). Doing so causes the application to switch printers but does not change the default printer. For example, assume a Post-Script printer is the default printer and you use Microsoft Windows Write's Change Printer command to switch to a LaserJet. If you then switch to another application—or even to a second instance of Write—and choose its Change Printer command, the PostScript printer is still listed as the default printer. The rule is this: The printer you choose as the default printer in Control Panel is the one Windows uses, unless you specify otherwise; and it remains so unless you return to Control Panel and change the default printer.

TIP 14: Minimizing MS-DOS Executive from WIN.INI

Following the *MouseSpeed* entry, your WIN.INI file may contain an entry named *MinimizeMSDos*, which tells Windows whether to minimize the MS-DOS Executive window when you run an application. If you've never used the Minimize MS-DOS Executive check box in the MS-DOS Executive's Run dialog box (on the File menu), your WIN.INI file won't contain this entry. But the first time you use the Minimize MS-DOS Executive option, MS-DOS Executive adds the entry to your WIN.INI file. You can disable the option in one of three ways: change the *MinimizeMSDos* entry to read *MinimizeMSDos=no*; delete the entire *MinimizeMSDos* entry; or choose Run from MS-DOS Executive's File menu, remove the check from the Minimize MS-DOS Executive check box, and then confirm the dialog box. (In this case, an application name doesn't have to appear in the Run dialog box; you're using the Run command simply to access the Minimize MS-DOS Executive check box.) To reactivate the option, choose Run, choose the Minimize MS-DOS Executive check box, and confirm the dialog box.

TIP 15: Using WIN.INI to Start an Application When You Run a Document

WIN.INI's *[extensions]* section contains the entries that allow Windows to run an application when you choose one of that application's documents to run (by double-clicking on the document's filename or by selecting the filename and then pressing Enter). For example, the entry *wri=write.exe ^.wri* tells Windows, "When someone chooses a file with the extension WRI to run, start WRITE.EXE and then pass that filename to Write so that it can open the document." The caret (^) is a wildcard character that represents the filename.

When you install a new Windows application, its installation program adds the application's extensions to this section. If an application doesn't include an installation program or if you install the application by simply copying it to your hard disk, Windows doesn't know about that application's extensions. If you subsequently choose one of that application's documents, MS-DOS Executive displays an alert message stating that it can't run the document.

You can specify additional extensions for an application by adding entries to the *[extensions]* section. Here is one useful addition:

```
wk1=excel.exe ^.wk1
```

This line, which can appear anywhere within the *[extensions]* section, tells Windows to run Microsoft Excel when you run a Lotus 1-2-3 WK1 file. Once Microsoft Excel opens, it opens the WK1 file you chose.

Another useful addition to *[extensions]* is the following line:

sys=notepad.exe config.sys

This entry lets you start Notepad and open CONFIG.SYS for editing by choosing CONFIG.SYS. Notice that the line doesn't contain the caret wildcard character. Instead, it explicitly names the CONFIG.SYS file, because many device drivers also end with the SYS extension. If this line used the caret wildcard and you chose SMARTDRV.SYS, Windows would run Notepad, and Notepad would attempt to open the file SMARTDRV.SYS. That attempt would produce the error message *Not a valid Notepad file.* (Notepad can open only ASCII text files.) By explicitly naming CONFIG.SYS in WIN.INI, you tell Windows, ''Whenever someone chooses a file ending in SYS, assume he or she wants to edit CONFIG.SYS and open it instead of the file he or she selected.''

Figure 8-9 contains several other useful *[extensions]* additions, each of which is preceded by a comment explaining its purpose.

FIGURE 8-9.

Other useful [extensions] *additions.*

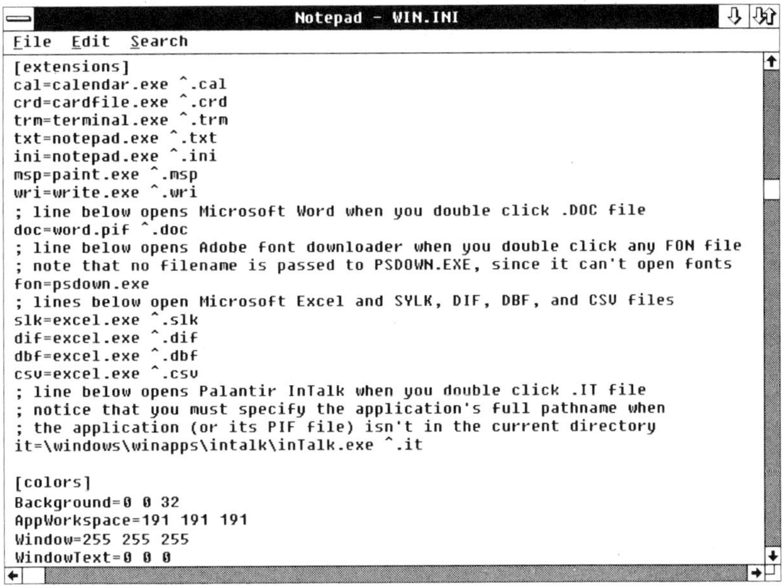

```
                        Notepad – WIN.INI
 File  Edit  Search
[extensions]
cal=calendar.exe ^.cal
crd=cardfile.exe ^.crd
trm=terminal.exe ^.trm
txt=notepad.exe ^.txt
ini=notepad.exe ^.ini
msp=paint.exe ^.msp
wri=write.exe ^.wri
; line below opens Microsoft Word when you double click .DOC file
doc=word.pif ^.doc
; line below opens Adobe font downloader when you double click any FON file
; note that no filename is passed to PSDOWN.EXE, since it can't open fonts
fon=psdown.exe
; lines below open Microsoft Excel and SYLK, DIF, DBF, and CSV files
slk=excel.exe ^.slk
dif=excel.exe ^.dif
dbf=excel.exe ^.dbf
csv=excel.exe ^.csv
; line below opens Palantir InTalk when you double click .IT file
; notice that you must specify the application's full pathname when
; the application (or its PIF file) isn't in the current directory
it=\windows\winapps\intalk\inTalk.exe ^.it

[colors]
Background=0 0 32
AppWorkspace=191 191 191
Window=255 255 255
WindowText=0 0 0
```

TIP 16: Specifying Output Devices in WIN.INI

The *[devices]* section of WIN.INI lists the output devices you've installed and the ports they're attached to. Windows displays the text to the left of the equal sign in an application's Change Printer or Target Printer dialog box. Normally, this text is specified in the printer-driver file, but you can change it by using Notepad. Assume you have two Post-Script printers—a LaserWriter attached to COM1 and a Linotronic typesetter attached to COM2. Instead of having to remember which printer uses which port, you can create a custom *[devices]* entry for each that lists each printer's name. To do so, follow the steps below. (These steps assume you've already installed the PostScript printer driver once. If you haven't, install it according to the directions in Chapter 6.)

1. Open Control Panel and choose Add New Printer from the Installation menu.

2. When asked for a disk containing a printer file, insert your Utilities 2 Disk in drive A and press Enter.

3. In the Available Printers list box, locate and select the Post-Script Printer entry. Then choose Add.

4. When Control Panel asks whether to *copy the associated printer driver file PSCRIPT.DRV?* choose No. Doing so tells Control Panel to create a new *[devices]* entry, but not to copy the driver file itself.

5. Choose Connections from the Setup menu. In the Printer list box, select the entry PostScript Printer on None. Then, in the Connection list box, select the appropriate port. Finally, choose OK to confirm the dialog box.

6. Choose Printer from the Setup menu, choose the new entry, and specify the appropriate print settings. (If this entry is for a Linotronic, for example, choose Linotronic 100/300/500 in the Printer list box.) Confirm the dialog box.

7. Open WIN.INI and use the Find command to locate the *[devices]* section.

8. Locate the entry for the PostScript printer. It reads *PostScript Printer=PSCRIPT,COM1:,COM2:* (although the port entries may

be different). This entry tells Windows that the PostScript driver is shared by two printers, one attached to COM1 and one attached to COM2.

9. Select the text *PostScript Printer* and type the name of the printer you attached to COM1. Next, delete the entry for COM2 at the end of that line. (Don't forget to delete the comma.) If you have a LaserWriter attached to COM1, your line reads *LaserWriter=PSCRIPT,COM1:* now.

10. Add a new line naming the printer you attached to COM2. For a Linotronic, add the line *Linotronic=PSCRIPT,COM2:* to the file. After you type the two entries correctly, save WIN.INI and exit Windows.

To admire your handiwork, restart Windows and run Write. When you choose Change Printer from the File menu, you see both printers, as shown in Figure 8-10.

Although this example used two PostScript printers attached to different ports, this technique works with any printers that share a common driver but use different ports.

FIGURE 8-10.

Change Printer dialog box listing different PostScript printers.

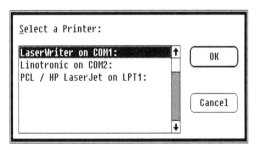

TIP 17: Specifying a Port in WIN.INI

You learned a little about the *[ports]* section of WIN.INI in Chapter 6 when you added the *PRINTFIL.PRN* entry to allow "printing" to a disk file. As you probably surmised, *[ports]* lists MS-DOS' standard port names, which appear in Control Panel's Connections dialog box. The serial port entries—COM1: and COM2:—also list the current baud-rate, parity, word-length, and stop-bit configuration of each port, as determined by the Communications Port command in Control Panel's Setup menu. If you specified hardware handshaking for a port, its entry ends with a lowercase p.

TIP 18: Setting up an Application-specific Section in WIN.INI

Windows applications can store configuration information in an application-specific section of WIN.INI. An application-specific section begins with the application's name surrounded in brackets, such as *[Draw]* for Micrografx Draw, *[PageMaker]* for Aldus PageMaker, or *[MSWrite]* for Microsoft Windows Write, as shown in Figure 8-11. An application's designers determine whether the application requires a configuration section, and if so, what the section contains. PageMaker, for example, uses its *[PageMaker]* section to list the directory containing its PM.CNF configuration file and to denote whether it displays ruler guides in color. Micrografx Draw uses its section to list its default directory for documents, the printer you last chose by using its Change Printer command, and the directory where Lotus 1-2-3 graphs are stored.

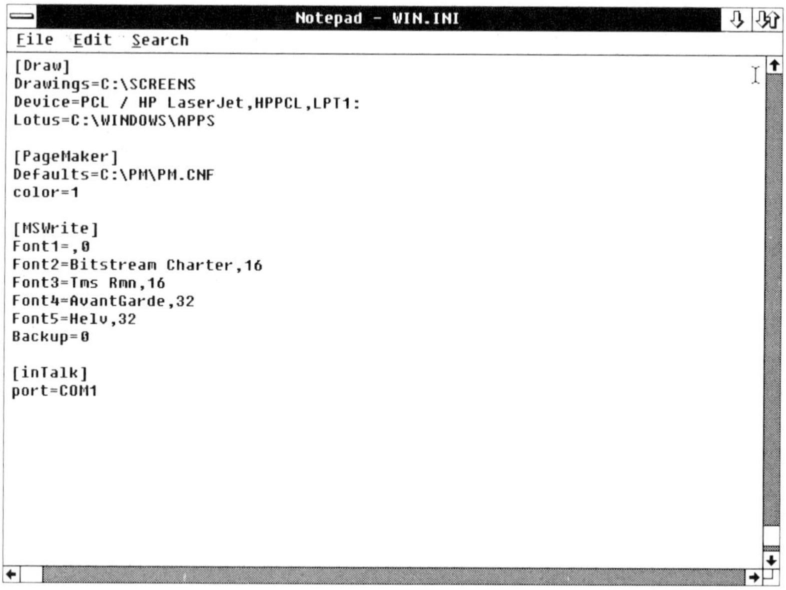

FIGURE 8-11.

Application-specific WIN.INI entries.

```
Notepad - WIN.INI
File  Edit  Search

[Draw]
Drawings=C:\SCREENS
Device=PCL / HP LaserJet,HPPCL,LPT1:
Lotus=C:\WINDOWS\APPS

[PageMaker]
Defaults=C:\PM\PM.CNF
color=1

[MSWrite]
Font1=,0
Font2=Bitstream Charter,16
Font3=Tms Rmn,16
Font4=AvantGarde,32
Font5=Helv,32
Backup=0

[inTalk]
port=COM1
```

PIFs AND STANDARD APPLICATIONS

Windows' ability to run standard applications and add clipboard support to them lets you enter the world of graphical operating environments without forsaking your existing applications. The bridge between applications of the past and Windows' graphical operating environment is the program information file (PIF). This chapter discusses PIFs and also examines how to use the clipboard with standard applications.

Looking at a PIF by Using PIFEDIT

Chapter 1 briefly described how a PIF works and how Windows runs a standard application, based on the information stored in its PIF. You learned that the entries in a PIF give Windows the information it needs to run the application efficiently and that Windows applications don't require PIFs because the information Windows needs to run them is coded directly into their program files. You start a standard application for which a PIF exists by selecting the application's program file or its PIF and pressing Enter or by double-clicking on the program file or the PIF. When you do, the Windows program named WINOLDAP.MOD swaps out to disk any other applications that are running, as well as some of Windows' code, in order to run the standard application. When you switch from a standard application back to Windows (or to another standard application), WINOLDAP.MOD swaps the currently running application to disk and then reloads into memory the code that was previously swapped to disk.

Let's examine PIFs more closely by looking at one with PIFEDIT, a Windows utility that lets you create and alter PIFs. Locate PIFEDIT in your WINDOWS directory, and start it. (If you can't find PIFEDIT in WINDOWS, look in the PIF directory.) Next, choose Open from the PIFEDIT File menu, enter the PIF subdirectory if necessary, and then locate and open the file WORD.PIF, a PIF for Microsoft Word, shown in Figure 9-1.

The options in a PIF fall into six categories:

Program information. This section includes options that Windows uses to locate the application's file and directory and to pass any parameters to the application. The four program-information options are: Program Name, Program Title, Program Parameters, and Initial Directory.

FIGURE 9-1.

WORD.PIF open in PIFEDIT.

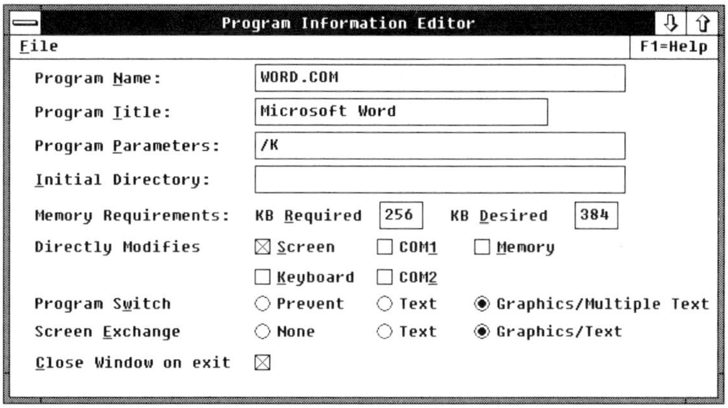

```
┌────────────────────────────────────────────────────────────┐
│ ▭              Program Information Editor              ⇩ ⇧   │
├──────────────────────────────────────────────────────────────┤
│ File                                                  F1=Help │
│                                                                │
│ Program Name:        [WORD.COM                           ]     │
│ Program Title:       [Microsoft Word                ]          │
│ Program Parameters:  [/K                                ]      │
│ Initial Directory:   [                                   ]     │
│ Memory Requirements: KB Required [256]  KB Desired [384]       │
│ Directly Modifies    ⊠ Screen   □ COM1    □ Memory            │
│                      □ Keyboard □ COM2                         │
│ Program Switch       ○ Prevent  ○ Text  ◉ Graphics/Multiple Text │
│ Screen Exchange      ○ None     ○ Text  ◉ Graphics/Text       │
│ Close Window on exit ⊠                                         │
└────────────────────────────────────────────────────────────┘
```

Memory information. This section, labeled Memory Requirements, tells Windows how much memory the application requires to run. The two memory-information options are: KB Required and KB Desired.

System-resource information. Listed in the section titled Directly Modifies is information that Windows uses to determine how the application accesses your computer's hardware. The options determine such details as whether an application can run in a window or takes over the entire screen. The options in the system-resource-information section are: Screen, COM1, Memory, Keyboard, and COM2. Note: This section is different in Windows/386. The differences are discussed in Chapter 12.

Switching information. The options in the section titled Program Switch determine whether Windows lets you switch from the standard application back to Windows or to other applications. The switching-information options are: Prevent, Text, and Graphics/Multiple Text.

Clipboard information. This section, titled Screen Exchange, indicates the ways in which you can access the clipboard while running the standard application. The clipboard-information options are: None, Text, and Graphics/Text.

Exit information. This one-option section, labeled Close Window on exit, determines what Windows does when you exit the standard application. When the box is checked, Windows closes the application's window when you exit. When it's unchecked, Windows leaves the application's window on screen, adding the text *inactive* to the window's title bar.

Program-information Options

Let's examine each option in the program-information section of the WORD.PIF file, shown in Figure 9-1.

Program Name. This option is the filename—including the extension—of the standard application. You should include the proper drive and pathname here if the application is not in the command path.

Program Title. The Program Title option is the descriptive text that appears beneath the program's icon when you select it and in the program's title bar. This text can be up to 29 characters long.

Program Parameters. This option allows for any parameters the program accepts when it starts up. The /c parameter for Microsoft Word invokes the program's character-display mode. To tell Windows to prompt you for parameters, put a question mark (?) in this section. Thereafter, when you start the application, Windows displays a dialog box asking for parameters. The latter approach is handy for applications such as WordStar or Microsoft Word, which can open a document you specify by name when you run the application.

Initial Directory. This option lets you enter the drive and directory containing the application and any data files or program overlay files it requires. (A program overlay file contains code that the program can load into memory as it runs.) If the application is in the current directory or is in a directory named in a Path statement, you can leave this entry blank. Figure 9-2 shows an example of an initial directory entry for MicroPro's WordStar, which I store in a directory named \WORDSTAR.

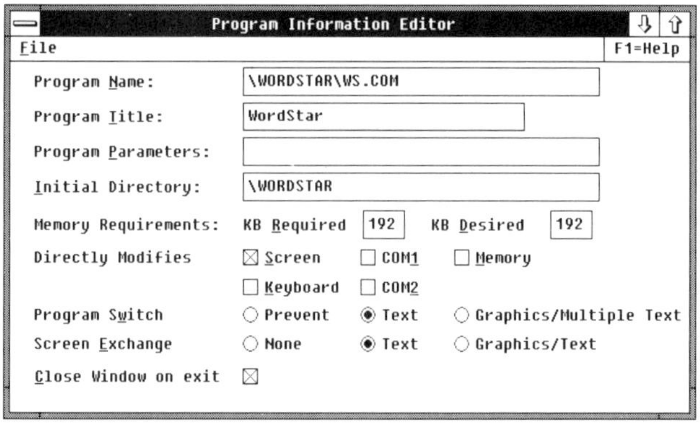

FIGURE 9-2.

PIF for WordStar stored in \WORDSTAR directory.

Memory-information Options

The Memory Requirements section of a PIF gives Windows two tidbits of information: KB Required and KB Desired. The KB Required option denotes the minimum amount of memory (in kilobytes) that the standard application requires to run. The KB Desired setting indicates the maximum amount of memory that the application can use. (You can determine this information by consulting your application's documentation.) As a general rule, the larger the KB Desired value, the better.

System-resource Options

A PIF's system-resource options indicate how the standard application accesses your computer's screen, keyboard, communications ports, and memory.

The Screen Option

The most important setting in this section is the Screen box, which indicates whether the program creates its screen displays by using standard MS-DOS system routines or by bypassing MS-DOS and accessing your computer's video memory directly. For Windows users, the former approach is better because it lets the program run in a window.

Most current standard applications—including some from Microsoft—weren't created with Windows users in mind; they bypass MS-DOS to access the screen directly. Direct screen access allows them to create screen displays faster, an important consideration for word processors, spreadsheets, and communications programs (which have to do a lot of scrolling) and programs that display graphics. But direct screen access also means the application can't run in a window.

For such applications, you must select the Screen box. Doing so lets the application take over the screen when you run it or switch to it. (You still can exchange data with other applications, as I'll explain later in this chapter.)

The Keyboard Option

The Keyboard system-resource option tells Windows whether the application directly accesses your computer's keyboard buffer, an area in memory where keystrokes are stored until they can be processed. Most applications don't directly access the keyboard buffer; indeed, of the dozens of PIFs included with Windows, only the one for XyQuest's

XyWrite word processor has this option selected. With this option selected, you cannot switch from the application using Alt+Tab or Alt+Esc, nor can you access the application's Control menu. Also, a PIF with the Keyboard option selected prevents the application from running in a window.

The COM1 and COM2 Options

The COM1 and COM2 options indicate whether the application accesses a communications port. When one (or both) of these options are selected, Windows does not run any other application that uses the same port because two applications can't access the same port at the same time. Generally, the only time you need to select one of these options is when the standard application is a communications program. However, you also need to select the one your application uses if the application uses a serial printer.

The Memory Option

The final system-resource option is Memory. Select this option for memory-resident applications (also called TSRs because they use the MS-DOS Terminate-and-Stay-Resident system call). This category includes pop-up software, such as Borland International's SideKick, as well as utilities, such as disk-caching programs and some network drivers. When you start an application for which this option is active, Windows swaps itself to disk when you run the application, allows MS-DOS to load the application into memory, and runs it. The application then modifies memory as needed (most TSRs, for example, relocate themselves in memory and then adjust certain MS-DOS memory pointers to reflect the amount of memory they used). Finally, the application uses the MS-DOS Terminate-and-Stay-Resident system routine to return control to MS-DOS, which swaps Windows back into memory from disk. If all went well, you are able to access the pop-up program using its hot-key sequence.

Program-switching Options

The option buttons in the Program Switch section of PIFEDIT determine whether you are able to switch between the standard application and Windows. The Prevent option disables switching; once you start the standard application, you're stuck there until you choose its quit command. The Text option enables switching and tells Windows to reserve 4 KB of memory to hold the contents of the screen when you switch from the application. When you switch back to the application, Windows restores the screen display by shuttling the data it saved back into your computer's video memory.

The Graphics/Multiple Text option also enables switching but tells Windows to reserve more memory (up to 36 KB, depending on your graphics adapter and on the graphics mode the standard application uses) to hold graphics screens.

Screen-exchange Options

PIFEDIT's screen-exchange options let you determine whether you can copy information from the standard application to the clipboard by using the Copy command on the Control menu or by using the Alt+PrintScreen key combination, which places a snapshot of the application's screen on the clipboard. Choosing None prevents you from copying anything from the application by disabling both the Alt+PrintScreen combination and the Control menu. Choosing Text lets you copy text information by using the Control menu or Alt+PrintScreen, and selecting Graphics/Text lets you copy both graphics and text.

Whether you actually are able to copy graphics screens, however, depends on your display hardware and on the amount of memory available when you press Alt+PrintScreen. If you have a Color/Graphics Adapter, Windows needs roughly 32 KB of memory to copy a low-resolution graphic screen. However, if you have an Enhanced Graphics Adapter, Windows needs approximately 112 KB. With the Video Graphics Array circuitry in an IBM PS/2 Model 50, 60, or 80, roughly 256 KB is required. If you press Alt+PrintScreen when there isn't enough free memory to copy the screen, Windows beeps.

The *[pif]* Section of WIN.INI

In addition to the PIF, Windows uses WIN.INI's *[pif]* section, shown in Figure 9-3 on the following page, for running standard applications. The first two entries in *[pif]*, *swapdisk* and *swapsize*, are especially important; they tell Windows which disk drive to use for swapping and how much memory to reserve for swapping.

Let's examine *swapdisk* first. Normally, this entry reads *swapdisk = ?* The question mark doesn't mean Windows is undecided as to which disk to use; rather, it tells Windows, "When you have to swap, swap to

FIGURE 9-3.

The [pif] *section*

of WIN.INI.

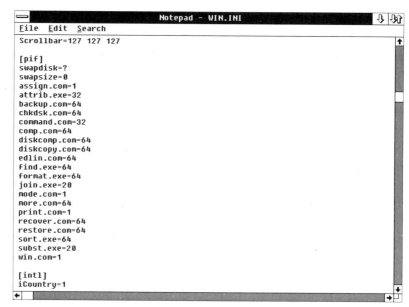

```
Notepad - WIN.INI
File  Edit  Search
Scrollbar=127 127 127

[pif]
swapdisk=?
swapsize=0
assign.com=1
attrib.exe=32
backup.com=64
chkdsk.com=64
command.com=32
comp.com=64
diskcomp.com=64
diskcopy.com=64
edlin.com=64
find.exe=64
format.exe=64
join.exe=20
mode.com=1
more.com=64
print.com=1
recover.com=64
restore.com=64
sort.exe=64
subst.exe=20
win.com=1

[intl]
iCountry=1
```

the disk named by the MS-DOS system variable TEMP or to the lowest-lettered hard disk in the system if no TEMP variable is set.''

The next entry in WIN.INI's *[pif]* section is *swapsize*, which lets you control how much memory Windows allocates to standard applications. The default *swapsize* value is 0, which tells Windows to use the value in the PIF of the first standard application you run. That's why you should try to run the larger of two standard applications first.

You can think of the remaining entries in the *[pif]* section of WIN.INI as mini PIFs. They tell Windows how much memory, in kilobytes, are required to run common MS-DOS programs such as FORMAT, EDLIN, BACKUP, and COMMAND.

TIP 1: Starting PIFEDIT and Opening a PIF in One Step

Normally, when you double-click on a PIF or select it and press Enter, Windows starts the PIF's application. If you're going to be doing a great deal of PIF editing, however, you might want to double-click on a PIF (or select it and press Enter) to start PIFEDIT and open the PIF. Adding the following line to the *[extensions]* section of your WIN.INI lets you do that:

```
pif=pifedit.exe ^.pif
```

When you've finished editing PIF, disable the line by reopening WIN.INI, adding a semicolon (;) to the beginning of the line, and replacing the equal sign with a space. Doing so turns the line into a comment. (Comments can't contain equal signs.) You could simply delete the line, but leaving it in as a comment lets you restore it in a flash for your next PIF-editing session. Remember that you must exit and restart Windows for your WIN.INI changes to take effect.

TIP 2: Giving an Application More Memory Than Its PIF Specifies

You can use one of three methods to give an application more memory than the Memory Requirements section of its PIF specifies: Use a blank KB Desired entry, enter −1 in KB Desired, or enter either 640 in KB Required or −1 in KB Desired and select the None option in the Screen Exchange section.

Using a blank KB Desired entry gives an application all available free memory—that is, the memory not in use by Windows or other applications. A blank KB Desired entry can benefit three types of applications: those that keep entire documents in memory, those that swap their own code in and out of memory as needed, and those that use expanded memory. Giving all the free memory to an application that keeps entire documents in memory, such as Ashton-Tate's Framework or IBM's Writing Assistant, lets you create larger documents. (Giving all free memory to an application that swaps portions of documents between memory and disk, such as Microsoft Word or Write, has no effect on the size of documents you can create because document size is limited only by available disk space.) Most of today's large applications don't load into memory all at once. Instead, they load in only as much code as is necessary to perform common tasks and swap other code in and out of memory as needed. Given all available free memory, they can load more code into memory and spend less time accessing the disk.

Entering −1 (a minus sign followed by 1) in an application's KB Desired entry tells Windows to swap nearly all of itself to disk when you start or switch to that program. (Normally, when Windows swaps, it swaps only a small portion of itself to disk, concentrating primarily on swapping other running applications.) When Windows swaps itself to disk, it suspends, or temporarily stops running, any other running applications. If any applications that use a serial communications port are running, Windows can elect not to swap itself to disk to avoid serial-port conflicts, such as an application changing the configuration of a port used by another running application.

Typing either *640* in the KB Required text box or *−1* in the KB Desired box *and* selecting None in the Screen Exchange section tells Windows not to set aside any memory to hold data from the standard application's screen (meaning you won't be able to copy any data from the standard application). If you find yourself resorting to this step, it's time to question whether you should even attempt to run the application under Windows. After all, being able to copy data from a standard application is one of the primary benefits of running it under Windows. You might be better off substituting a Windows application for the standard application or simply running the standard application from MS-DOS, particularly if the application can exchange data through files.

TIP 3: Determining Whether an Application Can Run in a Window

When can you run a standard application in a window? All the time, if you use Windows/386. If you use Windows 2.0, that isn't the case. However, if the application offers an installation option for use with Windows, IBM's TopView operating environment, or an ANSI device driver, chances are good that it can run in a window. The best way to find out is to experiment. When you create the application's PIF (or when you edit an existing one), be sure that the Screen box is not checked. Then try running the application. First be sure that no applications containing unsaved data are running because you may have to reset your computer. If only a blank window appears when you start the application, the application cannot run in a window. From this point, you may be able to quit the application if you know which keystrokes invoke its command for quitting. If not, reset your computer by pressing Ctrl+Alt+Del. Finally, return to the application's PIF and choose the Screen box.

Being able to run an application in a window does not necessarily mean that you should. There are benefits and a drawback to doing so.

On the plus side, because the application shares the screen with any other applications you may be running, you can switch between applications more conveniently and you can view data in the application while using other applications.

Most importantly, applications that run in a window can take advantage of Windows' multitasking capabilities. When you switch to an application that takes over the screen, Windows suspends all other running applications. But an application running in a window can share your system's processor with other applications. For example, I run Adobe Font Downloader utility in a window; doing so lets me select a set of fonts for downloading and then switch to other applications while the downloader transmits the fonts to the laser printer. If I ran the downloader as a full-screen application, I'd have to wait until the fonts were downloaded to switch to another application. If I switched to another application before all fonts were downloaded, the downloading would stop.

But there is a drawback to running a standard application in a window: Performance suffers. Because Windows must divide your computer's processing resources among all active applications, the application runs slower than it would if it had full control over the screen. With Adobe Font Downloader, for instance, downloading takes significantly longer. Most of the time, that isn't important, because I'm able to use the computer for other tasks during downloading. When I'm not willing to wait, I simply start the downloader by using a second PIF, one that has its Screen box checked.

TIP 4: Using TSRs That Use the Alt Key

If your Terminate-and-Stay-Resident program's hot-key sequence involves the Alt key, you may have trouble switching between applications and accessing menus within Windows. Because pop-up programs significantly alter the state of your system, loading and using them from within Windows is only slightly safer than breakdancing on a crate of nitroglycerin. Use Windows desktop applications instead; they provide similar or superior features without the risks. If you use non-pop-up, memory-resident applications such as network servers, disk caches, or expanded-memory managers, load them before starting Windows.

TIP 5: ## Using Program-switching Options with Large Standard Applications

Because the Text and Graphics/Multiple Text options consume memory, you may want to forego switching capability when running large standard applications. As a compromise, you can choose the Text option. Doing so will let you switch from the application when it's in text mode, but not when it's in graphics mode.

TIP 6: ## Setting Up and Using RAMDrive for Swapping

In most cases, your TEMP system variable in MS-DOS points Windows to a directory on your hard disk. However, if your computer has a few megabytes of memory and you're willing to set aside some of it as a RAM disk, you can decrease the amount of time required to switch between standard applications. To do so, use the RAMDrive utility included on the Windows' Utilities 2 Disk to reserve some of your system's memory as a RAM disk. (Instructions for using RAMDrive appear in Chapter 10.) Then, edit the *swapdisk* entry to point Windows to the RAM disk. For example, if your RAM disk is drive D (it is, unless your system has more than one hard disk), edit the *swapdisk* entry to read:

```
swapdisk=D:
```

On my IBM PS/2 Model 50, this approach speeds up swapping signficantly. Using the hard disk for swapping, it requires approximately 10 seconds to swap between Lotus 1-2-3 (release 2.01) and Microsoft Word (version 4.0). When I use a RAM disk for swapping, however, the time drops to less than 4 seconds.

A RAM disk used for swapping must be at least twice as large as the largest application you plan to swap, because two applications could end up on disk at the same time. For example, assume you are using Lotus 1-2-3 and Microsoft Word under Windows. You start 1-2-3, which requires 256 KB of memory. After running 1-2-3 for a while, you switch back to Windows and start Word, which also requires 256 KB. At that time, Windows moves 1-2-3 from its 256 KB memory partition into a temporary disk file and then loads Word into the freshly freed memory partition. The crunch for disk space comes when you switch from Word back to 1-2-3. At that time, Windows must move Word from memory to a temporary disk file and then move 1-2-3 from disk back into memory. For an instant—after Microsoft Word is swapped to disk but before 1-2-3 is swapped back into memory—both applications reside on disk in temporary files. *That's* why the RAM disk must be at least twice as large as the largest application you plan to swap.

To calculate the size of the RAM disk, add the Memory Required figures from the PIF for each pair of applications you plan to switch between, adding roughly 20 KB to each figure to hold the information Windows uses to restore the application when you switch back to it. Then double the resulting figure. If your standard application creates temporary files (as Word does), add more space to allow for them. So, for example, to swap between 1-2-3 and Microsoft Word, you need a RAM disk with slightly more than one megabyte free. If your RAM disk isn't large enough, Windows displays a message stating *Need more disk space* when you attempt to switch between applications.

TIP 7: Specifying a Minimum Amount of Memory for Swapping Standard Applications

By replacing the default 0 in the *swapsize* entry of WIN.INI's *[pif]* section with a specific amount (in kilobytes), you can reserve a minimum amount of memory for swapping.

Why bother? To find out, let's look at an example using Lotus 1-2-3 and MicroPro WordStar. Of those two programs, 1-2-3 has a larger Memory Required value (256 KB) than WordStar (version 3.3) (192 KB). Because Windows normally allocates memory for standard applications based on the first standard application you start, you should start 1-2-3 first to get the best performance when running both applications. To get optimum performance regardless of which program you start first, change your *swapsize* entry to 265. (It's a good idea to add roughly 10 KB to an application's memory requirements to allow for the extra information Windows stores regarding the application's state at the time of the swap.) Thereafter, Windows always allocates 265 KB of memory when you start a standard application—regardless of the values specified in the application's PIF.

TIP 8: Creating Your Own *[pif]* Entries in WIN.INI

You can create your own entries in the *[pif]* section of WIN.INI for standard applications that can run in a window, eliminating the need for a separate PIF. When you start a standard application, Windows first checks to see if the application is named in the *[pif]* section of

WIN.INI. If so, Windows uses the value adjacent to the application's filename as the Memory Required value and assumes the following information in place of the application's PIF:

Program Title. Windows uses the application's filename without the extension.

Initial Directory. The directory that is the current directory when the application starts is the initial directory.

Parameters. No parameters are passed to the application, nor are you able to specify any.

Memory Desired. Windows uses the value you enter in the application's *[pif]* entry.

Directly Modifies. Windows assumes the program does not directly modify the screen, the keyboard, the communications ports, or memory.

If you run a standard application that meets these requirements, consider listing it in the *[pif]* section. Doing so eliminates the need to create (and set aside disk space for) a separate PIF.

TIP 9: Copying from Standard Applications to the Clipboard

Windows does an impressive job of grafting clipboard support onto standard applications, which weren't designed with cutting and pasting in mind. I'll review the techniques for accessing the clipboard from standard applications, providing some additional comments and presenting some examples of their use. (Note that you must enable Program Switch and Graphics/Text in the Screen Exchange options in an application's PIF to use the following techniques.)

To copy an entire screen to the clipboard, press Alt+PrintScreen. Windows inverts your screen briefly to indicate it's copying the screen, a process similar to taking a snapshot. If your system doesn't have enough free memory to copy the entire screen, your computer beeps.

To copy part of a screen to the clipboard, press Alt+Spacebar to display the application's Control menu, as shown in Figure 9-4. Choose the Mark command. Next, use the direction keys to move the highlight to the beginning of the information you want to copy. Press Shift and then use the direction keys to select the information. (To cancel the selection, press Escape.) Finally, copy the information by pressing Alt+Spacebar to redisplay the Control menu and then pressing Y to choose the Copy command.

FIGURE 9-4.

Opening a
standard
applications
Control menu.

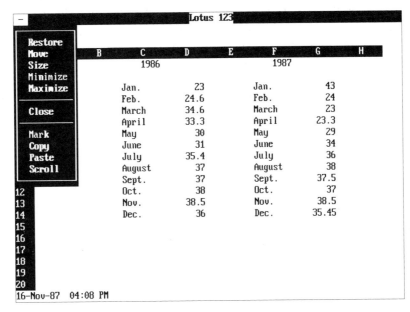

Graphics copied from standard applications are stored on the clipboard in bitmap format. Text is stored in two formats: text and OEM text. In OEM text format, the data is stored exactly as it appeared on the screen, in the characters present in your computer's native character set. In text format, the data is stored using the ANSI character set; if you copy special text characters such as double bars, Windows converts them into characters that mimic their appearance, such as equal signs. If you paste the data into a Windows application, Windows uses the text format. If, however, you paste the data into another standard application, Windows uses OEM text format, leaving the special characters intact if the standard application can display them.

Figure 9-5, on the following page, illustrates these concepts. The first screen shows some special characters being copied from Microsoft Word, which is running in its character mode. The second screen shows the characters pasted into Microsoft Windows Write. In the process of copying them, Windows translated them into ANSI characters; notice how Windows used characters that approximate the appearance of the originals. The third screen shows the characters pasted into a Microsoft Word document. Because Word is a standard application, Windows uses OEM text format, allowing the characters to appear in their original form. (Windows 1.04 could not render data from standard applications in two formats; instead, data copied from standard applications was always translated into ANSI format.)

FIGURE 9-5.

Pasting text in text and OEM text formats. (A) Special characters copied in Microsoft Word. (B) Special characters pasted into Microsoft Windows Write and translated to ANSI equivalents. (C) Special characters pasted into Word and remaining in OEM text format.

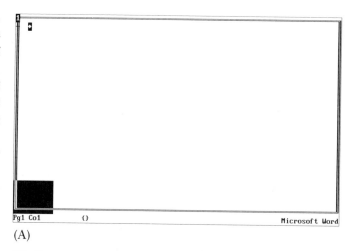

(A)

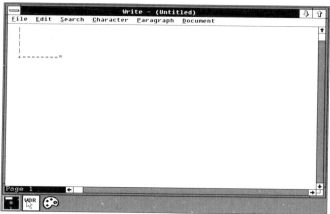

(B)

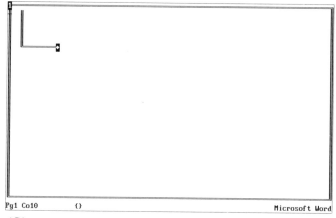

(C)

You can also paste text into standard applications. For example, to paste a table from a Lotus 1-2-3 spreadsheet into a Microsoft Word document, first use the Control menu's Mark command to select the table and its Copy command to copy it to the clipboard, as shown in Figure 9-6 on the next page. Next, start or switch to Microsoft Word (first quitting 1-2-3 if you like), position the cursor where you want the table to appear, and choose the Control menu's Paste command, as also shown in Figure 9-6. In this example, the columns are separated by spaces rather than tabs; to alter their spacing (and to print aligned columns on a printer that uses proportionally spaced fonts), you need to replace the spaces with tab characters and then use Word's Format Tab Set command to adjust the tabs as necessary.

FIGURE 9-6.

*Copying a table
from Lotus 1-2-3
to Microsoft
Word.
(A) Copying the
table in 1-2-3.
(B) Pasting the
table into Word.*

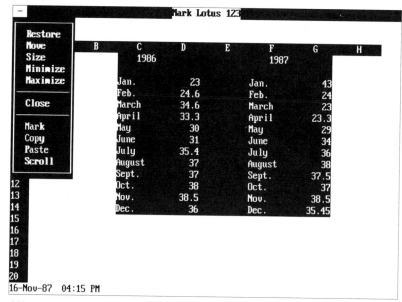

(A)

(B)

HARDWARE DECISIONS

Y ou need a system with five hardware elements to exercise the full power of Windows: a mouse, good graphics, a hard disk, sufficient memory, and a fast processor. Although you can control most Windows applications using the keyboard, a mouse is faster and more efficient for many tasks. If you use Windows on a computer with limited graphics, you can't enjoy Windows' color capabilities or fully appreciate its various fonts. If you use Windows on a machine without a hard disk, Windows starts and runs slowly, and you can't run multiple applications and switch among them without the tedium of swapping floppy disks. If you give Windows insufficient memory, you can't fully use its multitasking features. If you use Windows on a slow machine, you feel like you're trying to run wearing lead shoes.

This chapter examines the hardware options open to Windows users, with the goal of helping you assemble a system tailored to running Windows efficiently. I've included some brand names to give you a starting point for your quest, but I've generally avoided describing specific products in detail. Computer hardware evolves constantly, so detailed product descriptions would quickly make this book outdated. Instead, I've tried to provide the information that will make you a smarter shopper by presenting the factors involved in choosing each hardware component. Where appropriate, I've also included some technical background to help you understand how a given option works. Before you buy, visit local dealers and read reviews in computer magazines. (A list of reading resources appears in Appendix A.)

Mice and Other Pointing Devices

In Windows, it's not only polite to point, it's desirable. As discussed in Chapter 3, although you can perform nearly any operation with the keyboard, a mouse or some other pointing device is far more efficient for many tasks and is required equipment for many drawing and desktop publishing applications. As mentioned in Chapter 3, a mouse can streamline operations in every application. A mouse lets you choose dialog box options much faster than the keyboard does. It makes positioning a word processor's cursor or moving to a particular spreadsheet cell a one-click proposition. It lets you switch from one program to another by clicking in the second application's window, instead of pressing Alt-Tab until the desired application is active.

A mouse also makes short work of resizing windows, spreadsheet columns, and graphics. To resize a window with the keyboard, you choose the Size command from the window's Control menu and then tap the direction keys until the window is the desired size. To resize a window with the mouse, move the pointer to the window's border and drag. To resize a column in Microsoft Excel with the keyboard, you press Alt, T, and then C to choose the Column Width command; then you type the desired column width and press Enter. If the column is too wide or narrow, you repeat the entire process. With the mouse, simply move the pointer to the boundary between columns and drag left or right to change the column's width.

Of course, you can always use the keyboard when it's better to do so. Chapter 3 discusses when it's most efficient to use the keyboard, the mouse, or a combination of both.

The Two Mouse Types

Mice fall into two categories: optical and mechanical.

Optical Mice

An optical mouse, such as Mouse Systems' PC Mouse, operates by shining a light on a reflective mouse pad. The pad has a 6-inch to 8-inch square, metal surface covered with a grid of dots or lines. As you move the mouse, a sensor in it reads the light reflected from the grid and interprets the degree of mouse movement.

Mechanical Mice

A mechanical mouse, such as the Microsoft Mouse and IBM's PS/2 Mouse, contains a hard-rubber ball that rolls as the mouse moves. The ball rides against two metal rollers that are connected to shafts attached to encoders, round disks ringed with electrical contacts that translate the rotational movement into electrical signals. One roller-and-disk set measures horizontal movement; the other measures vertical movement. A mechanical mouse doesn't require a special pad, but its mechanical parts can wear out and are sensitive to dust and debris found on a normal desktop. These drawbacks are minor, however. A mechanical mouse has a life expectancy of about five years; chances are you will need to replace your computer before your mouse. And cleaning a mouse is a straightforward process: Simply remove the rubber ball according to the manufacturer's directions, rub it within a clean, lint-free cloth dampened with isopropyl alcohol, and then clean the mouse's internal rollers with the cloth and reassemble. If you work in a dusty environment, you might consider a mouse-cleaning kit such as Ergotron's MouseCleaner 360, which includes cleaning solution, a cloth, and a clever, velcro-covered ball that you moisten, insert in the mouse's ball chamber, and roll to clean the mouse's rollers.

A variation of mechanical mouse is the optomechanical mouse. An optomechanical mouse, such as one from Logitech Inc., uses technology from both camps. Like a mechanical mouse, an opto-mechanical mouse houses a rolling rubber ball attached to rods connected to round disks. The disks aren't ringed with electrical contacts, as those of a mechical mouse are. Instead, they're riddled with holes through which light from a light-emitting diode can pass and strike a photosensitive transistor.

How a Mouse Works

Internal differences aside, all mice work in the same way. They constantly generate electrical pulses that are transmitted to your computer and are interpreted by your mouse driver, which in turn communicates with Windows. Windows responds by performing certain tests, such as determining whether any buttons are pressed and whether the mouse has moved. If it has moved, Windows must determine how far it has moved, in units—the smallest degree of motion a mouse can register. Most IBM PC and PS/2 mice, including the Microsoft Mouse, register 200 units per inch. In theory, the more units per inch a mouse can register, the greater the mouse's resolution. In practice, however, most people can't discern minor differences in mouse resolution.

Serial Versus Bus Mice

Within the optical and mechanical categories are two additional categories: serial and bus. A serial mouse attaches to the computer's RS-232C serial port, and a bus mouse attaches to an expansion board that you install in a slot inside the computer. Although both cost about the same, each has advantages and drawbacks. A serial mouse uses a serial port that you could otherwise use for a modem, printer, or other serial device, while a bus mouse uses a slot that you could use for a memory board, internal modem, or other expansion board. Your decision depends on your system setup. If your serial ports are busy communicating with modems and printers, use a bus mouse; if your slots are jam packed but you've a port to spare, use a serial mouse. If you have an IBM PS/2 or other computer with a built-in port for a pointing device, your choice is easier; you can attach a mouse without using a slot or a serial port.

Microsoft InPort Mouse

If you don't have a PS/2 or a port or slot to spare, there's still hope. In July of 1986, Microsoft introduced its InPort device interface, an integrated circuit chip that does the same job as the logic circuits on the Microsoft Mouse bus board. Microsoft makes the InPort interface specifications and chip available to hardware developers who want to include InPort capabilities on their expansion boards. With an InPort-equipped expansion board, you can add a Microsoft bus mouse without having to sacrifice a serial port or dedicate a slot to the bus mouse's card. The Microsoft Mouse for IBM's PS/2 series is an InPort mouse; you plug Microsoft's cigarette-pack-size InPort adapter into the PS/2 and the mouse into the adapter. The Microsoft MACH 20 enhancement board, discussed later in this chapter, also provides an InPort connector, as do some other expansion boards.

Selecting the Right Mouse for You

As you hunt for a mouse, you might encounter species with varying numbers of buttons—anywhere from one to six, although two-button and three-button models are most common. With Windows, you need only two buttons. Indeed, most Windows applications use only one button, although some use the second for special purposes. Aldus Page-Maker switches between its actual-size and fit-in-window views when you press the alternate mouse button. Micrografx Designer lets you assign any menu command to the alternate mouse button, providing a convenient way to issue the command you use most often.

The availability of ports and slots on your system narrows your mouse search to a few candidates, which you should test before you buy. Ask yourself questions as you try each mouse. Does it feel comfortable in your hand? Does it roll smoothly? If you're considering an optical mouse, can you afford to donate six to eight square inches of your desk to its pad? Are the mouse's buttons large and easy to press, or are they small and stiff? Do the buttons emit an audible click when pressed? (These last two points might not seem important, but they are; like a keyboard, a mouse that provides good tactile and aural feed-back feels more responsive.) Does its pointer glide across the screen, or does it lurch and stick? Is its cable long enough? (Cable length is especially important if your computer's system unit is under or alongside your desk.) Do you like the way it looks? (Don't laugh— a mouse will become part of your desktop's decor, and I personally think some of the rodents on the market are ugly.) You will spend a great deal of time with a mouse; find one you're comfortable with.

Other Pointing Devices

If you've tried a few mice and just don't feel comfortable with them or if your desk lacks the few square inches of empty real estate a mouse requires, don't despair. Although a mouse is the best all-purpose pointing device, there are other ways to point.

Light Pens

One alternative is a light pen, a device that looks like a pen with a coiled cable coming out of its cap. For reasons I'll explore shortly, light pens aren't ideal for general Windows navigation tasks such as choosing menu commands and dialog box options. They're better suited to such specialized, touch-and-go applications as warehouse order entry and industrial control.

With most light pens, the cable attaches to your computer's Color/Graphics Adapter. If you use a different adapter (and you should with Windows), you must add an expansion board designed for the pen.

By touching the pen's tip to the surface of your monitor's screen, you can choose menu commands, select text or graphics, and draw. The pen's optical system contains a photosensitive transistor that generates a signal when it detects light coming from the video display's glowing phosphor. By measuring the intensity of the light and calculating how long it takes for the video tube's electron beam to reach the pen's sensor, the pen determines where you're pointing. The pen then sends a signal through the cable to your computer, where it's put into a form Windows can understand by the pen's software driver.

Light pens don't require desk space, but they have their own drawbacks. Unless you purchase their optional expansion boards, they can't accurately reflect small degrees of movement. With an expansion board, pens such as FTG Data System's FT-156 can resolve movement down to the single pixel level. And because you must constantly lift your arm up and down, picking up and putting down the light pen (as opposed to simply reaching for a mouse), using a light pen for an extended amount of time can be fatiguing. After hours of use, a light pen doesn't feel so light.

Graphics Tablets

Another mouse alternative is a graphics tablet, a flat pad roughly the size of a phonograph-album jacket. You draw on the pad with a stylus or a cursor. The stylus is a pen-like device; the latter is about the size of a mouse, with a circular opening containing crosshairs. The intersection of the crosshairs represents the current position on the screen. A tablet's stylus or cursor is connected to the tablet and transmits an electronic or magnetic signal that a receiving grid located in the tablet picks up and uses to calculate the stylus' or cursor's position. (Graphics tablets from Kurta Corporation, Pencept, and Summagraphics all operate in this way.) The tablet itself usually connects to your computer's serial port, although some may use their own interface boards.

Two variations on this theme are acoustic tablets and resistive touch pads. Acoustic tablets use a stylus that transmits high-frequency sound waves that microphones located at the tablet's edges use to determine the stylus position. Science Accessories Corp.'s GP-7 Grafbar Mark II Sonic Digitizer uses this approach to eliminate the tablet itself. Its microphones are located on a small receiver unit that effectively turns any flat surface into an electronic drafting table. Resistive touch pads, such as Koala Technologies' KoalaPad, contain two layers of conductive material, separated by a minute gap. When you exert pressure on the pad from a stylus or your finger, the two layers touch at that point, generating a signal.

Because they accurately mimic the pen-on-paper drawing process, graphics tablets are well-suited to computer drafting and drawing applications. You can also use them to trace existing artwork, which you can simply place on the tablet's surface. It's interesting to note a fundamental difference between graphics tablets and mice: A graphics tablet represents absolute movement; a mouse represents relative movement. Each point on a graphics tablet's pad corresponds to a specific screen location. With a mouse, no such one-to-one relationship between the device's physical position and the pointer's on-screen position exists; you can pick up the mouse and put it down anywhere on your desk.

A final point regarding alternative pointing devices: If you're considering one but you also use a mouse, be sure the device you buy can work along with a mouse. Some light pens or graphics tablets use a mouse driver and, therefore, can't work simultaneously with a mouse. And be sure the device is compatible with Windows.

Video Adapters and Displays

With graphical operating environments such as Windows, looks *are* everything. The greater the resolution of your computer's display and video-display circuitry, the better Windows looks. If you spend a great deal of time with Windows, it's in your best interest to have it looking its best.

Video Adapters

Better resolution means sharper text, especially in small sizes, and sharper graphics, with less apparent stair-stepping (jagged edges that appear on curves and diagonal lines). High-resolution graphics boards allow Windows to glitter with color graphics and sharp text; lower resolution boards give Windows a coarse, chunky appearance. Figure 10-1 lists the leading graphics standards in the MS-DOS world. (Resolutions are listed with number of horizontal pixels first and then the number of vertical pixels.)

FIGURE 10-1.

MS-DOS graphics standards.

Category	Resolution	Color in Windows	Rating for Windows use
Color/Graphics Adapter (CGA)	640 by 200	No	Poor
Hercules Graphics Adapter	720 by 348	No	Good
Enhanced Graphics Adapter (EGA)	640 by 200	Yes	Good
EGA with more than 64 KB memory*	640 by 350	Yes	Very good
Multicolor Graphics Array (MCGA)	640 by 480	No	Very good
Video Graphics Array (VGA)	640 by 480	Yes	Excellent

* Most non-IBM EGA-compatible adapters are in this category.

The graphics standards in Figure 10-1 are in ascending order of resolution and suitability for Windows, but the listing could almost be considered chronological. The resolution of graphic displays in the microcomputer world has constantly improved, and no end is in sight. One reason is memory: Each new generation of memory chips brings greater capacity at lower cost, and memory is a key player in determining graphics resolution.

How does memory affect graphics resolution? In a graphical operating environment such as Windows, everything you see—including text—is a graphic. Instead of creating text using the computer's built-in character-generating circuitry, Windows draws it using the Graphic Device Interface (GDI) discussed in Chapter 1. This twist allows Windows to display text in a vast array of sizes and styles. As mentioned in Chapter 7, graphics displays such as Windows' are called bitmapped displays because each pixel on the screen corresponds to (is mapped to) a bit in the computer's video memory.

Color bitmapped displays impose more memory requirements than monochrome displays; separate areas of video memory called bit planes are required to display multiple colors. A monochrome-display adapter provides only one bit plane and can, therefore, display pixels in one of only two values. In the monochrome world, there are no shades of gray or colors. (Shades of gray can be simulated, however, using a technique called dithering, in which groups of pixels are combined into patterns.)

When you add more bit planes, however, you gain the ability to assign additional bits of memory to each pixel. Those additional bits can be used to store color or gray-scale (shades of gray) information about the pixel.

To understand how additional bit planes allow for more colors, let's look at two ways in which the IBM Color/Graphics Adapter (CGA) can be used. This old standby provides 16 KB of video memory. That memory can be allocated in various ways, with each method providing different resolution and color capabilities. In one mode (mode 4), the adapter can create four-color displays with a resolution of 320 by 200 pixels. In this mode, the adapter's video memory is divided into two 8 KB bit planes. With two bit planes, a pixel can assume one of four colors. Two bits can represent four values because four different on-off combinations exist:

- One bit can be one and the second bit can be zero.

- The first bit can be zero and the second bit can be one.

- Both bits can be one.

- Both bits can be zero.

But 320 by 200 is too coarse for a graphical operating environment, so Windows does not use this mode.

In a different mode (mode 6), a CGA can display a resolution of 640 by 200 pixels. In this so-called high-resolution mode, all 16 KB of the adapter's memory is dedicated to a single bit plane. That means better resolution but no color because the CGA board has only enough memory to store one on-off combination for each pixel. If your computer has CGA video circuitry, Windows uses this mode.

The more video memory a computer has, the more pixels and colors it can represent. Figure 10-2 illustrates this; it's virtually the same table as in Figure 10-1, except that the columns titled "Color in Windows" and "Rating for Windows Use" are replaced with the amount of video memory and maximum number of colors that each adapter provides in its highest-resolution mode.

FIGURE 10-2.

Resolution, colors, and memory provided by MS-DOS video standards.

Category	Resolution	Number of colors	Amount of video memory
Color/Graphics Adapter (CGA)	640 by 200	2 (black and white)	16 KB
Hercules Graphics Adapter	720 by 348	2 (black and white)	64 KB
Enhanced Graphics Adapter (EGA)	640 by 200	16*	64 KB
EGA with more than 64 KB memory**	640 by 350	16*	128 KB or 256 KB
Multicolor Graphics Array (MCGA)	640 by 480	2 (black and white)	64 KB
Video Graphics Array (VGA)	640 by 480	16*	256 KB

* Windows displays only 8 colors because of the way it uses these adapters.
** Most non-IBM EGA-compatible adapters are in this category.

Display Monitors

Of course, you don't view an image on an adapter board. Your monitor is the real window into Windows, so it plays an influential role in determining how Windows looks.

In the past, choosing a monitor was fairly easy. For word processing and other text-oriented tasks, you would generally choose a monochrome monitor. For graphics applications such as drafting and business graphics, a color monitor was called for. After making that decision, you bought a monitor that provided the resolution matching that of your video adapter.

It's not that simple anymore. Graphics standards are evolving, with each generation bringing finer resolution. Thanks to the expandable nature of most MS-DOS computers, upgrading your video circuitry is a matter of plugging in a new display card. But what of your monitor? If you bought a monitor that was matched to a particular graphics standard, upgrading your video system means buying a new monitor too.

Multiscanning Monitors
Fortunately, monitor manufacturers have developed a powerful weapon against display obsolescence. Called multiscanning monitors, they contain special circuitry that allows them to sense and adapt to different graphics standards. NEC's MultiSync monitor pioneered the multiscanning concept; today, nearly a dozen multiscanning monitors are available from such manufacturers as Zenith, Sony, JVC, Magnavox, and Taxan.

Multiscanning monitors attain their versatility by being able to adapt to the various scanning frequencies that display adapters use. One such frequency is the horizontal scan rate, the speed at which the monitor's electron beams are guided across its tube. The CGA standard uses a 15.75 kHz horizontal scan rate, meaning the video adapter can sweep the electron beams across the display 15,750 times per second. The EGA standard boosts the horizontal scan rate to 21.85 kHz; VGA ups it to 31.75 kHz. The faster the horizontal scan rate, the better the horizontal resolution.

Multiscanning monitors can also adapt to different refresh frequencies, the speed at which the monitor can redraw the screen. The higher a monitor's refresh frequency, the better its vertical resolution can be. Most multiscanning monitors can adapt to refresh frequencies of between approximately 50 and 75 Hz, meaning they can redraw the screen at any rate between 50 and 75 times per second. Sony's Multiscan monitor (model CPD-1302) has a refresh range of 50 to 100 Hz. Because sharper graphics resolutions require faster refresh rates, a monitor with a higher maximum refresh rate provides a stronger fortress against obsolescence.

A factor that influences the sharpness of any color monitor—multiscanning or not—is the design of its video tube. The tube in a color monitor contains a shadow mask, a metal mask positioned between the tube's red, green, and blue electron guns and the screen's surface. A shadow mask is filled with minute holes, one for each screen pixel. The space between the holes is called the dot pitch. Generally, the smaller the dot pitch, the sharper the monitor's pixels. Most color monitors have a dot pitch of 0.31 mm—that is, less than a third of a millimeter is between each opening in the shadow mask. Some monitors, however, have finer dot pitches, which make for a potentially sharper image. IBM's 8513 Color Display for PS/2 systems has a 0.28 mm dot pitch. Sony's Multiscan has a 0.26 mm dot pitch. The size of each dot also influences sharpness, but few manufacturers list their products' dot-size specification.

Specialized Monitors

In addition to the standard adapter configurations, many specialized graphics adapters and displays are available. For desktop publishing or drafting applications, you might consider a large, monochrome-screen display such as Moniterm's Viking I or Sigma Designs' LaserView Display. Boasting 19-inch screens and resolutions of 1280 by 960 pixels for the Viking I and 1664 by 1200 for the LaserView, such displays show more of a page on screen at one time—indeed, up to two 8½-by-11-inch pages side by side. Seeing more of a page at one time means less scrolling and zooming, giving you a better overall impression of the page's appearance.

Large screen displays come with their own adapter boards, which usually contain their own microprocessors. These microprocessors send bits quickly from the adapter's video memory to the screen—a necessity when you consider that a 1664-by-1200 display requires nearly two million bits to create an image. Without a microprocessor on the adapter, a large screen display could monopolize your microprocessor's time, impairing the computer's performance.

But if your primary applications are word processing, spreadsheet analysis, or database management, you might find the wide-open space of a large monitor overwhelming. Although some wordsmiths and spreadsheet mavens prefer to see more of their documents on screen, I find it difficult to locate the cursor or the current cell on a large screen.

As this section has shown, numerous factors—many of them subjective—influence the purchase of a monitor. Nowhere does the phrase "try before you buy" apply more.

Hard Disks

A hard-disk drive is the single most important peripheral for running Windows. A hard-disk drive can transfer data far faster than a floppy-disk drive can, allowing your computer to start and run Windows and its applications faster. In addition, a hard disk provides enough storage space to hold dozens of applications, depending on its capacity. That means you can take advantage of Windows' ability to run multiple applications simultaneously without having to swap floppy disks. And because Windows uses a disk to swap data when running standard applications, a hard disk makes running standard applications under Windows far more practical and convenient.

Several factors work together to give a hard disk its speed and capacity. The disk, or platter, is made of highly polished, rigid metal. The computer can pack data more tightly on a hard disk than on a floppy disk. Most hard disks contain more than one platter, with one stacked above another. The platters spin far faster than a floppy disk—usually at 3600 revolutions per minute (RPM) as opposed to a floppy disk's 300 RPM. The platters and their read/write heads are sealed in an airtight enclosure that prevents dust and debris from entering and settling on a platter's surface, a potentially disastrous event. The drive's heads don't actually touch the platters; instead, the heads ride a fraction of an inch above the platters. A speck of dust on a disk platter can cause the head to bounce up and down on the platter's surface, causing permanent damage to the drive. (This bouncing can also occur if you jostle a hard disk while it's in use or while moving it. You can prevent the former problem by not moving or bumping your computer while it's in use. To prevent the latter problem, look for a hard disk with an automatic head-parking feature that moves the drive's heads to an unused portion of the disk when you turn your computer's power off.)

Many of today's MS-DOS computers include built-in hard disks. If yours doesn't, you can choose from dozens of drives, many of which you can install yourself. Installing an internal drive usually means plugging the drive's controller board into a vacant expansion slot, removing one of your system's floppy drives, mounting the hard disk in its place, and then connecting the hard disk to its controller board using flat, multiwire cable called ribbon cable. If your computer's case contains enough room, you may not need to remove a floppy drive to make room for a hard disk. You might also consider one of the increasingly popular hard-disk cards, marvels of miniaturization that combine a hard disk and controller circuitry on a single expansion card. The first such drive was Plus Development's HardCard; it's still considered by many to be the best.

When you shop for a drive, you should assess a drive's specifications in three important areas: capacity, transfer rate, and access time.

Capacity. The drive's storage space, or capacity, is usually measured in megabytes (millions of bytes). Drives of 5 and 10 MB used to be the standards, but today more users are opting for 20 MB and 40 MB models. When shopping for a hard disk, consider a drive's cost per megabyte. Large-capacity hard disks tend to cost less per megabyte than their lower-capacity counterparts. Of course, that's of little comfort if you can't afford to spend more money. Ultimately, your budget may be the last word.

Transfer rate. The transfer rate is the speed with which the drive's controller transfers data to or from the drive and your computer's bus, the freeway on which data rides among the computer's memory, microprocessor, and peripherals. The faster a drive's transfer rate, the better (assuming your computer's bus can accept the data from a faster controller).

Access time. Access time is the average amount of time, in milliseconds, required for the drive's heads to reach a given point on the disk. The lower a drive's access time, the better.

A more obscure specification you might encounter is the interleave factor, which refers to the organization of the drive's sectors—wedge-shaped, magnetic divisions on each platter. Generally, a one-to-one interleave factor is best; it means that the drive's controller is fast enough to read sectors consecutively. (As with the transfer rate, your system must be able to accept data as quickly as the controller supplies it.) With a two-to-one interleave factor, the drive's controller reads a sector and then must wait one complete revolution to read the next sector.

But specifications can be misleading. A drive manufacturer might team a drive with a lightning-fast, 30-millisecond access time with a slow controller that requires a two-to-one or three-to-one interleave factor. Another manufacturer might use a drive with a relatively slow 80-millisecond access time but combine it with a fast controller that allows a one-to-one interleave factor. If sheer speed is a paramount consideration, try to run some timing tests on several drives. Otherwise, read reviews in computer magazines and buy the drive that provides the best mix of performance, reliability, and value. Any hard disk is faster than a floppy, and in day-to-day use, the performance difference between many drives is barely noticeable.

Expanded and Extended Memory

Windows' memory-management techniques allow it to shoehorn as much code as possible into your computer's memory. In fact, Windows can squeeze more out of memory than any other graphical operating environment, including the Macintosh's. But that's of little comfort when you attempt to run more than one large application simultaneously and watch your system slow to a crawl.

The technical complexity of Windows' software and its ability to simultaneously run multiple applications give Windows a voracious appetite for memory. But you can satisfy that appetite by adding more memory. More memory allows you to run more applications simultaneously, and each application runs faster because Windows does not have to discard its code segments to free memory and then reload them from disk the next time they're needed.

But how much is "more?" Until recently, adding more memory meant expanding up to the 640 KB limit for IBM PC's and compatibles. For most users, 640 KB was a vast expanse of workspace that could never be filled. (Remember, the original IBM PC debuted with 64 KB of memory, and *that* gave people goosebumps back in 1981.) But as software grew increasingly complex, memory requirements rose along with users' demands. Now, for anyone creating colossal spreadsheets or using operating environments like Windows, 640 KB is constraining.

Expanded-Memory Specifications

Freedom came in the spring of 1985 at the COMDEX computer-trade show. There, Lotus Development Corporation and Intel Corporation, designer of the microprocessors around which MS-DOS computers are built, announced the Expanded Memory Specification (EMS), a software-and-hardware way around the 640 KB barrier.

EMS was originally created to give Lotus 1-2-3 users more room. Engineers at Microsoft, however, saw more promise in expanded memory and also recognized that Microsoft could and should have a say in such a significant enhancement of MS-DOS. Microsoft announced that it would support EMS and that a future version of Windows would be able to access expanded memory. Lotus, Intel, and Microsoft worked together to revise EMS, adding more support for multitasking operating environments. A new EMS emerged, dubbed the Lotus/Intel/Microsoft Expanded Memory Specification 3.2.

The expanded-memory waters were muddied, however, when AST Research, a manufacturer of expansion boards, joined forces with several software developers to create a new version of the specification, known as the Enhanced EMS, or EEMS. EEMS added important enhancements to EMS but did so at the expense of compatibility. The solution to that problem was unveiled in August of 1987 in the form of EMS 4.0, a new version of the specification that incorporated the EEMS enhancements and added some of its own.

How Expanded Memory Works

To understand how EMS works and how it benefits Windows users, let's step back and look at how MS-DOS computers use memory. Because of the design of its 8088 microprocessor, the original IBM PC has a 1 MB address space—that is, it can access a maximum of 1 MB of memory. Some of those memory addresses, however, are reserved for the video adapter's memory, for the computer's basic input-output services (the fundamental code that allows access to devices such as the keyboard and disk drives), and for other internal uses. A total of 384 KB is reserved for these vital functions, leaving a maximum user memory area of 640 KB. The user memory area is where MS-DOS, Windows, and application programs reside; for the sake of this discussion, I'll refer to it as main memory.

Today's top-of-the-line MS-DOS machines are based on Intel's 80286 or 80386 microprocessors, which can address far more than a mere megabyte of memory. The 80286 can address up to 16 MB, and the 80386, up to a whopping 4 gigabytes (GB). But MS-DOS is still built around the 8088's memory model (its way of dealing with memory) and remains limited to accessing a total of 1 MB, only 640 KB of which is main memory.

MS-DOS can't directly access memory above the 1 MB address space, but it can indirectly access it through some technical trickery called bank switching. Bank switching is a distant cousin of swapping, discussed in Chapter 9. You'll recall that swapping involves shepherding a chunk of code from memory to disk and then ushering code on disk into the newly freed memory.

With bank switching, however, program code or data isn't actually moved from one place to another. Instead, a software driver called the expanded-memory manager maps portions of expanded memory into and out of the 1 MB physical address space. The program code doesn't actually move. Rather, the expanded-memory manager tricks your system into believing that some code that was in main memory is now in expanded memory, and vice versa. This remapping requires far less time than actually swapping code, just as it's faster to change the street addresses of two houses instead of physically moving each house to the other's lot.

The EMS memory manager is loaded into your machine's memory when you start your computer. An entry in your CONFIG.SYS file loads the manager and configures it according to choices you make when you install the manager. (Most expanded-memory boards come with an installation program that lets you divide the memory in different ways; I'll provide more detail about this shortly.)

How Windows Uses Expanded Memory

Windows takes advantage of this pseudo-swapping to run applications from expanded memory. The following scenario illustrates how Windows uses bank switching.

Assume that you just started Windows from the MS-DOS prompt. When MS-DOS Executive loads, it requests and is given a chunk of memory in which to operate. Next, you start Windows Write. When you do, the expanded-memory manager banks out MS-DOS Executive and banks in free memory from the expanded-memory board. No data has actually moved; instead, the addresses of the memory where MS-DOS Executive resides and of the free memory are changed. When Write loads into this free memory, it's actually loading into expanded memory; your system has simply been fooled into treating the expanded memory as main memory.

Let's take the scenario a step further. You completed a document in Write and are ready to import it into PageMaker. To start Page-Maker, you use Alt+Tab to reactivate MS-DOS Executive. When you do, the expanded-memory manager banks out Write and banks MS-DOS Executive back in. (Again, neither Write's nor MS-DOS Executive's code actually moves; the memory manager simply changes their respective addresses so that the memory containing MS-DOS Executive is treated as main memory.) Next, you start PageMaker, causing the memory manager to bank MS-DOS Executive out once again, bank free memory in from the expanded-memory board, and load Page-Maker into it.

Incidentally, when you're using an application that can use expanded memory for data (such as Microsoft Excel or 1-2-3), the process is similar. Instead of banking program code into and out of expanded memory, the EMS memory manager banks data in and out.

There are many other expanded-memory technicalities. One concerns the size of the memory board's banking window, also called a page frame. A banking window isn't a window you see on the screen; it's the smallest unit of memory that can be banked in or out. The first expanded-memory specification provided for 64 KB banking windows. EMS 4.0 allows for up to 1 MB banking windows. Larger banking windows allow larger applications to reside in expanded memory.

Shopping for an Expanded-Memory Device

Fortunately, you don't have to understand how expanded memory works in order to benefit from it. You should, however, keep the following considerations in mind when shopping for an expanded-memory device.

- How much main memory does your system currently have? If it has less than 640 KB, be sure you can configure some of the expanded-memory board's memory as main memory.

- Is the board's EMS memory manager compatible with version 4.0 of the Expanded Memory Specification? As this book was going to press, some board manufacturers had yet to release their EMS 4.0 memory managers. Although you can use EMS 3.0 and 3.2 expanded memory as a RAM disk or disk cache (two subjects discussed in the section titled "RAMDrive and SMARTDrive"), neither of those memory applications are as useful as being able to run more programs at once.

- How much memory can the board house? The more, the better. Some boards, such as Cumulus Corporation's CuRAM series for the PS/2 Models 50 and 60, accept daughterboards that snap onto the main board, allowing it to house from 2 to 8 MB of memory. Microsoft's MACH 20 accelerator board (discussed later in this chapter) provides a similar arrangement that can add up to 3.5 MB of expanded memory to a PC, XT, or compatible.

- What configuration options does the board provide? If your board has more than a few megabytes of memory, reserving some of it as a RAM disk or disk cache improves Windows' speed. The most versatile boards include installation programs that let you divide their memory in various ways.

Extended Memory

One more point: As you shop for memory, you may hear the term extended memory. Don't confuse it with expanded memory. The two terms sound similar, but they couldn't differ more. IBM coined the phrase "extended memory" in 1984 to describe the memory above the 1 MB address space of a PC/AT. Today, the term applies to any non-expanded memory above 1 MB in any 80286 computer running MS-DOS. (By "non-expanded," I refer to memory not under the control of an EMS memory manager.) For example, with its base configuration of 1 MB of RAM, IBM's PS/2 Model 50 provides 384 KB of extended memory. (Remember, the 1 MB address space includes the main-memory area as well as the reserved addresses discussed earlier.)

Extended memory can't be directly accessed by MS-DOS, because MS-DOS runs the 80286 microprocessor in what is called its real mode, in which the microprocessor mimics the older 8088 all the way down to its 1 MB memory limitation. OS/2, by contrast, runs the 80286 in what is called protected mode; in this mode, the 80286 can access up to 16 MB of memory.

Again, we're getting into a world of technical jargon and complexities. Simply remember this: Under MS-DOS, extended memory isn't nearly as versatile as expanded memory. It does, however, have some uses; they're described in the section of this chapter titled "RAMDrive and SMARTDrive."

If you have trouble remembering the difference between expanded and extended memory, you might try the memory jogger I use: Lotus, Intel, and Microsoft *banded* together to create the ex*panded*-memory specification; ext*end*ed memory is a virtual dead-*end* for MS-DOS users.

Accelerator Boards

Windows doesn't run on the IBM PC or PC/XT, it walks. Graphical operating environments impose heavy demands on a computer, and IBM's earlier machines (and their compatibles) lack the processing speed required to give Windows the fast, responsive feel it deserves.

Windows runs best on computers based on the 80286 and 80386 microprocessors, such as IBM's PC/AT, the PS/2 Models 50, 60, and 80, and the COMPAQ DESKPRO 386. But that doesn't mean that the millions of PCs, PC/XTs, and compatibles can't run Windows. Within the vast selection of expansion boards for those computers are accelerator boards that boost performance into the PC/AT league by replacing the 8088 with an 80286 (or, in the case of Intel's Inboard 386/PC, an 80386).

When you install an accelerator board, you essentially perform a brain transplant on your PC or compatible. It sounds messy, but it's a straightforward, if delicate, job. Although installation steps vary among products, they generally involve plugging the accelerator board into a vacant slot and then carefully removing the machine's existing 8088 microprocessor and plugging a small connector from the accelerator board into its socket. Some products require you to install the 8088 in a socket on the accelerator board, where the chip is demoted to supervising input/output operations for your machine's new 80286. Completing the installation usually involves setting some jumpers or switches to configure your system. (Needless to say, this summary doesn't replace a board's instructions. Study them before starting. And be sure your body is free of static electricity: touch a metal radiator, metal light-switch plate, or, if your computer is plugged into a grounded outlet as it should be, its metal case.)

Microsoft MACH 20

When shopping for an accelerator board, don't buy one without looking at Microsoft's MACH 20 board. I say this not because someone at Microsoft told me to, but because the MACH 20 has several significant advantages over other accelerator boards. In addition to boosting the performance of a PC, XT, or compatible by two to six times (depending on how you use your computer), its built-in InPort connector lets you add a mouse without using a serial port or dedicating a slot to a mouse controller board.

Like many accelerator boards, the MACH 20 also contains cache memory, which holds recently used code and data. Because this cache memory resides on the MACH 20's 16-bit bus, your system can access data stored in this memory 16 bits at a time, just like an AT. (PCs, XTs, and compatibles have an 8-bit data bus—that is, they can transfer only 8 bits of data at a time. By contrast, 80386-based computers such as IBM's PS/2 Model 80 have a 32-bit data bus.) Many accelerator boards provide only 8 KB of cache memory; the MACH 20 provides 16 KB.

Moreover, the MACH 20 can accept optional expansion modules that let you squeeze more into a single slot. The Memory Plus module provides between 512 KB and 3.5 MB of expanded memory that, like the MACH 20's cache memory, is accessed 16 bits at a time. The memory board's circuitry also contains 30 register sets. In the world of expanded memory, a register set is a key player that keeps track of how the expanded-memory banks are mapped. When you switch from one application to another, the expanded-memory manager goes through a relatively time-consuming process in which it copies the contents of the register set into memory and then configures the register set for the application you're switching to. With the MACH 20's 30 register sets, this process is changed. Each of the register sets can be dedicated to a specific application, while a special selection register specifies which of the 30 register sets is the active one. When you switch applications, instead of manipulating one register set, the memory manager simply changes a single value in the selection register. (See the section of this chapter titled "Expanded and Extended Memory" for details on expanded memory.)

The MACH 20's Disk Plus module is a floppy-disk controller that lets a PC, XT, or compatible access 5¼-inch floppy-disk drives, as well as AT-style 1.2 MB floppy disks and 720 KB and 1.44 MB, 3½-inch disks (with the appropriate disk drives). Even if you don't use those disks, the Disk Plus board is a valuable add-on. By replacing your computer's existing floppy-disk-controller board, it lets you remove your existing controller and install the MACH 20 in its slot. Thus, even if your PC, XT, or compatible has no free slots, you can still add a MACH 20 by buying a Disk Plus module and replacing the existing floppy-disk-controller board. (For PC or XT compatibles that combine floppy-disk and hard-disk controllers on one board or whose floppy-disk controller is located on the machine's main board, this advantage doesn't apply;

the Disk Plus module doesn't replace a hard-disk-controller board. If your machine is a PC or XT compatible, verify with your dealer that the MACH 20—or any accelerator board you're considering—will operate in your machine.)

Perhaps most significantly, with a MACH 20 board, your machine can run OS/2. The hardware includes a task-switching clock tick—a steady heartbeat that OS/2's task scheduler requires to determine whether tasks need to be dispatched. And Microsoft is committed to providing an adaptation of OS/2 specifically for the MACH 20. As this book went to press, no other accelerator board manufacturer could claim OS/2 compatibility. Indeed, unless manufacturers develop clones of the MACH 20's OS/2-related hardware and also adapt OS/2, it's unlikely that any other OS/2-compatible accelerator boards will appear. The MACH 20 also supports an 80287 numeric coprocessor (discussed in the section in this chapter titled "Numeric Coprocessors").

Of course, OS/2 compatibility may not be important to you. It's altogether possible that your computing needs will be met by Windows running on your vintage PC, XT, or compatible equipped with a MACH 20 and a megabyte or two of expanded memory. And it's also possible that, if you decide to go with OS/2, even a MACH 20-equipped PC, XT, or compatible will not meet your needs.

Accelerator Board or New Machine?

That introduces an important question: With accelerator boards costing between $500 and $1,200, how do you decide between accelerating an 8088-based computer or selling it and buying an 80286 or 80386 machine? There is no cut-and-dried answer to that question, but there are some logical guidelines. For example, if your computer lacks a hard disk and contains a lowly Color/Graphics Adapter, an accelerator board will take you only one fifth of the way toward an ideal Windows machine. Conversely, if you're using a hard-disk-equipped XT or compatible with an EGA or VGA graphics board, an accelerator board could be the ideal fifth characteristic in the what's-needed-for-power-Windows quintet (a mouse, good graphics, a hard disk, sufficient memory, and a fast processor). In the end, you must assess your present and future needs and then determine whether they can be met by a souped-up (though aging) 8088-based computer or whether they require the big jump to a true 80286-based or 80386-based computer.

If you opt for the accelerator-board approach, what kind of performance gains can you expect?

Figure 10-3 shows the results of some timing tests performed by Microsoft on a hard-disk-equipped IBM PC/XT running PageMaker with and without a MACH 20 containing the Memory Plus option.

FIGURE 10-3.

Windows' performance without and with a MACH 20.

	Without MACH 20	*With MACH 20*
Switch from 75-percent view to fit-in-window view	4.1 seconds	1.32 seconds
Switch from fit-in-window view to actual-size view	7.82 seconds	2.19 seconds
Switch from fit-in-window view to 200-percent view	6.08 seconds	1.85 seconds

Numeric Coprocessors

A numeric coprocessor is a microprocessor with a penchant for number crunching; adding one to your machine can dramatically improve the speed and accuracy of the arithmetic calculations your machine performs. A numeric coprocessor acts as an assistant to the microprocessor, performing floating-point calculations far faster and more accurately than the microprocessor could, thus freeing the microprocessor to execute its next instruction. It then passes the result to the microprocessor.

One reason a numeric coprocessor performs calculations so quickly is that it contains seven built-in constants (values that don't change), such as 0, 1, pi, as well as several values used in working with logarithms. It also contains five standard transcendental operations used in trigonometric and logarithmic calculations. Numeric coprocessors obtain their accuracy by performing all calculations using 10-byte floating-point arithmetic—calculations are accurate to 18 decimal digits. (Without a numeric coprocessor, the computer's calculations are accurate to approximately either 6 or 16 decimal digits, depending on whether the coprocessor uses single-precision or double-precision math.)

Programs must be specially written to look for and use a numeric coprocessor. Generally, you'll find coprocessor support in spreadsheet programs (Microsoft Excel supports them), database managers, and specialized engineering applications. But a coprocessor won't speed up PageMaker or Reversi. Whether a coprocessor can help you, then, depends on how you use your computer.

A numeric coprocessor is designed to complement a specific microprocessor, so the chip you choose depends on the machine you use. For 8088-based PCs, XTs, and compatibles, use the 8087 coprocessor. For 80286-based machines, you need an 80287. Before you buy, be sure the chip you're considering can operate in your computer. For example, many 80287s are designed to operate at the AT's clock speeds of 6 or 8 MHz; they can't run in the 10 MHz PS/2 Models 50 or 60.

Scanners

Scanners are devices that turn drawings or photographs into electronic images. After you've scanned an image, you can alter it by using a graphics program and then include it in documents you create with other Windows applications. Scanners are especially popular among desktop publishers, who can use them to add photographs and other illustrations to publications. But they have other uses as well. If you use one with a database manager that can store graphics (such as Palantir Filer), you can scan employee photographs for a personnel database or house photographs for a database of real-estate listings. (Chapter 11 contains a sample real-estate database incorporating scanned photographs.) When used with optional optical character recognition (OCR) software, a scanner can convert—with varying degrees of accuracy—typed or typeset documents into text files that can be edited with a word processor.

Two primary categories of scanners exist: sheet-fed (also called platen-fed) and flatbed.

Sheet-fed Scanners

To scan a piece of artwork with a sheet-fed scanner, such as Microtek's MS-300A (a unit that's also sold under different names by Abaton and AST Research), you insert the original in a slot on the scanner, where it's pinched between sets of rubber rollers and rolled past the scanner's optical mechanism. The scanner contains a light source and a bank of photosensors that converts the varying degrees of light reflected from the original into voltage levels corresponding to shades of gray. The scanner's circuitry translates the voltage levels into a bitmap of the image. The image travels to your computer through the scanner's interface. (Most use their own adapter boards, but some use a serial port.) When the image is in your computer, you can alter it or save it in a variety of graphics file formats.

Flatbed Scanners

In a flatbed scanner, the artwork remains stationary while the scanner's optical mechanism moves across it. Flatbed scanners, such as the Datacopy 730, resemble a small photocopier; you place the original face-down on a glass surface, lower a hinged cover over it, and scan. Flatbed scanners can accept a wider variety of originals, including books, magazines, irregularly shaped artwork, and originals that are too small or too delicate to make the journey through a sheet-fed scanner. And flatbed scanners aren't susceptible to the image-skewing problems that can occur when a sheet-fed scanner's rollers are out of adjustment, when the rollers are unable to firmly grip the original, or when you simply don't insert the original perfectly straight.

Other Types of Scanners

In addition to these two standard categories, some nonstandard alternatives exist. Epson offers its Image Scanner Option Kit, a scanner that attaches to the printhead of its LQ-2500, EX-800, and EX-1000 dot-matrix printers, turning the printer into a scanner. You roll the original artwork into the printer as though it were a sheet of printout paper. The printer moves the scanner cartridge left and right, advancing the original slightly after each pass. The kit is limited to 180 dots-per-inch resolution (compared to the 300 dpi resolution of most flatbed and sheet-fed scanners). It's also far slower than a dedicated scanner, but it costs one-third to one-fourth as much.

AT&T's Overview scanner is another nonstandard offering. Resembling an overhead projector, it can scan three-dimensional objects up to one-inch thick. And products such as Aldus Corporation's SnapShot can capture images from video cameras or videotape recorders; such devices are well suited to applications involving three-dimensional objects.

Scanner Software

When shopping for a scanner, don't base your purchasing decision on the hardware alone. Nearly every scanner includes its own scanning software, which lets you define the size of the image to be scanned, adjust brightness and contrast, begin the actual scanning process, and alter the scanned image. That last category can be the most important, and it's where you'll find the most variation between products. The best scanning software lets you electronically retouch the scanned image using Paint-like tools such as a pencil and paint brush. It also lets you crop unwanted portions and provides a zoom-in mode for fine detail work.

If you plan to use the scanned images in documents created with other applications, be sure the product you buy can save images in the file formats you require. File incompatibility shouldn't be a problem, because most scanning applications support such common graphics formats as Paint, tagged-image file format (TIFF), and Encapsulated PostScript (EPS). (See Appendix B for descriptions of these and other common file formats.)

And of course, assess the software's convenience and ease of use. A program that runs within Windows saves you time by eliminating the need to exit Windows to run the scanning application. A scanning program that's a true Windows application is better still. Aldus SnapShot is a true Windows application, as is Hammerlab Corporation's ScanDo. Besides being able to control all popular scanners, ScanDo has impressive image-editing and retouching features, as shown in Figure 10-4.

Using Windows on a Network

A local-area network is an effective way to share information and expensive peripherals, such as hard disks and laser printers. Many networking products are available for MS-DOS computers; they run the gamut from low-cost, low-speed networks to expensive, high-speed file servers. Low-speed networks connect to each computer's serial port and let you access another computer's disk drives. Networks can also open the lines of communication between coworkers, allowing them to exchange electronic mail and access central message boards. File servers require an expansion board in each machine but can unite a building full of computers and act as central repositories of data.

Microsoft's technical-support staff reports that Windows operates with all popular network products available for MS-DOS computers. Their rule of thumb is that if standard MS-DOS applications, such as Lotus 1-2-3 or Ashton–Tate's dBASE III, operate with your network, Windows should too. This section examines the considerations you should observe if you plan to use Windows and Windows applications on a network.

FIGURE 10-4.

*Removing Grace
Kelly's necklace
using Hammerlab
Scan Do.
(A) Before.
(B) After.
(Photo by
David Ottenstein.)*

(A)

(B)

By performing a simple procedure, you can store one copy of
Windows on your network's file server, where it is available to all users
on the network. Multiple users can run that copy of Windows simultaneously, although Microsoft's standard licensing agreement prohibits
doing so unless you purchase a copy of Windows for each user or obtain a special site license. For information on the Windows licensing
agreement, contact Microsoft's Retail Group.

Installing Windows on a File Server

To install Windows on a network file server, run the Setup program and specify the network's hard disk as the destination drive for Windows. You must have read-write access to the network directory in order to install Windows on the file server. Most network software provides varying levels of access privileges to allow you to guard against unauthorized alteration of the file server's contents. See your network software's documentation for details on access privileges.

Once the setup operation is complete, create a copy of the WIN.INI configuration file on each machine that will run Windows. Giving each user his or her own WIN.INI file lets the user have his or her own Windows settings. After creating a copy of WIN.INI on each machine, you can delete the copy of WIN.INI from the file server, or you can leave it on the server to give users the option of running Windows using the network-wide settings. (I'll describe how shortly.)

Next, you must run the MS-DOS Attrib utility to designate the Windows files on the file server that are shareable, read-only files. To do so, change to the file server directory containing the Windows installation and then issue the command *attrib +r *.**. Finally, if you deleted the WIN.INI file from the file server, be sure that the directory containing the local copy of WIN.INI is named in each user's Path command. When a user starts Windows from the file server, Windows searches the directories in his or her path when it discovers that no WIN.INI file exists in its own directory.

If you didn't delete WIN.INI from the file server, you can run Windows by using the server's WIN.INI or by using your own WIN.INI. When it starts up, Windows uses the first WIN.INI file it finds in your computer's path. You'll recall from Chapter 4 that the search along a path begins in the current directory. If a file isn't in the current directory, MS-DOS searches the directories named by the Path command, in the order in which they're listed. Thus, to use your own WIN.INI file, start Windows from the directory containing your copy of WIN.INI— that is, change to that directory using MS-DOS' Change Directory (chdir) command, type *win*, and press Enter. To use the network's WIN.INI file, make the file-server directory containing Windows your current directory and then start Windows.

As an alternative to changing to the directory containing your WIN.INI file, you can edit your Path command so that the directory containing your WIN.INI is listed before the file-server directory containing Windows. With this approach, Windows uses your WIN.INI unless you start Windows from the file-server directory.

Other Network Considerations

It's likely that the computers in your network differ in their video-display or pointing-device configurations. If that's the case, you must install a separate copy of Windows for each configuration. Create separate directories on the file server and follow the steps just outlined to install a copy of Windows in each directory. Give each directory a name that reflects its Windows configuration, such as VGAPS2 for a VGA installation of Windows that is used on a PS/2. To save disk space on the file server, you might want to delete Write, Paint, and the Windows desktop applications from each installation's directory and store only one copy of each of them in a separate directory, where all users can access them. Don't forget to use Attrib to designate the applications as shareable, read-only files, and remember to list this directory in each user's Path command.

For machines in the network that lack hard disks, you might want to change the swapdisk entry in WIN.INI's [pif] section to reflect the network's file server. For example, if the file server is designated as drive D, change the swapdisk entry to read:

```
swapdisk=D:
```

Doing so lets Windows use the file server for standard application swapping. Bear in mind, however, that this increases the traffic on the network, and that could slow the file server's performance.

In the hard copy department, whether you can access a shared network printer from Windows depends on your network software. Some software, such as Microsoft Networks and Ungermann–Bass' Net/One, lets you redirect one of your LPT or COM ports to a network printer. After doing so using the appropriate network command, you can connect to the network printer using Control Panel's Connections command on the Setup menu and then print as if the printer were connected directly to your machine.

Other products, such as Novell's Netware, require a two-step process that involves printing to a disk file and then using a network utility to send the disk file to the network printer. Instructions for creating and using print-to-disk files appear in Chapter 5. Because printing features and techniques vary between network products, consult your network software's documentation for printing information.

RAMDrive and SMARTDrive

If your computer has any expanded or extended memory, you can use either of two utilities—RAMDrive or SMARTDrive—to squeeze an extra measure of performance out of Windows.

RAMDrive, which uses the device driver RAMDRIVE.SYS, lets you turn part of your system's temporary memory (random-access memory, or RAM) into a pseudo disk that exists in memory and retains its contents only as long as your computer has power. Because a RAM disk has no moving parts, it's faster than a hard disk. If your RAM disk is large enough, you can copy Windows and its applications into it upon starting up your computer. After that, you can change to the RAM disk, start Windows, and load applications as quickly as your machine can access its memory.

SMARTDrive, which uses the device driver SMARTDRV.SYS, also boosts performance by substituting memory for a predominantly mechanical disk, but it does so in a different way. SMARTDrive is a disk-caching program; it stores in expanded or extended memory the data that was most recently read from or written to the disk. If the information is needed again, SMARTDrive supplies it directly from memory rather than from disk. To take advantage of SMARTDrive's performance-boosting benefits, you don't need to copy files or perform any special steps after starting up. However, because it stores only information that has already been read from disk, SMARTDrive's benefits don't appear immediately. Instead, they surface over time, as you start, exit from, and switch between applications. These activities normally cause Windows to access your hard disk. When the data or program code Windows needs is in memory, however, SMARTDrive supplies it in a flash.

For example, when I use SMARTDrive on my PS/2 Model 50, Microsoft Excel takes 11 seconds to load and run. If I exit and then restart Microsoft Excel, however, it opens in only 6 seconds. By contrast, if I run Microsoft Excel and Windows from a RAM disk created using RAMDrive, it starts in 7 seconds the first time and every time thereafter.

Because they both perform special tricks with memory, you can't use RAMDrive and SMARTDrive simultaneously. Which one you choose depends on how you use Windows. If you want a specific application to fly from the moment you start it, RAMDrive is best, provided you're willing to copy the application (and Windows, if memory permits) into the RAM disk before starting Windows. (Add the appropriate Copy command in your AUTOEXEC.BAT file to have MS-DOS do the job for you when you start up your computer.) But be forewarned: Don't use a RAM disk for document storage. If your power goes, your documents do too.

On the other hand, you should use SMARTDrive if you're unsure of which applications you will be running during your Windows session. SMARTDrive is also preferable if you frequently switch between numerous applications. In such cases, you probably wouldn't have enough memory to create a RAM disk capable of holding all the applications you will be running. Instead of attempting to hold every byte of every application, SMARTDrive works quietly behind the scenes to keep only the most recently accessed areas of the disk in memory. And unlike some disk-caching programs, SMARTDrive always copies new or modified data to disk. (A disk cache that always copies modified data to disk is called a write-through cache.)

Installing and Using SMARTDrive

Because SMARTDrive is an MS-DOS device driver, you install it by adding a line to your CONFIG.SYS file. A SMARTDrive command line has the following form (text within brackets is optional):

    device=[d:][path]smartdrv.sys [size][/a]

The [size] value tells SMARTDrive how much memory you want to allocate to the disk cache. If you omit this value, SMARTDrive receives 256 KB. Use the /a switch if you have expanded-memory or if you want to use an extended-memory board as expanded memory. For example, the line:

    device=c:\dos\smartdrv.sys 1024 /a

gives SMARTDrive 1 MB of expanded memory and tells MS-DOS to look in the DOS directory on drive C: for the SMARTDRV.SYS driver. The line:

    device=c:\dos\drivers\smartdrv.sys

gives SMARTDrive 256 KB of extended memory, and tells MS-DOS that SMARTDRV.SYS is stored on drive C: in the \DOS\DRIVERS directory.

You can use Notepad to add the SMARTDrive command line to your CONFIG.SYS file. If you use an expanded-memory board, be sure to place the command line after any command lines that load an expanded-memory driver into memory. (Such a line might read *device=emm.sys.*) Also, delete any command lines pertaining to other disk-caching or RAM-disk software that you may have tried; unlike non-Microsoft disk-caching or RAM disk utilities, SMARTDrive is designed to work with Windows.

After adding the SMARTDrive command line to CONFIG.SYS, save the file, exit Windows, and restart your computer. When it loads, SMARTDrive displays a message listing how large its disk cache is. When the MS-DOS prompt appears, you can use your computer as you normally would. If an error message appeared instead, consult the list of SMARTDrive error messages in Appendix C of the *Microsoft Windows User's Guide.*

Installing and Using RAMDrive

The steps for installing RAMDrive are identical to those needed to install SMARTDrive. RAMDrive even accepts identical parameters in its command line. If you use expanded-memory, remember to place RAMDrive's command line after any command lines used to load an expanded-memory driver. Save your CONFIG.SYS file after adding the RAMDrive command line, exit Windows, and restart your computer.

After RAMDrive loads, MS-DOS recognizes a new drive letter—the next letter following the lowest-lettered physical drive in your system. For example, if your lowest-lettered drive is drive C, RAMDrive creates a RAM disk labelled drive D. You can use the RAM disk as you would a physical disk drive (although you should avoid using it for document storage). When you start Windows, the RAM disk's icon appears in the MS-DOS Executive window.

WINDOWS APPLICATIONS

This chapter presents a sampling of currently available and soon-to-be-available Windows software. I've tried to convey the personality of each application rather than present a detailed analysis, so don't base a purchasing decision on these descriptions alone. Moreover, this chapter isn't intended to be a complete guide to Windows applications, so don't limit your search to the products described here. More Windows applications are under development than ever before, so it's likely that each program discussed here will soon have competition (if it doesn't already). Use this chapter as a starting point for your software shopping.

Discussion of the applications is organized by task: word processing, spreadsheet analysis, desktop publishing, drawing and drafting, database management, and telecommunications. Many of the discussions include a scenario that offers a way in which you could use the product discussed. The text spotlights each application's key features, and an accompanying figure shows the application in action. The company name, address, and phone number for each product discussed appears in Appendix A.

Word Processing

Word processing is the most popular computer application—and for good reasons. Whether you write letters, memos, proposals, or novels, you can benefit from the ease of revision and the formatting options that a word processor provides.

Microsoft Windows Write

You might not need to shop for a Windows word processor once you've bought Windows. Microsoft Windows Write, included with Windows, is an ideal word processor for writing tasks that don't require complex document formatting capabilities. (I wrote much of the manuscript for this book with it.)

Write fully supports the clipboard, so your documents can contain graphics or text created in other applications. (Chapter 5 presents several examples of exchanging data with Write.) It also contains mouse-oriented editing shortcuts. For example, you can move or copy text quickly and without replacing the contents of the clipboard. To move text from one spot to another, select the text, hold down the Shift and Alt keys, point to the text's destination, and click. To copy text elsewhere, select the text, hold down Alt, and click where you want the copy to appear.

Palantir Windows Spell

If you're a lousy speller, consider pairing Write with a spelling checker such as Windows Spell from Palantir Software. Spell uses a 65,000-word dictionary, which you can supplement by adding words to a user-defined dictionary, as shown in Figure 11-1. Spell can proofread text-only (ASCII) files, as well as documents created with Write, Microsoft Word, and Micrografx Draw and Designer. It can also check the contents of the clipboard, allowing you to proofread text from any application that can access the clipboard.

Spell also exploits Windows' multitasking capabilities by checking documents while you work in other applications. In its background mode, Spell minimizes itself into an icon as soon as you open a document and then checks the document's spelling while you perform other tasks. Each time it encounters an unknown word, Spell's icon flashes to grab your attention.

FIGURE 11-1.

Palantir Windows Spell. (A) When Spell locates a misspelled word, choose Search to tell it to scan its 65,000-word dictionary. (B) You can accept one of its suggestions or tell it to remember the word as you originally spelled it.

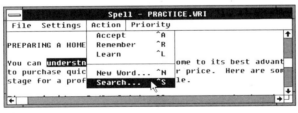

(A)

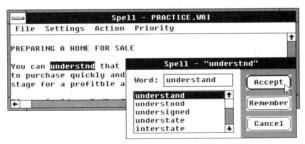

(B)

High-End Word-processing Applications and the Clipboard

Write is adequate for many users' needs, but it lacks the document formatting features required for complex jobs such as manuals, proposals, executive summaries, and reports. These applications often require features for creating tables of contents and indexes, footnotes, table columns containing leader dots that guide the eye across a line of text, and style sheets for automating repetitive formatting chores.

At this writing, Windows is ill-equipped for this upper tier of word slinging. No Windows word processor exists that offers the aforementioned features. Fortunately, Windows has the ability to run standard applications and add clipboard support to them. All of today's powerhouse word processors can run within Windows; Windows includes PIFs for Microsoft Word, XyWrite, and WordPerfect.

Microsoft Word and Microsoft Pageview

Although Windows adds limited clipboard support to standard applications, it can't add features to a program. None of these programs supports Windows' ability to paste graphics into word-processing documents. However, if you use Microsoft Word, you can add graphics to documents using Microsoft Pageview. Pageview is a Windows application that lets you open Word documents, preview and change the appearance of each page, and add graphics created in other applications and pasted from the clipboard. Figure 11-2 shows an example of a Pageview display.

Incidentally, because Word and Write use similar file formats, you can use Pageview to open Write documents. To do so, simply choose Pageview's Open command from the File menu and type *.wri* in the filename portion of the Open dialog box. Although you don't need Pageview to add graphics to Write documents, you can use it to preview pages and conveniently adjust margins and page breaks.

Text Retrieval

Regardless of the word processor you use, if you do a great deal of writing, you probably occasionally can't remember which document contains a certain piece of text. Rather than laboriously opening and closing document after document in search of that key phrase, consider a text-retrieval application.

FIGURE 11-2.

*Inserting a graphic and enlarging the display in Microsoft Pageview.
(A) The original document, before inserting a graphic from the clipboard.
(B) After inserting a graphic in Zoom mode.*

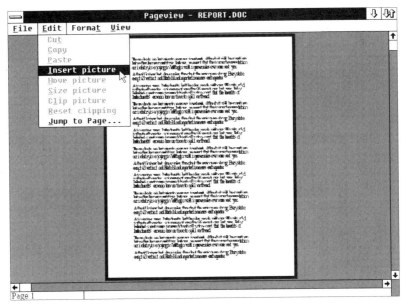

(A)

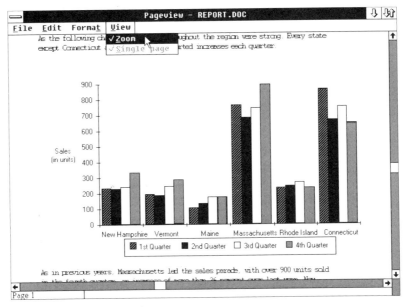

(B)

One such Windows text-retrieval application is Dragnet from Access Softek.

Dragnet searches text files (or spreadsheets or databases) based on keyword patterns that you specify. An architect, for example, might use the keywords *historic AND renovat** to locate all proposals for projects involving renovation of historic buildings. The asterisk wildcard lets Dragnet find related words like *renovation, renovating,* and *renovate.* An attorney might use the keywords *divorce AND settlement NOT custody* to locate legal briefs describing divorce settlements that did not involve custody suits. The words AND and NOT are logical operators— special commands that you use to describe the relationships between the keywords in a search.

You can tell Dragnet to search only certain files or directories, or you can specify your entire hard disk as its hunting ground. When Dragnet locates your search text, it copies it into a text-only output file along with the context and the name and location of the file in which it appears. In its interactive mode, Dragnet pauses each time a match is found. It then displays the matched text and asks if you want to save it in the output file. In its continuous mode, Dragnet presents a dialog box that shows your search keywords and Dragnet's progress. In its icon mode, Dragnet conducts its search in the background while you work in other Windows applications.

Version 1.0 of Dragnet runs only under Windows/386; it does not run under Windows 2.0. Access Softek was developing a version of Dragnet that runs under Windows 2.0 as this book went to press.

Spreadsheet Analysis and Graphing

Electronic spreadsheet programs provide a ledger-booklike framework containing storage slots called cells for storing text and numbers. By combining the ability to store numbers with the ability to calculate them, spreadsheet programs provide an excellent environment for analyzing numbers. You specify the relationship between the numbers you enter by creating formulas. Once you've created the formulas, you can explore any number of "What if?" scenarios. Asking questions like "What if our fourth quarter sales doubled?" or "What if my interest rate dropped to 10 percent?" becomes as easy as typing new values. And because a picture is worth a thousand cells, spreadsheet programs team up well with business graphics applications, which turn tables of numbers into charts that let you spot trends at a glance.

Microsoft Excel

If you're going to ask "What if?", Windows is an ideal place to ask it, thanks to Microsoft Excel. If you've used Lotus 1-2-3 or other non-graphical spreadsheet programs, many aspects of Microsoft Excel will seem foreign. The basic row-and-column spreadsheet format is the same, but Microsoft Excel puts it within the framework of Windows' interface. On the basic level, that means less typing, more formatting options, easy data exchange, and great graphics. On a more complex level, it means sophisticated data exchange opportunities using Dynamic Data Exchange (described in Chapter 5), as well as the ability to develop custom applications with their own menus and dialog boxes and the ability to automate repetitive tasks by using macros.

Figure 11-3 on pages 214 and 215 shows the steps that a national sales manager might take to create a simple quarterly sales spread-sheet. In Step 1, the columns are resized with the mouse, not with a half-dozen keystrokes as would be the case with a non-Windows spreadsheet. In Step 2, notice how Microsoft Excel lets you access Windows' typographic capabilities to format text attractively.

Step 3 illustrates the process of creating a formula in Microsoft Excel. The sales manager wants to determine the total of each division's sales but can't remember which function to use. Rather than riffling through a manual, he chooses Paste Function from the Formula menu and chooses the desired function from the list of built-in functions. If he isn't sure which function he needs, he can use Microsoft Excel's context-sensitive help system to obtain capsule descriptions of each one.

He chooses the SUM, or additions, function. Microsoft Excel pastes it into the formula bar, positioning a blinking insertion point between the function's parentheses, where the function's argument appears. Instead of typing the argument (which, in this case, is the range of cells for each division's sales results), he drags the mouse pointer across the range of cells. As he does, Microsoft Excel inserts the range in the formula bar. He clicks the Enter icon (a check mark) in the formula bar to indicate that the formula is complete, and Microsoft Excel calculates and stores the formula.

FIGURE 11-3.

Creating a worksheet in Microsoft Excel. (A) Resizing columns with the mouse. (B) Formatting column headings as boldface. (C) Pasting a function by using the Paste Function command. (D) The completed worksheet, with grid lines hidden and cell borders activated.

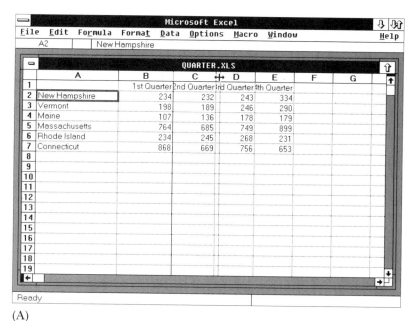

(A)

(B)

(continued)

FIGURE 11-3.

continued

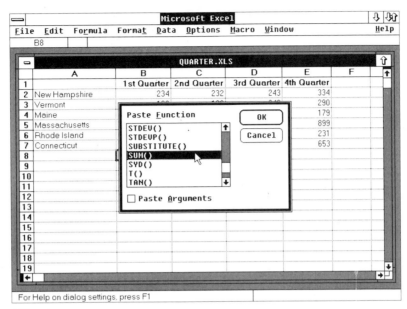

(C)

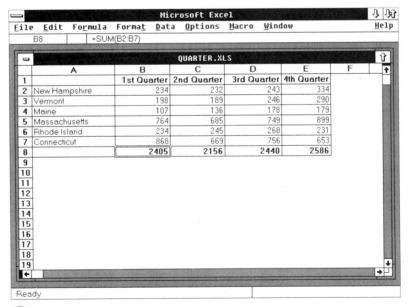

(D)

The sales manager completes the spreadsheet by adding SUM functions to the remaining columns, this time typing the formula directly into the formula bar. When it's complete, he uses Microsoft Excel's Display and Border commands to hide the on-screen grid lines and to create borders around the table. Finally, he saves the spreadsheet on a network file server, where it will be opened later by his firm's vice president of sales.

When the vice president sees the spreadsheet, she realizes that its data would be easier to interpret if it appeared in chart form. She's new to Microsoft Excel, but she's a veteran at creating graphs in 1-2-3. As Figure 11-4 on the next two pages shows, Microsoft Excel lets her use her 1-2-3 experience. She chooses the Lotus 1-2-3 command from Microsoft Excel's Help menu and enters the keystrokes for the 1-2-3 graphing command she knows so well: /ga. Microsoft Excel's help system swings into action, displaying the steps required to create a new chart.

She learns that those steps involve selecting the spreadsheet data, choosing New from the File menu, and selecting Chart in the subsequent dialog box. Those few steps create the basic chart, which she then polishes by adding a legend and axis labels, again using the Lotus 1-2-3 command from the Help menu to guide her. Before printing the chart in full color on a plotter, she uses Microsoft Excel's Print preview capability to see on the screen a representation of how it will appear on paper.

Because this fictitious vice president uses Microsoft Excel's help system often, she doesn't close the help window when she's finished reading about a topic. Instead, she makes the window inactive by clicking within Microsoft Excel's main window. When she does, Microsoft Excel's window moves to the front. When the Microsoft Excel window isn't maximized, a portion of the help window remains visible at the bottom of the screen, and she can reactivate the help system by simply clicking within the window or by pressing Alt+Tab or the F1 key. When the Microsoft Excel window is maximized, she returns to the help system by pressing Alt+Tab or F1 or by choosing Index or Keyboard from the Help menu.

Microsoft Excel as a Database Manager
Next, let's look at Microsoft Excel's database-management prowess by illustrating how a sales representative might store and retrieve client information. (For a capsule lesson in database-management terminology, see the section of this chapter titled "Database Management.")

FIGURE 11-4.

Creating a graph in Microsoft Excel. (A) Using Microsoft Excel's Lotus 1-2-3 command from the Help menu. (B) Selecting underlined items displays additional help. (C) An additional help screen. (D) The completed chart with legend and axis label.

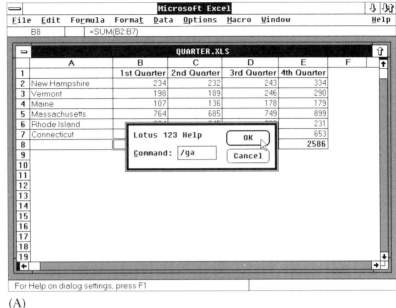

(A)

(B)

(continued)

FIGURE 11-4.

continued

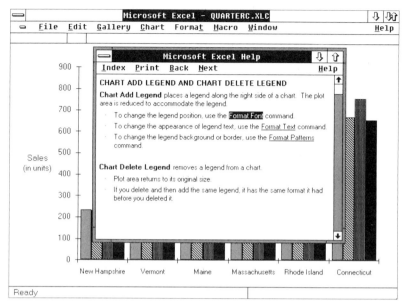

(C)

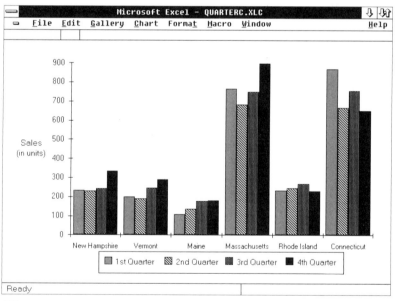

(D)

Figure 11-5 on the following page outlines the steps involved in using Microsoft Excel's database-management features. Starting with a blank spreadsheet, the sales manager creates column headings that will serve as field names. Next, he selects the field names and a blank row below them and defines that area as a database. (Because he included blank rows in the selection, Microsoft Excel will expand the database range when he inserts new records.) Finally, he chooses the Form command from the Data menu to display a data-entry form that will make it easier to enter and retrieve data.

Microsoft Excel creates a default data-entry form in which field names appear to the left of their contents. (Microsoft Excel's macro language, however, offers statements that let you create customized forms.) The sales manager types each field item, pressing Tab to move from one field to the next and pressing Enter to store a record in the database (actually, to add data to the spreadsheet as a new row).

As he works with the database, the sales manager presses Alt+P to display the previous record, Alt+N to display the next record, and Alt+D to delete unwanted ones. To locate records meeting specific criteria, he selects the Criteria button and then types his search criteria in the field names. When search criteria are in effect, Microsoft Excel displays only those records meeting them. He can also sort the records and, by entering criteria in other cells, extract certain records and copy them elsewhere in the spreadsheet.

Microsoft Excel Macros
Microsoft Excel also is a powerful programming environment for developing spreadsheet-based applications containing their own custom drop-down menus and dialog boxes. A well-designed Microsoft Excel application can be used by spreadsheet novices, even those who have never used Microsoft Excel.

As Figure 11-6 (on page 221) and Figure 11-7 (on page 222) show, the heart of Microsoft Excel's programming environment is its macro language. Macros are stored in a spreadsheet called a macro sheet. In Figure 11-6, our fictional sales manager has created a macro to replace Microsoft Excel's standard menu bar with a custom one. Figure 11-7 shows a macro that displays a custom data-entry form. The custom menu commands will be the gateway to the sales manager's database, allowing him—and, more importantly, his assistant, who has never used a spreadsheet—to perform queries and retrieve data by simply choosing the appropriate commands.

FIGURE 11-5.

Microsoft Excel as a database manager. (A) Defining a database range. Column headings become field names. (B) Microsoft Excel's preset database form. Choose New to enter the current record into the worksheet.

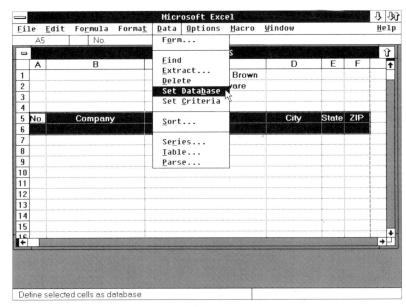

(A)

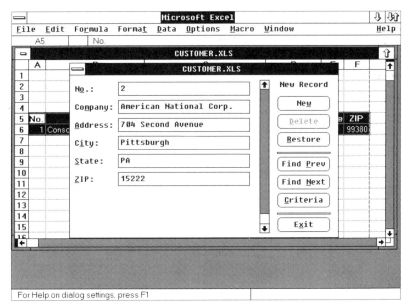

(B)

FIGURE 11-6.

Creating a custom-menu macro.

(A) A macro for a custom menu.

(B) The menu it displays.

Cells that specify the menu title and items

Macros that run when commands are chosen

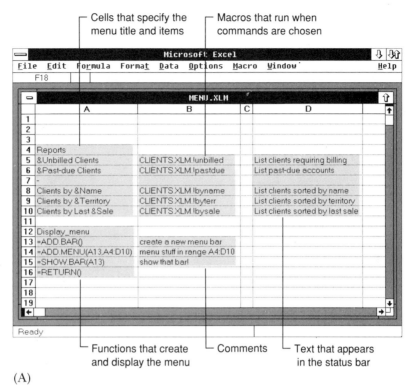

Functions that create and display the menu

Comments

Text that appears in the status bar

(A)

(B)

FIGURE 11-7.

Creating a
custom-form
macro.
(A) A macro for a
custom data-
entry form.
(B) The form it
displays.

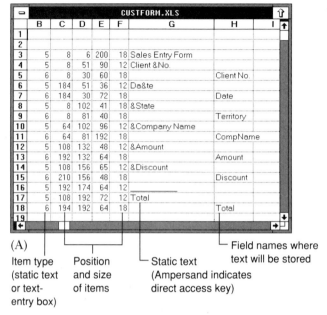

(A)

Item type
(static text
or text-
entry box)

Position
and size
of items

Static text
(Ampersand indicates
direct access key)

Field names where
text will be stored

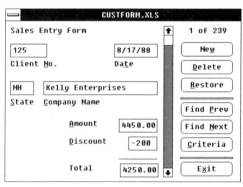

(B)

But macros need not be complex programming routines for creating dialog boxes or menus. They can also be simple time-savers that automate repetitive tasks. The macro in Figure 11-8 is one example: With one key combination (Ctrl+B), it formats the text in the selected cells in Helv Bold and left-aligns the text. Such time-savers can be created using Microsoft Excel's macro recorder, which peers over your shoulder as you use Microsoft Excel, translating your actions into statements for future playback.

FIGURE 11-8.

*Microsoft Excel
macro for
formatting a
selection as
boldface.*

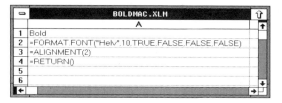

Spreadsheet and Graphing Alternatives

You might not need Microsoft Excel's sophisticated features. Or
perhaps you're running Windows on an 8088-based computer. In
either case, you might consider Win Calc, which, at this writing, was
under development by Palantir Software. Next to Microsoft Excel, Win
Calc promises to be a spreadsheet lightweight, but it will be quite adequate for such tasks as personal finance management.

An ideal supplement to Win Calc—or, for that matter, to
Microsoft Excel—is Micrografx Graph. Graph offers many of the
same graphing features as Microsoft Excel, plus a few more, such as
the ability to add depth to a graph to create a three-dimensional look.
Graph is also stronger at drawing, with commands for adding lines,
rectangles, and other shapes to a graph. Its on-screen rulers simplify
sizing and positioning of elements and are especially useful for creating graphs of a specific size for inclusion in other documents. Graph
can also open PIC-format graphics documents created by Micrografx's
other graphics products, Draw and Designer (described in the section
of this chapter titled "Painting and Drawing"), allowing you to
superimpose graphs over images. Graph works similarly to Designer
and Draw; if you've used either of the latter two, you're well on your
way to knowing how to use Graph.

With its drawing and graphics orientation, Graph is an ideal application to use for creating presentation graphics, such as overhead
transparencies. If you pair Graph with Micrografx's MGX/port utility,
you can create stunning color slides using film recorders—hardware
devices that create their output on photographic film.

Figure 11-9 on pages 224 and 225 shows the steps that the eastern
sales manager for a chain of electronics stores might take to create a
three-dimensional sales chart. First, the store manager uses Graph's
Open command to open a picture containing a map of her sales terri-
tory. She created the picture in Micrografx Draw, using a United
States map from Micrografx's clip-art series as a starting point.

FIGURE 11-9.

Creating a graph in Micrografx Graph.
(A) A map based on a Micrografx clip-art image.
(B) Entering data in Graph's worksheet window.
(C) Choosing a column graph.
(D) The completed graph after adding depth, a legend, and graphic embellishments.

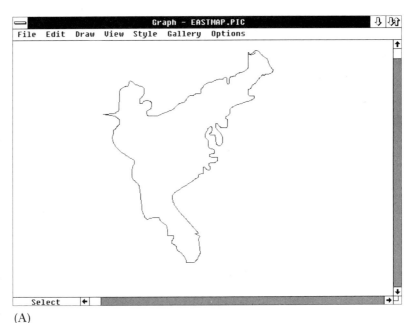

(A)

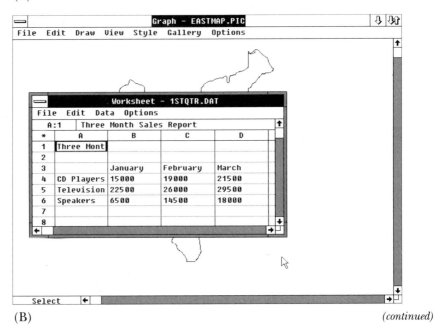

(B)

(continued)

FIGURE 11-9.

continued

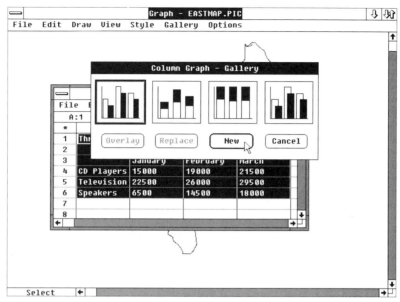

(C)

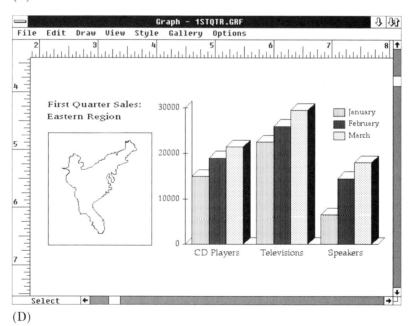

(D)

Next, she uses Graph's built-in spreadsheet window to enter the categories and sales figures that will form the graph's axis. (If those figures were stored in a DIF file, a SYLK file, a Lotus 1-2-3 WKS file, or a comma-delimited ASCII file, she could open them directly using the spreadsheet window's Open Data command.) The spreadsheet window isn't a full spreadsheet, but it provides a row-and-column framework for holding graph data and can also perform four-function math and calculate percentages.

After entering the data, she selects it, activates Graph's main window, and chooses Column from the Gallery menu. She chooses the desired column chart from the subsequent dialog box, and Graph creates the chart. Next, she uses the Projection command from the Options menu to add a three-dimensional look to the chart and the Legend command to add a legend. Then she chooses the Style menu's Fonts command to reformat the chart's text. Finally, she saves the chart in two formats: in Graph's GRF format, in which the chart remains linked to its worksheet data; and in PIC format, in which the chart is stored as a Windows metafile that can be included in a publication she's creating with Aldus PageMaker.

Graph supports Windows' Dynamic Data Exchange features, so it can work hand-in-hand with other DDE-supporting applications, including Microsoft Excel. In addition to supporting dynamic links between a Microsoft Excel spreadsheet and Graph's spreadsheet window, Graph contains several DDE functions that allow other applications to instruct it to open files; to clear its spreadsheet or graph; and to set its updating mode, which controls when Graph redraws a chart—either each time the data changes or only when explicitly instructed to. Micrografx includes several Microsoft Excel macros with Graph.

Desktop Publishing

With its "what you see is what you get" operating style, its typographic talents, and its mouse support, Windows is an ideal foundation for desktop publishing. While several publishing programs are available for MS-DOS computers, two of the best—Aldus Pagemaker and Ready, Set,Go! from Manhattan Graphics—run under Windows.

Aldus PageMaker

Aldus PageMaker was the first Windows-based publishing program, debuting in early 1987. One year later, PageMaker 3.0 was unveiled, offering significant new features while retaining the original version's straightforward operating style. (PageMaker 3.0 was in the final development stage as this book went to press.)

Figure 11-10 on pages 228 and 229 illustrates the steps a graphic designer might take to produce a display advertisement in PageMaker version 1.0a. He begins by specifying the basic characteristics of the publication: its page and margin dimensions, orientation, and so on. PageMaker's pasteboard—an electronic version of a layout table— appears, showing the page's size and margins. If he were creating a multipage document such as a book or newsletter, he might create left and right master pages, whose contents appear on every page in the publication.

The designer begins laying out the advertisement by using Page-Maker's Place command to open the graphic of the piano keyboard, which he created in Micrografx Designer (described in the section of this chapter titled "Painting and Drawing"). The Place command is PageMaker's gateway to text and graphics documents created in other applications. When he chooses the document to be placed, Page-Maker's mouse pointer changes shape from its standard arrow shape to resemble a small paint brush to indicate that it's loaded with, or carrying, the graphic. He places the graphic on the page by pointing to the page and clicking.

After fine-tuning the graphic's position, the designer activates PageMaker's text tool and types the headline, using the Type Specs command to specify its type size and style. Then he creates a two-column grid—a framework indicated on screen by dotted lines—and places a text document created in Microsoft Word within it. Page-Maker imports text from all popular word processors and retains most formatting attributes. PageMaker 3.0 also imports and interprets Word style sheets, which allow you to automate complex formatting chores by assigning formatting attributes to a single command and then applying those attributes to a text passage by issuing the command. You can also create style sheets directly within PageMaker to automate the production of lengthy publications.

FIGURE 11-10.

*Creating a
publication
with Aldus
PageMaker
version 1.0a.
(A) Placing a
graphic in
PageMaker.
After you choose
a file to place, the
pointer assumes
a different shape.
(B) The newly
placed graphic.
(C) Placing a
column of text.
The plus sign
indicates more
text remains.
(D) The
completed
publication.*

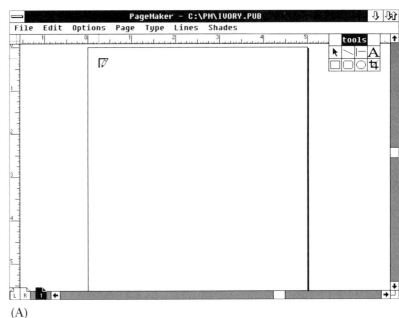

(A)

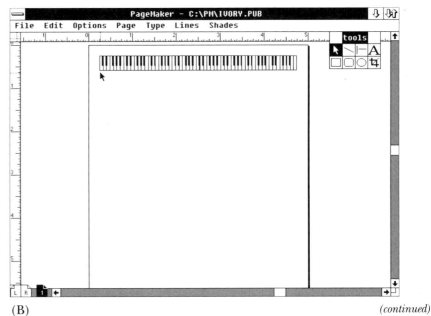

(B)

(continued)

FIGURE 11-10.

continued

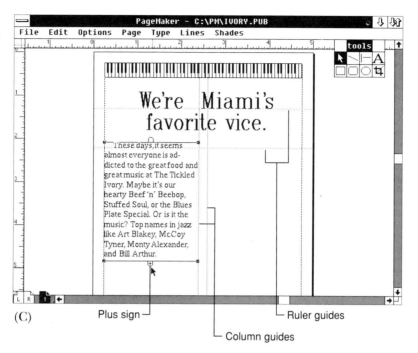

(C)

Plus sign ⌐   Ruler guides

Column guides

(D)

PageMaker places text in much the same way that it places graphics: After you choose a file, the pointer changes shape to resemble a small column of text to indicate that it's loaded with text. The designer then points to the first column on the page and clicks, and the text flows into the column, stopping at the bottom. In this example, the entire document did not fit within the first column; Page-Maker indicates that more text remains by placing a plus sign at the bottom of the text block. To place the remaining text, the designer clicks on the plus sign. Again it assumes its loaded appearance. When he moves the pointer into the second column and clicks, the remaining text appears.

PageMaker knows that the two text blocks contain the same document and establishes an invisible link between them. As the designer resizes, reformats, or edits the text blocks, the text reflows within them. Anyone who's made a minor editing change on a conventional layout and then had to painstakingly peel and repaste strips of type to accommodate the change can tell you that automatic text reflow is one of a desktop-publishing program's great strengths. Whether the linked text blocks are adjacent to each other on a page or 50 pages apart, changes made in one block make the text reflow throughout all blocks linked to it.

PageMaker also includes export filters that allow you to copy altered text from PageMaker into separate word-processing documents that you can open with a word processor. Using export filters, you can make editing and formatting changes within PageMaker and then export the edited or reformatted text to ensure that the original files remain current. PageMaker 3.0 includes export filters that allow it to create Microsoft Word 4.0 and DCA-format documents, and the program can directly swap publication files with the Apple Macintosh version of PageMaker.

Desktop publishing often involves importing scanned images. All publishing programs let you crop and resize imported graphics, but PageMaker 3.0 also offers contrast and brightness controls for altering the appearance of bitmapped graphics. (See Chapter 10 for information on scanners and image-processing programs.) PageMaker also lets you wrap text around irregularly shaped graphics.

If you aren't a designer, you'll find useful the 20 predesigned templates included with PageMaker, which cover such typical publications as newsletters, brochures, proposals, calendars, price lists, slides, overhead transparencies, and company directories. You simply open the desired template and replace its canned, placeholder text with your own text.

Aldus goes a long way toward educating publishing neophytes in the fine points of design and typography. PageMaker includes a basic guide to design, and Aldus offers an extensive library of instructional materials and predesigned publication templates. If you lack design experience, take advantage of these teaching aids. Designing a printed page is like playing a musical instrument: Inexperience shows.

Ready,Set,Go! from Manhattan Graphics

Another Windows desktop publishing program, Ready,Set,Go!, is under development by Manhattan Graphics at this writing and is scheduled for release in mid-1988. If you want to see Ready,Set,Go! before it's actually available, visit an Apple dealer and ask to see the Macintosh version. Manhattan Graphics reports that the Windows version will offer identical features and commands.

Ready,Set,Go! has features similar to PageMaker but in a slightly different form. For example, you don't place text by choosing a Place command and clicking a loaded icon on the page. Instead, you place it first by drawing text blocks as if you were drawing boxes on the page. To link one text block to another for text reflow, you activate a linking tool and then click the mouse pointer within each text block to be linked.

PageMaker makes no pretense at being a word processor. Its text-editing features are rudimentary: You can type and edit text directly on the layout, but that's all. Ready,Set,Go!, on the other hand, includes search-and-replace features, a spelling checker, and a glossary feature for one-key entry of frequently used words and phrases. These extra features don't make Ready,Set,Go! a word processor, but they do make extensive text editing within the program far more practical.

Publisher's Type Foundry from ZSoft Corporation

If you need special characters missing from your current fonts, investigate Publisher's Type Foundry by ZSoft Corporation. Publisher's Type Foundry lets you create printer fonts for PostScript printers and for Hewlett-Packard LaserJet Plus and Series II printers. You can also create bitmapped fonts for use with ZSoft's PC Paintbrush and Publisher's Paintbrush. A Windows version of PC Paintbrush is included with Publisher's Type Foundry. (PC Paintbrush is described in the section of this chapter titled "Painting and Drawing.")

In Figure 11-11, a graphic designer is creating a special character, a small version of Windows' Minimize icon, that will be used to mark the ends of articles in a Windows newsletter. In this example, the designer is adding the character to an existing font—12-point Charter, a downloadable LaserJet Plus font from Bitstream's Fontware library (described in Chapter 7). He begins by translating the LaserJet Plus font into Publisher's Type Foundry font-description format using

FIGURE 11-11.

Using Publisher's Type Foundry. (A) The bitmap editor lets you create fonts for the Hewlett-Packard LaserJet. (B) The outline editor lets you create fonts for PostScript printers.

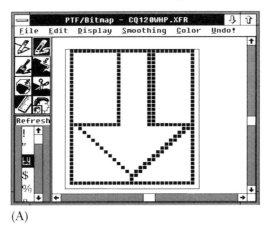

(A)

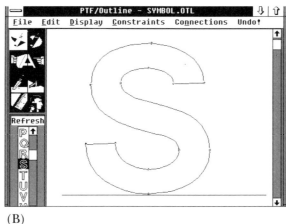

(B)

a utility included with Publisher's Type Foundry. Next, he loads the font description into Publisher's Type Foundry's bitmap font editor and clears an unnecessary character (the pound sign), leaving a blank character box that will hold the new character.

He then draws the new character using Publisher's Type Foundry's drawing tools, zooming in and out as needed for detail work. When the character is complete, he saves the font. He then creates a new LaserJet Plus printer font using the same utility he used to translate the original into Publisher's Type Foundry format. Finally, he creates a new printer font-metrics file using the PCLPFM utility that accompanies Windows. (PCLPFM also is described in Chapter 7.)

If the designer switches to a PostScript printer in the future, he can transfer the bitmapped font description to Publisher's Type Foundry's outline font editor. The outline editor lets you draw and adjust the lines and curves that form the foundation of PostScript fonts.

Although this example used Publisher's Type Foundry to create a single character in an existing font, you can also use it to create new fonts. If you have the patience of a surgeon and the artistic eye of an architect, you might try designing a typeface from scratch. A faster and less demanding approach involves expanding or condensing an existing font. Making a font 20 percent wider or narrower can give it an entirely different personality. Publisher's Type Foundry's Global Change command makes it easy to perform such alterations, as well as to create slanted, or oblique, fonts.

Another way to create new fonts is to scan a font from a public-domain type-specimen book, paste the bitmapped images of each character from the clipboard into Publisher's Type Foundry's bitmap editor, and then use the editor's tools to touch up the resulting characters. Remember, however, that commercial typefaces are protected by copyright laws. Dover Books publishes several volumes of ornamental and display typefaces that can be used and copied freely. They're available at graphics and art supply stores, as well as by mail. For a catalog, write to Dover Publications, Inc., 180 Varick St., New York, NY 10014.

Painting and Drawing

Considering Windows' graphic orientation, it isn't surprising that
the painting and drawing category of applications offers the widest
selection. Whether you want to use the program as an electronic paint
canvas, create precise technical illustrations, or simply use and modify
clip-art images for desktop publications, a Windows graphics application can meet your needs.

Two basic categories of graphics programs exist: bitmapped and
object-oriented. Bitmapped programs such as Microsoft Windows
Paint and ZSoft's PC Paintbrush treat an entire drawing as a series—a
map—of bits in your computer's memory. Object-oriented programs
such as Micrografx Draw and Designer treat a drawing as a series of
objects—circles, rectangles, lines, arcs, and so on. Each object has a
corresponding description for GDI, Windows' library of graphics routines. Bitmapped-graphics programs are often called painting programs; object-oriented applications are called drawing programs.
(Chapter 5 mentions these points in discussing clipboard formats.)

Bitmapped programs are best for rendering fine shading and
details; scanners also create bitmapped images. Object-oriented programs are best for creating line drawings such as floor plans, architec-
tural illustrations, maps, diagrams, and schematics. Object-oriented
programs also give you the advantage of producing resolution-
independent images. Because each object is stored as a GDI description, rather than as a series of bits, an object-oriented graphic can
take advantage of all the resolution your printer can offer. A bitmapped graphic always prints at the resolution at which it was created,
but an object-oriented picture prints at whatever resolution your
printer provides, no matter whether it's a 70 dots-per-inch (dpi)
dot-matrix printer or a 2450 dpi Linotronic PostScript typesetter.
Finally, object-oriented graphics can be resized without distortion,
because Windows needs only to modify each object's description to
reflect its new size. Figure 11-12 summarizes these and other differences between painting and drawing programs.

Microsoft Windows Paint

Microsoft Windows Paint is a monochrome (black-and-white) painting
program.

Because Paint is included with Windows, it's an excellent way to
sample the world of electronic painting. If you already own a copy of
Windows, chances are you've already tried Paint; therefore, I won't

FIGURE 11-12.

Summary of differences between painting and drawing programs.

Painting programs	Drawing programs
Images stored as a series of bits; each dot corresponds to a bit in memory.	Images stored as a series of GDI commands; each command draws an object, such as a line, circle, or box.
Images are tied to a fixed resolution and always print at the same number of dots per inch, regardless of your printer's capabilities.	Images are resolution-independent; they can take advantage of all the resolution a printer provides.
Images are subject to distortion when resized.	Objects can be resized without distortion because the program needs to update only the object's GDI command.
Best for representing fine details and shading; images can be edited bit by bit in zoom-in mode.	Best for line art and technical drawings, which are usually discrete shapes. Images are edited object by object, not bit by bit.

describe a typical application here. Chapter 5 contains examples of how you can include graphics created with Paint in documents created with other Windows applications.

PC Paintbrush from ZSoft Corporation

PC Paintbrush for Windows (I'll call it PC Paintbrush from now on, though you should not confuse it with ZSoft's non-Windows version of the program by the same name) is a full-color painting program.

Figure 11-13 on the following page shows a PC Paintbrush screen reproduced in black and white. PC Paintbrush provides the same basic drawing functions as does Paint, although many tool names and icons are different. For example, in Paint, you use the selection net to select an irregularly shaped region; in PC Paintbrush, you use the scissors. And instead of providing an array of patterns to choose from, PC Paintbrush provides a palette of colors. You can mix custom hues by double-clicking on an existing color and using red, green, and blue scroll bars to mix the three primary colors. Other PC Paintbrush tools are tailored to the task of working with colors. The color eraser, for example, lets you erase the color currently selected.

PC Paintbrush works well with Paint. You might, for example, begin a painting in Paint because you need the perspective tool as

FIGURE 11-13.

*PC Paintbrush
graphic from
ZSoft
Corporation.*

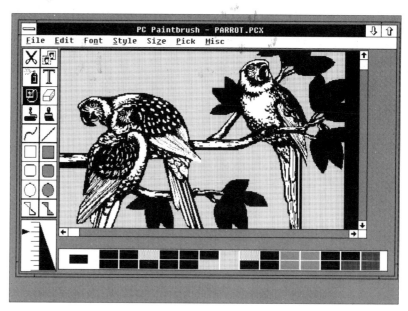

well as certain patterns; then you might open the image with PC
Paintbrush to color it. PC Paintbrush provides more printing options
than does Paint, including the ability to print portions of the graphic
and multiple copies.

Micrografx Draw

The first Windows drawing application was Micrografx Draw. (Indeed,
as you might recall from Chapter 1, Draw actually made it to market
before Windows itself.) Micrografx remains a leading supplier of
graphics-oriented Windows applications with three applications: Draw,
Designer, and Graph. (The latter is described in the section of this
chapter titled "Spreadsheet Analysis and Graphing.") All three programs share similar file formats, allowing them to team up well. You
might, for example, create a bar chart in Graph and then import it
into Draw or Designer for further embellishment. Micrografx also
offers a library of more than 1000 clip-art images—object-oriented
graphics that you can use exactly as they are or that you can modify
for inclusion in your own drawings or in desktop publications.

Figure 11-14 on the next two pages illustrates how a designer for a
national airline might use Draw to modify a Micrografx clip-art image
to create a route map for the airline's in-flight magazine.

FIGURE 11-14.

Micrografx Draw.
(A) Selecting the original clip art in Draw.
(B) Preparing to draw lines connecting cities after having deleted some.
(C) Zooming in for detail work.
(D) The completed map after drawing lines and adding a box and drop shadow.

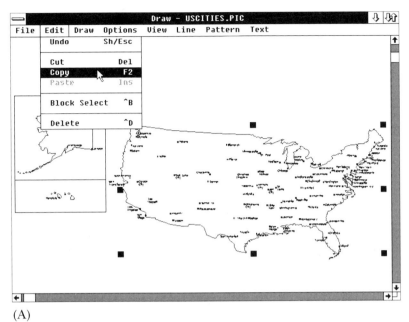

(A)

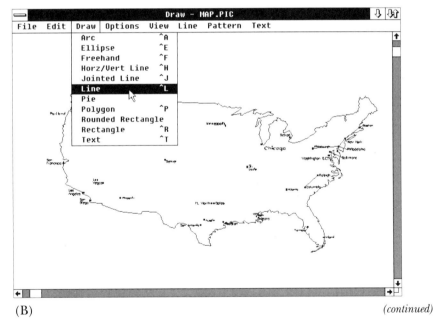

(B)

(continued)

FIGURE 11-14.

continued

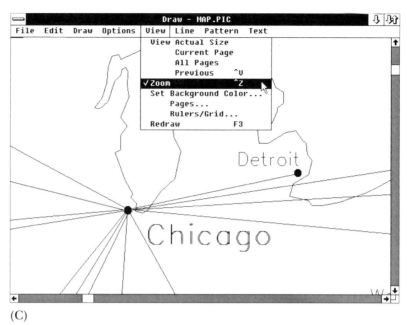

(C)

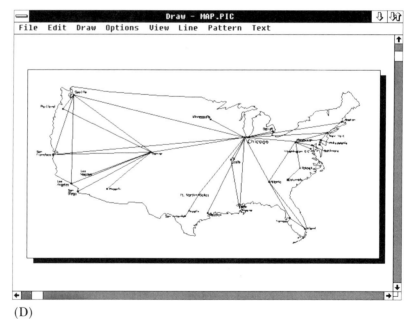

(D)

First, she opens the clip-art file, selects the United States map by clicking on it, and then copies it to the Clipboard. Next, she opens a new, untitled document, pastes the map into it, and then deletes the cities that won't appear in the final map. Finally, she draws lines between the remaining cities, encloses the map in a shadowed box, and saves the document as a PIC file, which she'll import into a PageMaker publication. (And because Draw images are object oriented, she'll also be able to resize the map without distortion to fit into a schedule booklet and service brochure.)

Micrografx Designer

Draw and Designer offer many similar features, but Designer is the more powerful of the two programs. Draw is designed for light-duty drawing—for creating organizational charts, simple floor plans, and flowcharts or for modifying clip art. Designer is intended for computer-aided design and drafting applications and for producing complex illustrations for desktop-publishing jobs. Many of Designer's menu commands are similar to those of Draw, making it easy to move between the two programs.

Figure 11-15 on the next two pages shows one approach a technical artist might use to draw an exploded parts diagram using Designer. This example showcases one of Designer's many unique features—its ability to assign descriptions to the objects in a drawing and then create a parts list showing each object's description as well as the number of times it appears in the drawing. You can print the resulting parts list directly from Designer or save it as a text file to import into a spreadsheet, a word-processing document, or a desktop publication. Better still, you can use a Microsoft Excel macro to establish a link between a parts list and a spreadsheet. Micrografx is developing macros for Designer that will do just that. One macro starts Designer, opens a drawing, displays a parts list, copies it to the clipboard, pastes it into a spreadsheet (which contains a database that lists each part and its price), and then prints a formatted bill-of-materials report.

FIGURE 11-15.

Creating a technical illustration in Micrografx Designer. (A) Drawing the base plate. (B) Creating and naming a symbol. (C) The completed drawing. (D) Saving the parts list for inclusion in another application.

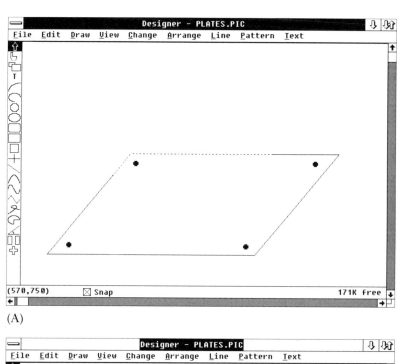

(A)

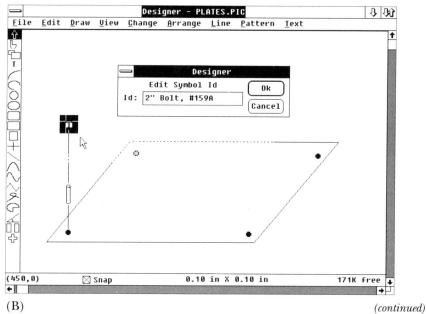

(B)

(continued)

FIGURE 11-15.

continued

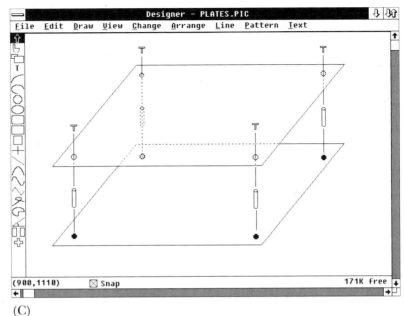

(C)

(D)

Desktop publishers can use Designer to create line art by tracing bitmapped graphics. In Figure 11-16, a designer creating a pet store logo for PageMaker-produced business cards, letterhead, and invoices has imported a scanned image of a dog into Designer. He traces the image to create an outline. Designer's curve-drawing tool allows him to create smooth curves, while its freehand tool lets him render irregular shapes.

Designer offers far more features than can be described here. It boasts advanced color capabilities, including color-mixing commands that give you access to 3.6 million different colors. It also lets you rotate objects in 0.1-degree increments, edit and define your own fill patterns, and create drawings of up to 168 by 168 inches.

Pro3D from Enabling Technologies

Pro3D is a three-dimensional modeling application from Enabling Technologies. Using Pro3D is different from using other Windows graphics applications. Instead of creating images with paintbrushes or shape-drawing tools, you combine basic geometric shapes, called primitives, with objects drawn using Pro3D's tools. Pro3D adds shading and perspective effects to the resulting framework to create impressive three-dimensional images.

In Figure 11-17 on pages 244 and 245, a graphic designer is using Pro3D to create a three-dimensional wine glass. To define the basic shape of the glass, she uses Pro3D's lathe tool. Like a woodworker's lathe, Pro3D's lathe tool lets you create radially symmetrical objects such as glasses, bottles, and baseball bats. (Pro3D's other drawing tool, the profiler, is an electronic jigsaw, used for creating irregularly shaped objects.) After she specifies the outline of the glass using the lathe, Pro3D creates the glass. She fine-tunes the image's lighting using the commands in Pro3D's Light menu. Next, she uses Pro3D's rotate and revolve icons to produce different views of the glass, each of which she saves as a PIC file.

Note: Version 1.0 of Pro3D had several compatibility problems with Windows 2.0. At this writing, Enabling Technologies was developing a new version that will fix the incompatibilities and add several new features.

FIGURE 11-16.

Using Designer to trace scanned images.
(A) Trace the image to create an outline.
(B) Copy the outline to PageMaker and position it.

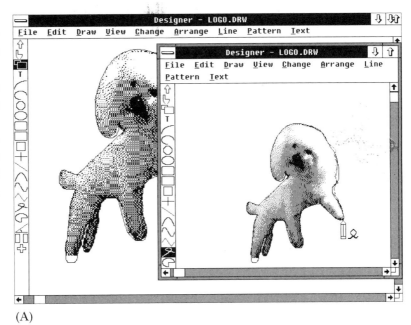

(A)

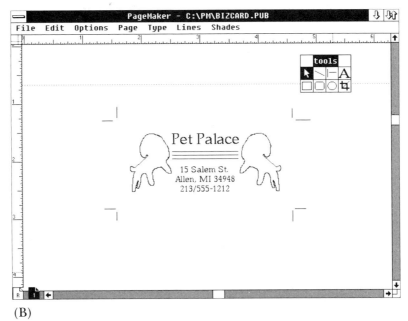

(B)

FIGURE 11-17.

*Using Pro3D
from Enabling
Technologies to
create a
three-dimensional
object.
(A) Creating the
wine glass by
using the lathe.
(B) The 3-D
rendition.
(C) Rotating
the glass.
(D) A "wire
frame" view
showing the
components.*

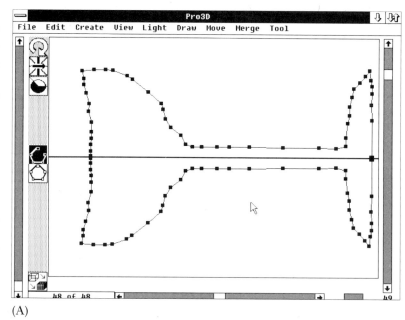

(A)

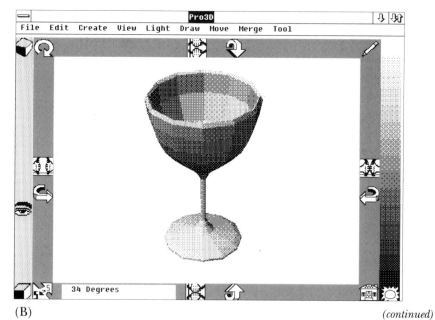

(B)

(continued)

FIGURE 11-17.

continued

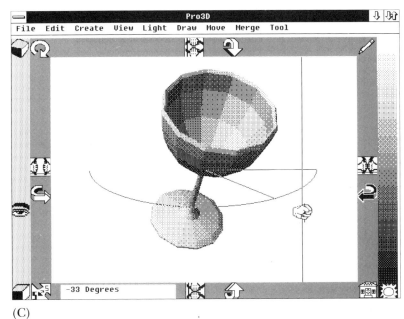

(C)

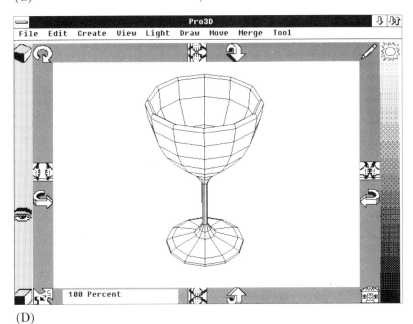

(D)

Database Management

Because computers are particularly adept at sorting and storing information, database management ranks alongside word processing and spreadsheet analysis as one of computing's most popular applications. Database managers store and retrieve information that is organized in a specific format. The building blocks of a database are fields and records. In this regard, a database is like an address book: A field in a database corresponds to an item of information (a name, an address, a city, and so on) for one person in an address book. Taken together, the fields for one person form a record. Database managers let you enter information into one or more on-screen data-entry forms that you create. You retrieve the information by displaying records on screen or by printing reports, in which the information in the database is presented in row-and-column form, usually sorted according to criteria you specify.

Better database managers let you create customized data-entry forms that resemble their paper counterparts. A personnel database, for example, might use a form that resembles your company's paper personnel form. Or, your company's sales-invoice database might use a form that resembles your company's invoice. Forms that mimic the appearance of paper forms help make data entry less tedious and intimidating, especially for database beginners.

To create customized forms, you need a database manager that lets you position field names anywhere on screen, instead of forcing you to use a preset field layout. (Ideally, you should be able to position a field by clicking and dragging it, rather than by typing spaces to move it to the right or by deleting spaces to move it to the left.) Better still is a database-management program that takes advantage of Windows' typographic capabilities by allowing you to format fields and other text in different fonts and styles. If you combine such a program with a laser printer, you can print forms and reports that look as if they were typeset.

Two basic types of database managers exist: filers and relational database managers. A filer, sometimes called a flat-file database manager, lets you work with one data file at a time. Filers are generally used as electronic replacements for simple paper filing systems such as address books or index-card boxes. A filer is like an index-card box;

a relational database manager is comparable to a cross-referenced filing system. A relational database manager lets you work with multiple files, establishing links, or relations, between them. The primary advantage for doing so is efficiency: By linking separate files, you can access information from both files without having to enter it separately. One application for a relational database is an invoicing and inventory system for a mail-order business. Such a database might use two separate but related files: a customers file and an inventory file. When a purchase is made, the database manager can create an invoice by combining the customer name from the customers file with the item names, descriptions, and prices from the inventory file, as shown in Figure 11-18. At the same time, the inventory file is updated to reflect the sold items.

FIGURE 11-18.

Combining data from separate files of a relational database to produce an invoice. The customer-address file comes from the clients file; item numbers, descriptions, and prices come from the inventory file. The database manager calculates the totals.

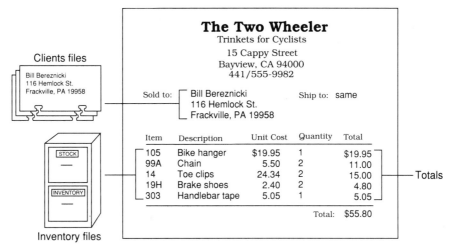

Palantir Filer

Palantir Software's Filer is, as you might guess, a filer. Figure 11-19 on the following page shows how a real-estate agent could use Filer to store information on available properties. This application takes advantage of Filer's ability to store graphics by storing a scanned image of each property. Prospective buyers can browse through the database, searching for—and seeing—houses that meet their needs.

Because the data files that Filer creates share an identical format with Ashton–Tate's dBASE III, Filer can directly read and update files created with dBASE III or dBASE Mac. And, of course, that also means you can open Filer databases using Microsoft Excel or open Microsoft

FIGURE 11-19.

Palantir Filer.

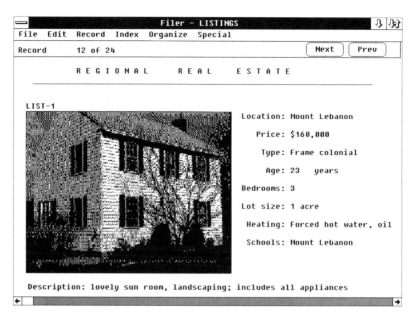

Excel databases in Filer by saving the data as a DBF file. (Chapter 5 describes data-file exchange techniques in greater detail.) When a Filer database contains graphic fields, Filer keeps each graphic in a separate disk file and stores pointers to the appropriate disk files in the database. This separation of text and graphics lets you use Filer databases containing graphics in applications that don't support text and graphic databases, such as the dBASE series and Microsoft Excel.

Filer doesn't allow you to format reports in various fonts or sizes, but you can export data to a text file and then use Write to format it in different fonts or to add graphics such as a company logo. Finally, at this writing, the latest version of Filer (3.01) has several compatibility problems with Windows 2.0, most of them cosmetic. You may not mind Filer's limited typographic features, but you should verify that the program has been updated to work with Windows 2.0.

Omnis Quartz from Blyth Software

Omnis Quartz from Blyth Software takes advantage of the Windows interface to simplify the task of creating complex relational databases. Omnis Quartz also provides application-development features and a built-in programming language for creating database-management applications with their own menus and dialog boxes. Consultants and developers can use these programming features to create complete applications that even newcomers to database management can use.

Designing an Omnis Quartz application is usually a five-step process. First, you create the data files, specifying each field name and the type of data (text, numbers, dates, and so on) it will hold. Next, you design layout formats and report formats. Layout formats are windows that enable users to enter and retrieve the information in the data files. Report formats describe how information in the database will appear when printed. You might also design search formats, which let users retrieve data according to certain criteria. Finally, you tie everything together with custom menus and sequences, Omnis Quartz's term for programming procedures. A sequence specifies what happens when a custom menu command is chosen.

Figure 11-20 shows part of a personnel and payroll application created in Omnis Quartz. The menus at the top of the screen are custom menus; each command on the menus activates a corresponding sequence that opens a layout window or prints a report. The option buttons and check boxes in the data-entry form also are customized. They improve the database's accuracy by reducing the amount of typing required during data entry.

FIGURE 11-20.

A personnel-entry screen in Omnis Quartz from Blyth Software.

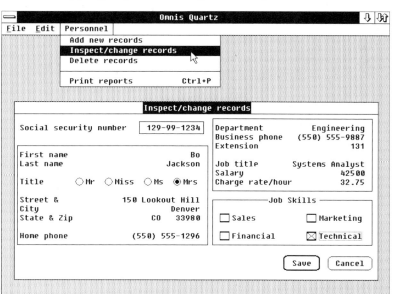

Figure 11-21 demonstrates an Omnis Quartz sequence. This sequence, which was created entirely by pointing and clicking within Omnis Quartz's sequence-editing window, swings into action when you choose the Delete Pay Period command from the Payroll menu. Because you can't recover a deleted pay period, the sequence's first job is to display a dialog box that warns you accordingly. That dialog box appears in Figure 11-22. If you click its Yes button, the sequence opens a data file named PAYROLL, which holds the data for the last pay period and then clears its contents. If you click the No button, the sequence displays a custom dialog box that reassures you by letting you know nothing was deleted.

Figure 11-23 illustrates a different Omnis Quartz application—a customer-invoice system. This application uses multiple files to create invoices: The customer's name comes from one file; the item descriptions and unit prices come from another. The invoice form layout also illustrates the use of calculated fields. Each item's total price is determined by Omnis Quartz, which multiplies the unit price for each item by the quantity ordered.

FIGURE 11-21.

Creating an Omnis Quartz sequence.

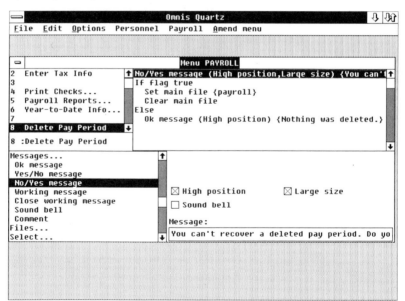

FIGURE 11-22.

An Omnis Quartz custom dialog box.

FIGURE 11-23.

An Omnis Quartz invoicing application.

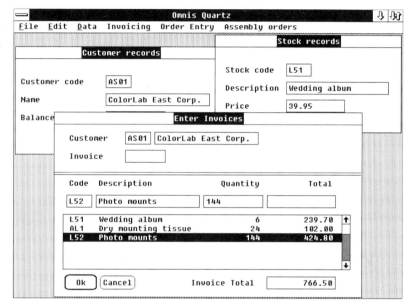

Beneath Omnis Quartz's friendly veneer is a powerful database manager that can work with files of up to 2.5 gigabytes, containing up to 120 fields of up to 2400 characters each. Omnis Quartz also can import and export ASCII, dBASE, Lotus 1-2-3 WKS, and DIF files. Blyth has announced plans to deliver a multiuser, DDE-supporting version of Omnis Quartz during the first quarter of 1988. A version that can access databases created with Blyth's Omnis 3 Plus, a Macintosh database program that's similar to (but not as sophisticated as) Omnis Quartz, is scheduled for delivery in the second quarter of 1988.

Telecommunications

A telephone modem and a telecommunications program can lead you into a vast world of up-to-the-minute news and business information, electronic mail, free software, and much more.

Palantir inTalk

Palantir inTalk is a full-featured telecommunications program that is ideal for accessing electronic mail services such as MCI Mail; general-purpose information services such as CompuServe, The Source, or GENie; and bulletin boards—homespun information services run by user groups and dedicated computer hobbyists.

In Figure 11-24, inTalk is being used to write and send an MCI Mail communique. Note the buttons at the bottom of the screen; when clicked, each transmits a text command to MCI Mail. These function keys, as inTalk calls them, help take the typing tedium out of communications. With inTalk, you can create up to 32 function keys, switching between sets of 8 by clicking the numbered buttons in the lower-right corner of inTalk's window. A function key can transmit a

FIGURE 11-24.

Palantir inTalk.

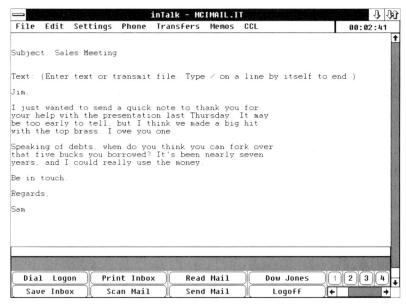

simple text string, such as your user name or password, or it can instruct inTalk to execute a script of commands programmed in CCL, inTalk's communications-control language. CCL statements let you automate communications sessions. For example, the statement:

WAIT STRING "Password:", SEND "swordfish"

tells inTalk to pause until the text *Password:* is received, then transmit the text *swordfish.*

A CCL script can be as simple as the preceding one line or as complex as an automatic mail retriever that signs on after 11:00 PM (when phone rates drop), retrieves any waiting mail, saves it in a disk file, and then signs off. You create CCL scripts using inTalk's built-in text editor, which is also useful for composing and reading electronic mail and other text files.

The inTalk program supports all popular file-transfer protocols, including Xmodem, Kermit, and Crosstalk, and provides its own transfer protocol that allows easy file exchange with other inTalk users. When two inTalk users exchange files under the inTalk protocol, one user can begin a file transfer by choosing the Send Binary File or Receive Binary File command. That user's copy of inTalk communicates with the copy of inTalk at the other end of the line, instructing it to receive or send a file. The inTalk protocol can also transfer Macintosh binary files, which use a special format that cannot be sent by other MS-DOS transfer protocols. This feature, combined with the fact that Palantir sells a nearly identical version of inTalk for the Macintosh, makes inTalk an excellent choice if you use MS-DOS computers and Macintoshes.

You can copy incoming text to the clipboard and paste it into other Windows applications. (Chapter 5 shows how.) Palantir also plans to include DDE support in inTalk version 2.0, scheduled for delivery in the first quarter of 1988. Using DDE, you can establish a link between inTalk and a stock-market graph created with Microsoft Excel or Micrografx Graph; as the incoming stock data changes, your graph is updated accordingly.

WINDOWS/386

Windows/386 is a version of Windows designed for computers based on Intel's 80386 microprocessor—machines that include the IBM PS/2 Model 80, the COMPAQ DESKPRO 386, and the Tandy 4000. Although Windows/386 looks and works very much like Windows 2.0, there are some significant differences, especially when you run standard applications. This chapter explores the internal and external differences between Windows 2.0 and Windows/386.

How Windows/386 Works

In Windows/386, Microsoft combined Windows' multitasking talents with a special operating mode of the 80386 microprocessor to create an operating environment that offers the same platform for graphical applications as does Windows 2.0 and that provides far superior support for standard applications. Windows/386 provides these benefits by taking advantage of a special operating mode of the 80386 called the virtual 86 mode. In virtual 86 mode, the 80386 can act like a number of separate 8086 microprocessors, the predecessors to today's 80286 and 80386 microprocessors. Windows/386 uses virtual 86 mode to create as many virtual machines—pseudo machines, each capable of running a standard application—as your computer's memory allows.

Virtual DOS Machine Manager

The component of Windows/386 responsible for creating and controlling virtual machines is called the Virtual DOS Machine Manager (VDMM). When you start Windows/386, the file WIN386.COM loads the VDMM into your system's extended memory. (As explained in Chapter 10, extended memory is memory above the 1 MB MS-DOS physical address space.) Next, VDMM creates a virtual machine with 640 KB of memory, copies portions of MS-DOS into it, and then loads a special version of Windows 2.0 into the virtual machine. Next, the VDMM passes control of your system to Windows 2.0, which reads its own WIN.INI file and runs MS-DOS Executive.

When you start a standard application, the VDMM creates a new virtual machine, copies MS-DOS and other important system data into it, and then loads the application into the new virtual machine. The size of the new virtual machine is controlled by the application's PIF. If the application lacks a PIF, Windows/386 attempts to allocate 640 KB to the virtual machine. At the same time, Windows/386 loads the contents of the file WINOLDAP.MOD. This file is comparable to the WINOLDAP.MOD file in Windows 2.0: It contains code that lets standard applications run in their own windows and that lets you copy and paste data from or to standard applications. Each time you start a new standard application, Windows/386 creates a new virtual machine by using these steps. Thus, if you have five standard applications running, your computer actually contains six virtual machines: one containing each application and one containing Windows 2.0.

Windows/386 takes an entirely different approach to starting Windows applications. Instead of creating new virtual machines when you start Windows applications, Windows/386 loads them into the first virtual machine—the one containing Windows 2.0. The machine's 640 KB size doesn't restrict the number of applications you can run, because Windows 2.0 is able to store Windows applications in expanded memory, letting it load as many Windows applications as you have room for in expanded memory. (For this reason, you shouldn't disable or reduce the amount of expanded memory if you often run numerous Windows applications simultaneously.)

The Windows/386 Approach to Multitasking

As stated in Chapter 1, Windows' approach to multitasking is a cooperative effort among all Windows applications currently running. In Windows 2.0, a Windows application grants control to other Windows applications when checking its queue for messages. Windows' multitasking approach is called non-preemptive multitasking because Windows never interrupts an application to allow another application to run. But multitasking grinds to a halt when you run a standard application that takes over the screen.

Windows/386 works differently. Multitasking doesn't grind to a halt when you run a standard application full-screen, unless you run the application in exclusive mode by modifying its PIF or using the Settings command in its Control menu, as described later in this chapter. Windows/386 divides your computer's resources among all the standard applications you run by using a multitasking scheduler tied to an internal heartbeat that ticks slightly more than 18 times per second. Your computer uses this heartbeat, which is generated by a quartz crystal, for timing-intensive tasks, such as refreshing its

memory chips—a job it must perform periodically, lest the chips lose
their contents. Every few heartbeats, Windows/386 interrupts the currently running application and turns its attention to a different
virtual machine, allowing its application to run. The number of beats
an application gets depends on the tasking options you've specified
for it and on the total number of applications running. Thus, Win-
dows/386's approach to multitasking *is* preemptive. As soon as an application receives its allocated number of ticks, it's put on hold so that
another application can get its share.

But this preemptive approach to multitasking doesn't extend to
Windows applications. Because they run in one virtual machine under
the control of Windows 2.0, they run exactly as they would if you were
using a true copy of Windows 2.0—that is, non-preemptively. Thus, if
you're running only Windows applications, the VDMM's multitasking
talents are unused. Conversely, if you're running only standard applications, Windows 2.0's non-preemptive multitasker sits idle.

In essence, Windows/386 is a hybrid form of Windows. By taking
Windows 2.0 and encasing it in the VDMM, which works intimately
with MS-DOS and the 80386, Windows/386 provides the best of both
worlds. It gives you full compatibility with Windows applications *and*
it provides true multitasking support for standard applications, with
none of the little quirks and workarounds found in Windows 2.0. It's
the ultimate version of Windows—and the most flexible MS-DOS
operating environment.

Running a Standard Application in a Window

Windows/386 takes advantage of the 80386's capabilities to allow standard applications—even applications that might be called ill-behaved,
ones that bypass MS-DOS and directly access hardware components—
to run in their own windows. Instead of having to take over the screen
and suspend other running applications, a standard application can
coexist on the screen with other standard applications and with Windows applications.

When you start a standard application for which no PIF exists,
Windows/386 runs the application full-screen. When running an
application full-screen, you can switch back to Windows/386 by using
the Alt+Esc combination, and you can copy information to the clipboard by pressing Alt+Spacebar to display the Control menu and then

using its Mark and Copy commands. (Chapter 9 contains examples of copying information from standard applications.)

Displaying a Standard Application in a Window

Unlike Windows 2.0 users, Windows/386 users can tell Windows/386 to display a full-screen application in a window by pressing Alt+Enter. For example, Figure 12-1 shows Microsoft Word running in a window. When a standard application is in its window-display mode, you can move and size the window as you would with a Windows application. If you have a mouse, you can use it to select information in the window for subsequent copying to the clipboard. However, if the application supports a mouse (for choosing commands, as does Microsoft Word, for instance), you cannot use the mouse to choose commands within the application's window unless it's running full-screen. That's because Windows/386 interprets any mouse click within an application's window as the beginning of a selection operation. If you accidentally click within a window to choose a command, simply press Esc to cancel the selection operation.

Terminating a standard application is done the same way in Windows/386 as it is in Windows 2.0. First, choose the application's quit command. Then, if the application was running in a window, close its

FIGURE 12-1.

Microsoft Word running in a window.

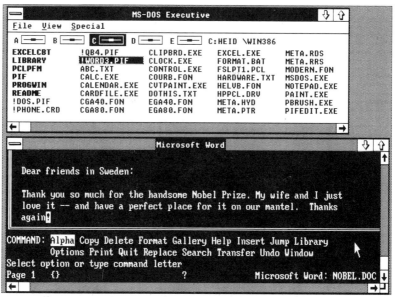

window. If the application's PIF specified that the application's window closes upon exit, the second step is unnecessary. (Windows/386 PIFs are examined later in this chapter.) In those rare cases when an application has crashed and refuses to terminate, you can force it to terminate by choosing Settings from the application's Control menu and using the Terminate button. For reasons described shortly, however, use the Terminate button as a last resort only.

The Settings Command on the Control Menu

Beyond the basics of running a standard application in a window, Windows/386 provides additional options that let you tap its enhanced multitasking talents. The gateway to those options is the Settings command that appears in a standard application's Control menu. When you choose Settings, the dialog box in Figure 12-2 appears.

The Display Options section of the Settings dialog box lets you specify whether the standard application runs in a window or runs full-screen. You probably won't use these buttons very often because it's more convenient to use the Alt+Enter combination to switch between full-screen and window display modes.

The Tasking Options buttons let you control how (and whether) Windows/386 divides your computer's processing time between the standard application and other standard applications that might be running. The Tasking options let you tailor the attention Windows/386 gives to each running application, letting you get the best performance from your system. The tasking settings are:

Foreground. In foreground mode, the standard application runs only when it's displayed full-screen or when its window is the active window. Otherwise, the application is suspended. When you start a standard application for which no PIF exists, Windows/386 runs the application in foreground mode.

FIGURE 12-2.

Settings dialog box.

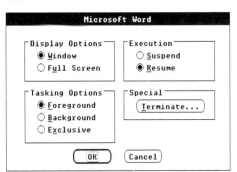

260

Background. Selecting this option tells Windows/386 to run the application in the background when it is not the active application. The background option is especially useful for applications that perform time-consuming operations. For example, a telecommunications program running in the background can check your electronic mailbox at regular intervals while you perform other tasks. A database manager can sort a large file. A word processor can send a file to a printer or perform a lengthy search-and-replace operation. When you select the background option, Windows/386 allocates two-thirds of the microprocessor's time to the foreground application (the active application) and divides the remaining third among all the open background applications. Because processor time is taken away from the active application, it runs slower than if it were an exclusive application.

Exclusive. Selecting this option causes Windows/386 to devote all your computer's time and resources to the application. When an application runs in exclusive mode, all other applications—including Windows applications—are suspended. (In this regard, exclusive mode resembles the way Windows 2.0 runs a standard application that can't run in a window.) Exclusive mode is best when you need maximum performance from an application and you don't need to run other applications in the background. You can still switch to other applications using Alt+Tab or Alt+Esc; when you do, Windows/386 suspends the exclusive application and displays it as an icon. If you have multiple exclusive applications open, Windows/386 suspends all but the active application.

The Execution section of the Settings dialog box contains buttons for suspending and resuming an application. The Suspend button lets you put a background application on hold to gain more processor time for other background applications.

The final section of the Settings dialog box, Special, contains one button labeled Terminate. As mentioned earlier in this chapter, the Terminate button is a last-resort panic button; you use it to regain control of the computer when a standard application has crashed and ignores your keystrokes, thus prohibiting you from quitting it normally. When you choose Terminate, a dialog box appears warning you that termination may put MS-DOS in an unstable state. Heed its warning: After using the Terminate button, save any unsaved documents that are open in any other applications, exit Windows/386, and restart your computer.

Using PIFs in Windows/386

In Windows/386, PIFs don't play as vital a role as they do in Windows 2.0. In Windows 2.0, a PIF is required if you want to be able to switch between a standard application and Windows or if you want to run a standard application in a window. Windows/386 provides these capabilities without requiring PIFs. You can, however, use a PIF to fine-tune the way Windows/386 runs a standard application. Specifically, you can control how much memory Windows/386 gives to a standard application and whether Windows/386 runs the application in its exclusive or background tasking modes.

As Figure 12-3 shows, the Windows/386 PIF Editor looks much like its Windows 2.0 counterpart. The workings of the Program Name, Program Title, Program Parameters, and Initial Directory entries are identical. (These entries are described in detail in Chapter 9.) The Memory Requirements entries are also similar, although you need to be aware of two subtle differences if you convert from Windows 2.0 to Windows/386. First, Windows/386 cannot swap itself to disk when running a standard application. Therefore, typing −1 in the Memory Desired box has no effect. Second, if you leave the Memory Desired and Memory Required boxes blank, Windows/386 allocates 640 KB to the standard application. In Windows 2.0, leaving the Memory Required entry blank tells Windows to allocate all available memory to the application.

One unique aspect of a Windows/386 PIF is its Usage Control entries. The Full Screen setting controls whether the application takes over the screen when you run it or whether it runs in a window. The

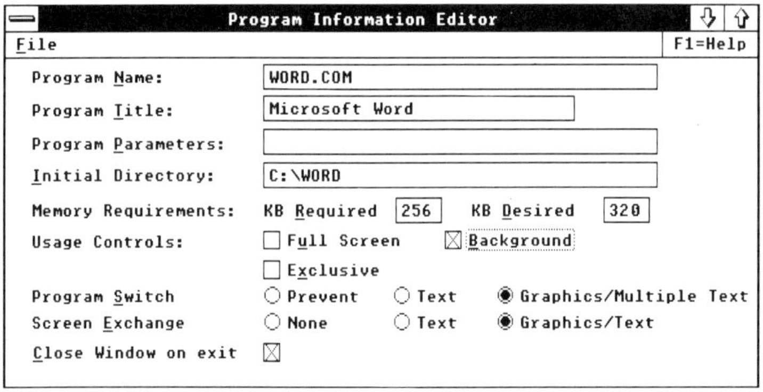

FIGURE 12-3.

Windows/386 PIF Editor.

Background and Exclusive settings let you specify whether Windows/386 runs the application in the background or in its exclusive mode; they correspond to the Background and Exclusive buttons in the Settings dialog box.

Below the Usage Control entries are the Program Switch, Screen Exchange, and Close Window on Exit settings. Because you can always switch between standard applications under Windows/386, you can ignore the Program Switch setting.

The Screen Exchange option works similarly to its Windows 2.0 counterpart, in that it lets you control how much memory Windows/386 reserves for saving the screen image when you use the Alt+PrintScreen combination to capture a screen image and store it on the clipboard. Generally, you don't need to specify a Screen Exchange option; Windows/386 allocates memory as needed to capture a screen image. However, if you're running low on memory, you can conserve some memory by choosing the Text setting.

Note: Another feature of Windows/386 that isn't available in Windows 2.0 is the ability to paste bitmaps into standard applications. With Windows/386 any bitmap you can load into Clipboard can be pasted into any standard application that accepts bitmaps. As noted in Chapter 9, Windows 2.0 can paste only text and OEM text into standard applications.

The Close Window on Exit setting works identically to its 2.0 cousin with one exception. If you don't set this option, a full-screen application changes to a windowed application when you issue its quit command. At that point, the application becomes inactive, but its display remains behind in the window, which you can close by choosing the Control menu's Close command.

Although Windows/386 handles standard applications well without PIFs, you might want to use one if you have certain operating preferences for an application. For example, if you always run an application in the background, create a PIF for it and choose its Background option. Doing so eliminates the need to use the Settings command each time you start the application. Or you might want to use your computer's memory more efficiently. If an application uses only 320 KB of memory, you waste memory if you let Windows/386 allocate its default value of 640 KB. Create a PIF for the application, specifying its memory requirements in the Memory Required and Memory Desired boxes.

You might even want to create multiple PIFs for a single application, with each PIF tailored to a particular task. For example, for those times when you sort colossal files with a database manager, you might want to create a PIF that lets the application run in the background. For data-entry sessions, when you want fast response to your keystrokes, create a PIF that lets it run in exclusive mode.

Using a Terminate-and-Stay-Resident Utility under Windows/386

In addition to its support for standard applications and its unique PIF options, Windows/386 differs from Windows 2.0 in other areas. One difference concerns terminate-and-stay-resident, or pop-up, software such as Borland's SideKick. With Windows 2.0, you must load any pop-up programs that you plan to use before you start Windows. Microsoft discourages the use of pop-up applications because they often access the keyboard in nonstandard ways that prevent them from working under Windows, unless you're running a standard application that has taken over the screen.

In Windows/386, you must load pop-ups *after* starting Windows. If you load them before starting Windows/386, they won't run reliably under Windows/386. To load a pop-up after starting Windows, run COMMAND.COM and then load the pop-up from the MS-DOS prompt. You can use the pop-up utility any time the COMMAND.COM window is displayed on the screen. If you use a particular set of pop-ups with a given application, create a batch file that loads the pop-up and then the application.

Using WIN.INI under Windows/386

Windows 2.0 and Windows/386 also differ in their WIN.INI configuration files. A Windows/386 WIN.INI file contains a *[win386]* section, with entries that control how Windows/386 uses your system's memory and keyboard. The *windowmemsize* entry determines how much memory Windows/386 allocates to running Windows applications. (More specifically, *windowmemsize* determines the size of the virtual machine that contains Windows applications.) The default *windowmemsize* value is 640 KB; however, if you use Windows/386 strictly for running standard applications, you can save memory by decreasing that value to as little as 420 KB.

The *[win386]* section can also contain an optional entry, *emmsize*. The *emmsize* entry controls how much of your computer's memory Windows/386 treats as expanded memory. (The basics of expanded memory are discussed in Chapter 10.) Without an *emmsize* entry, Windows/386 reserves up to half of your computer's available memory, if necessary. Depending on the types of applications you run, that may be too much memory. For instance, many standard applications reserve a fixed amount of expanded memory for holding data but don't relinquish the memory to other applications when it isn't needed. They're like a selfish child who takes a toy just because another kid wants it. In such cases, you can restrict the amount of expanded memory available to an application by using an *emmsize* entry. To set aside 384 KB of memory as expanded memory, for example, add the following line:

    emmsize=384

to the *[win386]* section. You can disable Windows/386's expanded-memory support altogether with the following line:

    emmsize=0

But because Windows/386 can use expanded memory to store Windows applications, this drastic step limits the number of Windows applications you can run simultaneously.

The *[win386]* section also includes five entries that let you override how special Alt-key sequences work with Windows/386. These are *altescape, altenter, altspace, alttab,* and *altprintscn.* In most cases these sequences should be set to *on* so that Windows can trap and use them. If a sequence is important in an application you use often, set it to *off* so that Windows ignores it and passes it on to the application.

RESOURCES

L isted in this appendix are the names, addresses, and telephone numbers for the hardware and software manufacturers whose products are mentioned in this book. Following these is a list of books and magazines that are excellent sources of information about MS-DOS and Windows.

Pointing Devices

FTG Data Systems *(FT-156 High Performance Light Pen and PXL-350 Hi-Res Light Pen Board)*
10801 Dale St.
Suite J-2
P.O. Box 615
Stanton, CA 90680
(800) 962-3900 Customer service
(714) 995-3900

IBM Corp. *(IBM Personal System/2 Mouse)*
Old Orchard Rd.
Armonk, NY 10504
(914) 765-1900

Koala Technologies Inc. *(Koala Pad+ Touch Tablet)*
269 Mount Hermon Rd.
Scotts Valley, CA 95066-4029
(800) 877-7844 Customer service
(408) 438-0946

Kurta Corp. *(IS/ONE Series Tablet)*
4610 S. 35th St.
Phoenix, AZ 85040
(800) 445-8782 Marketing/sales line
(602) 276-5533

Logitech, Inc. *(LogiMouse)*
6505 Kaiser Dr.
Fremont, CA 94555
(415) 795-8500

Microsoft Corp. *(Microsoft Mouse)*
16011 NE 36th Way
P.O. Box 97017
Redmond, WA 98073-9717
(800) 426-9400 Consumer response/marketing
(206) 882-8088 Customer service
(206) 882-8089 Product support

MSC Technologies, Inc. *(PC Mouse from Mouse Systems)*
2600 San Tomas Expressway
Santa Clara, CA 95051
(408) 988-0211

Pencept Inc. *(Pencept Penpad Model 320)*
39 Green St.
Waltham, MA 02154
(617) 893-6390

Summagraphics Corp. *(SummaSketch 1201)*
777 Commerce Dr.
Fairfield, CT 06430
(800) 243-9388 Customer service
(203) 384-1344

Ergstrom, Inc. *(Mouse Cleaner 360)*
P.O. Box 17013
Minneapolis, MN 55417
(612) 854-9116
(800) 328-9829

Monitors

JVC Information Product Co. of America *(GD-H3214)*
Division of JVC Corp.
Western Regional Sales
1011 W. Artesia Blvd.
Compton, CA 90220
(213) 537-6020

Moniterm Corp. *(Viking 1)*
5740 Green Circle Dr.
Minnetonka, MN 55343
(612) 935-4151

NEC Home Electronics *(MultiSync series)*
1255 Michael Dr.
Wood Dale, IL 60191
(312) 860-9500

Sigma Designs *(LaserView)*
46501 Landing Parkway
Fremont, CA 94538
(415) 770-0100

Sony Corp. of America *(Multiscan)*
9 W. 57th St.
New York, NY 10019
(212) 371-5800

Taxan USA Corp. *(Super Vision 770)*
18005 Cortney Ct.
City of Industry, CA 91748
(800) 772-7491
(818) 810-1291

Memory Boards

AST Research, Inc.
2121 Alton Ave.
Irvine, CA 92714-4992
(714) 863-1333

Cumulus Corp. *(PS/2 boards only)*
180 Basswood
Cleveland, OH 44022
(216) 247-2236

Intel Corp.
Personal Computing Enhancement Operation
5200 NE Elam Young Parkway
Hillsboro, OR 97124
(800) 538-3373

AppleTalk Expansion Boards

Apple Computer, Inc.
20525 Mariani Ave.
Cupertino, CA 95014
(408) 996-1010

Tangent Technologies, Ltd.
5990-K Unity Dr.
Norcross, GA 30071
(404) 662-0366

TOPS *(TOPS for MS-DOS)*
2560 Ninth St.
Suite 220
Berkeley, CA 94710
(800) 222-TOPS from outside California
(800) 455-TOPS from inside California
(415) 549-5900

Hard Disks

Plus Development Corp. *(Hard Card)*
1778 McCarthy Blvd.
Milpitas, CA 95035
(408) 946-3700

Laser Printers

Apple Computer, Inc. *(LaserWriter)*
20525 Mariana Ave.
Cupertino, CA 95014
(408) 996-1010

Hewlett-Packard Co. *(LaserJet)*
1820 Embarcadero Rd.
Palo Alto, CA 94303
(800) 752-0900

QMS, Inc. *(QMS-PS 800+, QMS-PS 810)*
P.O. Box 81250
Mobile, AL 36689
(205) 633-4300

Software

Access Softek *(Dragnet)*
3204 Adeline St.
Berkeley, CA 94703
(800) 222-4020
(415) 654-0116

Adobe Systems *(downloadable PostScript fonts)*
1585 Charleston Rd.
Mountain View, CA 94039-7900
(415) 961-4400

Aldus Corp. *(PageMaker)*
411 First Ave. S.
Suite 200
Seattle, WA 98104
(206) 622-5500

Bitstream Inc. *(Fontware downloadable fonts for LaserJet Plus and Series II printers, PostScript printers, and numerous dot-matrix printers)*
Athanaeum House
215 First St.
Cambridge, MA 02142
(800) 522-3668 Marketing
(617) 497-6222

Blyth Software *(Omnis Quartz)*
1065 E. Hillsdale Blvd.
Suite 300
Foster City, CA 94404
(415) 571-0222

Enabling Technologies, Inc. *(Pro 3D)*
600 S. Dearborn
Suite 1304
Chicago, IL 60605
(312) 427-0386

Manhattan Graphics Corp. *(Ready,Set,Go!)*
401 Columbus Ave.
Valhalla, NY 10595
(914) 769-2800

Micrografx Inc. *(Draw, Graph, Designer)*
1820 N. Greenview Ave.
Richardson, TX 75081
(214) 234-1729

Microsoft Corp. *(Windows, Word, Pageview)*
16011 NE 36th Way
P.O. Box 97017
Redmond, WA 98073-9717
(800) 426-9400 Consumer response/marketing
(206) 882-8088 Customer service
(206) 882-8089 Product support

Palantir *(Filer, inTalk, WinSpell)*
12777 Jones Rd.
Suite 100
Houston, TX 77070
(713) 955-8880

Word Perfect Corp. *(Word Perfect)*
288 W. Center St.
Orem, UT 84057
(801) 225-5000

XyQuest, Inc. *(XyWrite)*
44 Manning Rd.
Billerica, MA 01821
(617) 671-0888

ZSoft Corp. *(PC Paintbrush, PC Paintbrush+, Publisher's Paintbrush, Publisher's Type Foundry)*
450 Franklin Rd.
Suite 100
Marietta, GA 30067
(404) 428-0008

Reading Resources

PC Magazine
One Park Ave.
New York, NY 10016

PC World magazine
Publish! magazine
Windows magazine
PCW Communications, Inc.
501 Second St.
San Francisco, CA 94107

Running MS-DOS by Van Wolverton
Microsoft Press
16011 NE 36th Way
Box 97017
Redmond, WA 98073-9717

SOME COMMON
FILE FORMATS

S tandards are sparse in microcomputing, but several common formats do exist for document data files. Many programs can open and create documents in one or more of these formats, so you might find them useful for transferring files between applications. The following file formats are ones you're most likely to encounter in your work with Windows.

Format: DCA.
Stands for: Document Content Architecture.
Developed by: IBM.
Application: Word processing.
Description: The DCA format, also called Revisable Form Text (RFT) format, was developed for exchanging formatted word-processing documents between different word-processing and office-automation systems. In the microcomputer world, it's supported by IBM's Display Write 3 word processor and by many other word processors, including Samna Word III, Volkswriter 3, and WordStar 2000. You can also convert Microsoft Word files to DCA format by using the Word Exchange file translation utility from Systems Compatibility Corporation.

Format: DIF.
Stands for: Data Interchange Format.
Developed by: VisiCorp.
Applications: Spreadsheet analysis, database management.
Description: The DIF file format debuted with VisiCorp's pioneering VisiCalc spreadsheet program. It is still supported by most spreadsheet applications and by many database managers. A DIF file consists of ASCII text records that represent a row-and-column grid of unformatted numeric and text values.

Format: EPS.
Stands for: Encapsulated PostScript.
Developed by: Altsys Corporation, a developer of font utilities and a PostScript drawing program for the Apple Macintosh.
Applications: Illustration, image scanning, and desktop publishing, where the final product is printed on a PostScript printer.

Description: EPS files contain programs in the PostScript page-description language and are usually used to add illustrations or special text effects to desktop publications. Many programs that accompany scanners can save images in EPS format. A full EPS file contains not only the PostScript code that creates a given image but a Windows metafile that allows the desktop-publishing program to display an approximation of the effect on screen. Whether an EPS file contains a metafile depends on the application that created it. If an EPS file doesn't contain a metafile, your desktop-publishing program instead probably displays a box that indicates the PostScript image's boundaries.

Format: SYLK.
Stands for: Symbolic Link.
Developed by: Microsoft Corporation.
Applications: Spreadsheet analysis, database management.
Description: Like DIF files, SYLK files are intended primarily for exchanging row-and-column-oriented data, such as spreadsheets and databases. Unlike DIF files, however, SYLK files provide some data compression and can also represent some formatting information, such as alignment, commas, and column widths.

Format: TIFF.
Stands for: Tagged-Image File Format.
Developed by: Aldus Corporation, with assistance from leading scanner manufacturers, primarily Hewlett-Packard. Responsibility for maintaining the standard was turned over to Microsoft in 1987.
Applications: Desktop publishing, image scanning and processing.
Description: TIFF files are used primarily to store graphics created by image scanners. TIFF files contain tags that describe an image's height and width, resolution, gray scale or color, and the type of data compression scheme used. TIFF also allows high-resolution graphics to be stored more efficiently by using run-length compression. Run-length compression substitutes groups of identical (all white or all black) pixels with a code that uses less disk space. In a way, you use a method similar to run-length compression when describing how many eggs are in a carton: Instead of saying ''egg'' twelve times, you

say "a dozen eggs." TIFF files use a slightly modified run-length compression standard with the catchy name CCITT Group 3. TIFF isn't tied to a brand of machine or type of microprocessor, and it's designed to handle many different images, from line art to halftones to color, in a variety of resolutions.

Format: RTF.
Stands for: Rich-Text Format.
Developed by: Microsoft Corporation.
Applications: Word processing, desktop publishing.
Description: Like DCA files, RTF files are used to exchange formatted text between word processors or other text-handling applications. RTF, however, maintains far more formatting information. A DCA file, for example, cannot contain point-size information. RTF works by using control words—strings of characters such as \margl for left margin and \plain for plain text. RTF can also encode color and graphics and is designed to support high-resolution printers. (The measuring system in RTF is a twip; one twip equals $1/20$ of a point, or $1/440$ of an inch.) RTF is a standard Windows clipboard format; applications that support RTF can exchange formatted text.

INDEX

Jim Heid

A resident of Peterborough, New Hampshire, Jim Heid writes for a variety of magazines, including *PC World, Publish!* and *Macworld,* where he is the "Getting Started" columnist. Heid is also the author of several books, including *dBASE Mac in Business.* He has also served as a technical editor for Wayne Green Books and *Microcomputing* magazine.

The manuscript for this book was prepared and submitted to Microsoft Press in electronic form. Text files were processed and formatted using Microsoft Word.

Cover design: Ted Mader and Associates

Interior text design: Darcie S. Furlan

Principal typographer: Lisa G. Iversen

Principal production artist: Peggy Herman

Text composition by Microsoft Press in New Baskerville with display in Helvetica Light, Helvetica Black, and New Baskerville Bold, using the MAGNA composition system and the Linotronic 300 laser imagesetter.